Praise for

SPEAKING U

"Through its impressive national scope, *Speaking Up* sheds new light on the history of minority-majority relations in the country. With a subtle understanding of the concerns of linguistic groups, primarily French and English, but also including Aboriginal and other languages, Martel and Pâquet deliver an engaging and convincing exploration of ethnic identities, schooling conflicts, and communication politics in a complex country."

> – Colin M. Coates, Director, Robarts Centre for Canadian Studies,
> York University

"*Speaking Up* is an indispensable guide for anyone seeking to understand the place of language in Quebec politics. It is impossible to understand this province, or the desire of some here for independence, without an understanding of the historical context that defines the Québécois identity. Meticulously researched and comprehensive in scope, *Speaking Up* provides exactly that context. It should be required reading for English-Canadian pundits, most of whom so profoundly misunderstand this province."

> – Ethan Cox, Montreal-based writer, activist and political
> commentator, and the Quebec correspondent for *rabble.ca*

SPEAKING UP

A History of Language and Politics in Canada and Quebec

Marcel Martel and Martin Pâquet

Translated by Patricia Dumas

BETWEEN THE LINES
Toronto

**Speaking Up: A History of Language and Politics
in Canada and Quebec**

First published in French as *Langue et politique au
Canada et au Québec: Une synthèse historique*
©2010 Éditions du Boréal
English translation ©2012 Patricia Dumas

First published in English translation in 2012 by
Between the Lines
401 Richmond Street West
Studio 277
Toronto, Ontario M5V 3A8
Canada
1-800-718-7201
www.btlbooks.com

**Library and Archives Canada Cataloguing
in Publication**

Martel, Marcel, 1965-

    Speaking up : a history of language and
politics in Canada and Quebec / Marcel Martel and
Martin Pâquet.

Translation of: Langue et politique au Canada et au
Québec.
Includes bibliographical references and index.
Issued also in electronic format.

ISBN 978-1-926662-93-0

    1. Language policy–Canada–History. 2.
Language policy–Québec (Province)–History. 3. French
language–Political aspects–Canada–History. 4.
Canada–Languages–Law and legislation–History.
I. Pâquet, Martin, 1963- II. Title.

P119.32.C3M3813 2012   306.440971   C2012-903709-5

Cover design by Jennifer Tiberio
Front cover photo: Demonstration against Bill 22 in Quebec,
1974 (BANQ, centre d'archives de Québec, Fonds du ministère
des Communications, E10, S44, SS1, D74-698, P14).
Text design by David Vereschagin/Quadrat Communications
Printed in Canada

RECYCLED
Paper made from
recycled material
FSC® C103567

Between the Lines gratefully acknowledges assistance for
its publishing activities from the Canada Council for the
Arts, the Ontario Arts Council, the Government of Ontario
through the Ontario Book Publishers Tax Credit program and
through the Ontario Book Initiative, and the Government of
Canada through the Canada Book Fund.

We acknowledge the financial support of the Government of
Canada, through the National Translation Program for Book
Publishing for our translation activities.

Canada Council
for the Arts

Conseil des Arts
du Canada

Canada

ONTARIO ARTS COUNCIL
CONSEIL DES ARTS DE L'ONTARIO

To Normand Pâquet
To Georges-Henri Martel
To Sarah Courtemanche-Pâquet

Speech is a conquest of life.
A red glow bursting into the realm,
Sliding through cracks of silence, filling dreams.
Walls quiver with the vivid clamour of voices.
Thousands call for the return of Babel,
From far-distant times, where the word was born.

Contents

INTRODUCTION

Comment abolir les siècles qui séparent les langages des significations?
- Pierre Perrault, *Le Grand Jeu des miroirs*
  (*Irréconciliable désir de fleuve*)

In 1974 the Royal Canadian Mounted Police asked its officers in Quebec to gather information on individuals and groups advocating for French unilingualism in the province. In doing this, the police force was not only attempting to assess support for the cause, but also trying to determine the potential for violence among citizens who had taken part in public demonstrations.

The language demonstrations taking place at that time were not the first of their kind in Canada. By the end of the 1960s several groups had already mobilized around language issues—not just in Quebec but elsewhere in Canada, in particular Ontario and New Brunswick. The issue of language was inspiring many people to speak up—to raise their voices in resistance and seek power in the public sphere. In this way the issue of language was helping to define the common interests of an entire political community.

If some policy-makers believed in 1974 that they were facing a new problem on the language front, they were deluding themselves. The 1960s had been characterized by a sense of anxiety about the place of the French language in the public sphere and as the common language of Quebec. Moreover, by that time the language issue had been influencing political life and public debates for several decades—even several centuries. From the arrival of the first settlers in New France, the king of France had promoted linguistic uniformity in an effort to establish French as the common language in the colony. After the British conquest of 1760 introduced the use of English, the status of French remained contested by advocates of ethnic and linguistic uniformity, first within the British North American provinces and later within the Dominion of Canada. Resistance to the arbitrary power that these advocates exercised over language led to a series of political crises throughout the nineteenth and twentieth centuries. Intimately linked to nation-building, these crises were a potential threat to public peace because they questioned dominant socio-economic relations and inequalities based on language. To ensure public order, community elites and policy-makers— whether elected members of legislatures or federal and provincial civil servants—employed a number of methods to reduce the potential for unrest. These varied methods—part of an overall policy designed to recognize and manage diversity—ranged from language-planning policies to court actions, and included various symbolic gestures. As it turned out, RCMP surveillance was just one of the many interventions set in place.

The relation between language and politics

This book—as a contribution to the history of political culture—explores the historical relation between language and politics in Canada and Quebec, from the first language edict passed by the king of France in 1539 to the twenty-first century. We hasten to add that it does not present a history of language-planning policies, although such policies have occupied a decisive place in the history of Canada and Quebec since the arrival of Europeans.

What we mean by the word "language" in the phrase "language and politics" is not simply a matter of the system of signs—whether words, sounds, graphics, or gestures—that people use to communicate with each other. Rather, we use "language" to refer to the manifestations of social relationships and practices—including goals and rules—that change over time. For example, the French used at the court of Francis I or the English employed at the court of Elizabeth I is not the same as the French used today by Michel Garneau and Patrice Desbiens or the English used by Leonard Cohen and Gordon Downie. Not only have the vocabulary and grammar changed; but the socio-historical contexts, and the values and meanings expressed by the languages, are no longer the same.

Consequently, in this historical study of the relationship between language and politics, our approach to language is three-dimensional. First of all, we see language as the mode of communication that social actors use to exchange meaning in their interactions. Second, we see it as an identity symbol through which individuals express both inwardly and outwardly, to others, their specific characteristics and sense of social belonging. Third, we see language as a political issue when it becomes the discourse of speakers who convey the aspirations, divisions, alliances, rivalries, and neutrality of their communities. Language is a political issue because political actors assign it intrinsic value. Indeed, French, English, and indigenous languages in Canada and Quebec are not neutral modes of communication. On the contrary, they put into words fundamental concepts about common interests, sealing the social bond; this explains their particularly sensitive nature. Language is also a political issue because, beyond the limits of any given discourse in which individuals tend to become trapped, languages reveal the socio-historical reality of struggles, relations of domination, and inequalities within society. Language is political because it embodies the human relationship to the real world.

A study of the relation between language and politics must also raise the question of governance, which we understand as how a state goes about managing social divisions and determining how people will live together in the future. In the case of the language issue in Canada and Quebec, such a study implies the three dimensions analysed by political scientists David Cameron and Richard Simeon, among others: the *vouloir-vivre collectif* (will to live together), *devoir-vivre collectif* (duties of living together), and *comment-vivre ensemble* (how to live together).

The first dimension, the will to live together—which hearkens back to Ernest Renan's famous formula for defining a nation—is based on a feeling of belonging to a historical community, the sharing of cultural references, and the desire to connect a shared past to a shared future. Whether in 1755, 1912, or 1977, the use of French in Acadia, Ontario, and Quebec does not indicate a similar desire to live together because the socio-economic contexts and political frameworks of each time and place are different. As for the duties of living together, these conditions are determined by the imperial power of political institutions—from the older kingdoms of France and Great Britain to the newer federal and provincial states. The second dimension—the duties of living together—emanates from the setting of standards aimed at homogenizing the population within a given territory in order to ensure civil peace despite social divisions. Since 1539—the year in which King Francis I established French as the administrative language of his realm—various language laws, court decisions, and appeals for linguistic quality standards have shaped the duties of living together. The third dimension—how to live together—depends upon the political ramifications of power given that people in a particular society or social milieu do not all have access to the same resources or share the same dominant socio-economic positions. An Aboriginal person on a reserve or a federal civil servant, a Franco-Ontarian activist in 1927 or one in 2002, an Italian-speaking parent in Saint-Léonard or a supporter of French unilingualism: these actors will all perceive the issue of how to live together differently.

The question of *how to live together* involves exercising power and resisting it; it entails developing various strategies that can be used in negotiations or confrontations, alliances or rivalries, pacification or reconciliation. For people throughout the centuries in Canada and Quebec, the will to live together, the duties of living together, and the question of how to live together have intertwined to shape the issue of language.

When viewed as a political issue, then, language becomes intimately linked to questions of how people live together in time and space. The language issue insinuates itself into the history of relations between individuals; it reflects the standards and power relationships within society; it also reveals the aspirations of a community. Language and politics combine in their relations to determine the past, present, and future of a community. In Canada and Quebec the language issue, in all its facets and across history, has been at the very heart of political interactions.

General trends in the language issue

Through more than four and a half centuries in Canada and Quebec, several general trends in the relationship between language and politics have developed, endured, or faded depending on how deeply they have been linked to the broader contexts. But one permanent feature in public policies has remained, rooted in the basic requirements of the duties of living together: the need to homogenize the population as a means of exercising power within a given territory. Homogenization necessitates the adoption of measures that govern communications between individuals and political jurisdictions, whether they are colonial or state-controlled. For the authorities, the efficient exercise of power requires that a population share common characteristics, including, potentially, the use of a given language.

Until the French Revolution, the main criterion of homogenization within a territory was religious denomination. Whenever and wherever legal and political regulations were established, the language issue was subordinate to religion because allegiance to the sovereign was a matter of faith—and the tragic deportation of Acadians in 1755 serves as a demonstration of what happens when a people have an adherence to what is considered the wrong religion in the wrong place. With the toppling of the ruling estates in Europe and the development of new political models based on concepts of nation, the language issue was redefined. From then on, language was tightly connected to nationhood. In the case of the English language, the British, faced with the threat of the French Revolution, retreated into an ethno-cultural concept of nation that spread to the colonies across the Atlantic; while the French language in Lower Canada became a symbol of national identity after the crushing of the Patriotes' rebellion of 1837–38 and the rejection of the republican ideal. Confronted by the clearly expressed will of some English Canadians to assimilate them, French Canadians would in future integrate the French language as an inseparable element of their will to live together. It became the very definition of their nation.

With the development of the modern state and the rise of the bourgeoisie to positions of power in the nineteenth century, the language issue took on new dimensions. In the North American British provinces, mirroring the hegemony of the liberal order, as historian

Ian McKay points out, the language issue exemplified the relationship between capital and work, with the industrial and commercial bourgeoisie expressing themselves mainly in English and many workers and farmers knowing only French. To mitigate social conflicts arising from the proximity of various ethno-linguistic communities, the state, or its ruling elites, adopted an approach of mutual accommodation based on the concepts of law, order, and good government. The promotion of harmony between the majority and minorities took place through informal relations established between members of the French- and English-speaking elites. While some minorities, such as the French Canadians and Acadians, were part of the political community, others, such as the Aboriginal peoples, were excluded. The state did not necessarily act as a mediator in the fulfilment of this ideal of *bonne entente*, rooted in the firm requirements of *how to live together* and aimed at controlling potential conflicts. Still, the rhetoric of harmony did not prevent major crises from breaking out, such as the resistance surrounding Ontario's Regulation 17, which was issued in 1912 and restricted French as a language of instruction to the first two years of schooling. The law was not repealed until 1927.

After the Second World War, the mutual-accommodation approach crumbled under the rise of individualism, the development of communication technologies, the acceleration of international migratory movements, and greater access to education. From then on, social relations came under the yoke of a new political culture whose formal standards were to become preponderant in the 1960s. As members of various communities began to speak out publicly—sometimes in a disorderly manner—disassociating themselves from the elites, the definitions and guidelines previously used to contain conflicts no longer worked. In the case of the language issue per se, language—a mark of cultural identity as well as a cultural reality—was at the very core of the *will to live together* of francophones and of Aboriginal peoples. From then on, confronted by potentially explosive situations—such as conflicts over the language used in schools in Saint-Léonard in 1967–68 and student protests over an increase in tuition fees at the Université de Moncton in 1968–69—elites were forced to ask for the intervention of the federal and provincial governments, which had the resources necessary to set formal standards.

At first those resources included the scientific expertise required to assess the kinds of intervention needed. Based on the works of various commissions of inquiry set up at the turn of the sixties and seventies, the federal and provincial governments made specific choices with regard to language planning—bilingualism or unilingualism—in order to reduce the outbursts of violence created by social conflict and turmoil. The choices made reflected how the political leaders perceived the public's interest. The English-Canadian leaders favoured a bilingual and multicultural Canadian society rooted in individual rights. Quebec leaders favoured a model of society in which French unilingualism would be an instrument of socio-economic development and collective emancipation. For their part, the political leaders of French-speaking minority groups viewed language as an indicator of the vitality of their community. They saw that vitality as being essential to their survival. Indigenous peoples similarly saw it as being essential to their future well-being.

By the 1980s the government approach in this area came increasingly under the mantle of the law and its legal arsenal. Following the example of the international legal regime that took shape after the Universal Declaration of Human Rights of 1948, Canada and Quebec each contributed in their own way to the promotion of rights, including language rights. The repatriation of the Constitution in 1982 brought about the entrenchment of the Canadian Charter of Rights and Freedoms, whose articles were regularly referred to in the numerous language cases brought to court. Language was transformed from a political problem to a legal dispute. Furthermore, with regard to language matters, the rulings of judges were no longer based solely on the clauses pertaining to the *duties of living together*. Indeed, the courts became the preferred theatre of operations for strategies on *how to live together*, with the various protagonists seeking to have their respective concepts of the language issue prevail. Although the concepts basically reflected the primacy of individual rights, they did not as such exclude compliance with collective rights, as demonstrated by recent Supreme Court rulings or the management of disputed Aboriginal claims.

Finally, the hegemony of the marketplace altered the linguistic relationship between capital and work. The increasing globalization of cultural exchanges and interactions, the economic concept of social relations, and its ancillary—the promotion of a common language for commerce—gained in popularity, to the detriment of other aspects of living together and of the *will to live collectively*, including cultural and linguistic diversity.

The six phases of a movement

The general trends shaping the language issue emerged, then, in six phases spanning the years from 1539 to the twenty-first century.

During the first phase, from 1539 to 1848, the linguistic issue fell within the jurisdiction of French and British political authorities. In the colonies, language policies put into words the metropole's requirements for, first, religious and, then, national homogenization. The approaches showed major similarities from one colony to the next, in particular with regard to maintaining law and order. By the turn of the nineteenth century citizens were developing resistance strategies, including efforts to make French a distinctive element of the *will to live together*.

During the second phase, from 1848 to 1927, the language issue caused a series of major conflicts. School crises in New Brunswick, Manitoba, the Northwest Territories, and Ontario bear witness not only to the determination on the part of the authorities and special-interest English-Canadian groups to homogenize culture and language within the Canadian territory, but also to the resistance of citizens to these attempts. In using the state, and in particular the school system, as an instrument to achieve their goals, the English-speaking interest groups and political actors demonstrated how little they cared about what Acadians and French Canadians considered to be their linguistic and cultural rights. In an increasingly tense climate that reached its peak with the crisis surrounding Regulation 17, requirements regarding the *duties of living together* promoted by those in charge of government clouded the terms and conditions of the *will to live together*.

From the Regulation 17 crisis to the Quiet Revolution of the 1960s, the language issue went through a period of relative calm, during which French-Canadian and Acadian citizens developed strategies to regain their linguistic rights. These strategies did not lead to any spectacular public mobilization, which is a measure of the precariousness of the accommodations surrounding *how to live together.* With members of the French-Canadian and Acadian elite being wary of provoking negative reactions among anti-francophone groups, the claim for language rights unfolded timidly. For its part, the federal government granted a few concessions but failed to develop an overall language-planning policy officially promoting French as a language of use in the country.

In the 1960s the movement for change sped up, and the following three phases evolved rapidly. The language issue experienced a major revival in debates within English-Canadian and Québécois public spaces. The years 1963 to 1969—the fourth phase—witnessed a strong moment marked by the voice of the people. Many citizens equated the use of English in the public sphere and the workplace with a deeply rooted injustice—the cultural colonization of the French-Canadian and Acadian nations—a condition reflecting relations of dominance. The issue became increasingly pronounced with the massive anglicization of immigrants. In a spirit of emancipation the revaluation of the status of French was put forward as a remedy. At the same time, basically following the precautionary principle inherent in political action, the federal and provincial governments made efforts to channel the voice of dissenting citizens and reduce the risks of social turmoil, setting up commissions of inquiry mandated to analyse the ins and outs of the new language crisis.

After a period of reflection the federal and provincial governments opted for legislative action. This fifth phase, from 1969 to 1982, was marked by the implementation of policies promoting French as a language of use. Reshaping their internal symbolic order,[1] governments took aim at ensuring citizens' approval and stifling further agitation around the language issue. With its Official Languages Act in 1969, Ottawa implemented bilingualism. After vacillating, Quebec adopted unilingualism in 1977 with its Charter of the French Language. The other provinces opted for various administrative measures, but, given the hostility more or less rampant towards the French fact—apart from New Brunswick, where the Acadians were heard loud and clear—most refused to declare themselves officially bilingual.

The sixth and last phase, beginning in 1982, became characterized by the rule of law. The entrenchment of the Canadian Charter of Rights and Freedoms in the Constitution set the foundation for a new symbolic order in Canada. From then on, the Charter stated the terms and conditions of the *duties of living together*. Therefore, citizens now resorted increasingly to courts when seeking to assert their language rights regarding both the terms and conditions of *how to live together* and the management of linguistic diversity. Although French-speaking minority groups registered gains, the issue of the vitality of the French fact remained. In Quebec, the government's efforts to francize some immigrant communities and otherwise promote the French language led to a fragile political consensus on the language issue. Still, the issue of the quality of the language taught and spoken remained sensitive; and the complex issue of the status and well-being of indigenous peoples, which by the 1980s had once again become part of the agenda, left open the question of the survival and preservation of their languages and cultures.

CHAPTER 1

FROM RELIGION
TO LANGUAGE

1539-1848

*That legislator [Justinian] had composed his Institutes, his
Code, and his Pandects, in a language which he celebrates
as the proper and public style of the Roman government, the
consecrated idiom of the palace and senate of Constantinople,
of the camps and tribunals of the East. But this foreign
dialect was unknown to the people and soldiers of the Asiatic
provinces, it was imperfectly understood by the greater part of
the interpreters of the laws and the ministers of the state.*
  - Edward Gibbon, *The History of the Decline and Fall of the
    Roman Empire,* 1776

In Europe at the end of the Middle Ages the issue of language
use did not have anything like the same political dimension
that it would acquire in modern times. Although language was
already a part of the homogenization of people living within
certain territories, the sharing of a common tongue also meant
adhering to existing systems of justice, which at the time were
firmly established on religious foundations. A political community—marked by allegiance to a king or prince—was understood
as a matter of sharing a common faith. Later, during the Age of

Revolution, when the ancient order was toppled, different relations of domination took shape and new stakes emerged in the use of language. For states wanting to ensure the homogenization of the population within territories they controlled, language became tied to the goal of nationalization—a process that unfolded until the middle of the nineteenth century in the British North American colonies.

The king's language and faith

Among other factors, the use of language is a function, on one hand, of the political battles waged to gain dominance over a given territory and, on another, of establishing civil peace around common standards. For our purposes, the propagation of French represents a significant example of this tendency. At the end of the Middle Ages the growth of the kingdom of France took place through conflicts and the implementation of various strategic alliances. With the end of the Hundred Years War in 1453, the English abandoned the region of Guyenne in what is now southwestern France; it was an area that had belonged to the English Crown for three centuries. In 1477 Picardy and the Duchy of Burgundy fell under the suzerainty of the kings of France. When King René died in 1480, Louis XI seized Provence. In 1491 the marriage of Anne of Brittany and King Charles VIII drew Brittany closer to the kingdom of France; the states of Brittany entered into a Treaty of Union with France in 1532. Following the bloody interlude of the religious wars of the sixteenth century, the expansion continued: parts of Savoy in 1601; part of Alsace with the treaties of Westphalia in 1648; Artois and Roussillon were acquired in a peace agreement with Spain in 1659; Franche-Comté and the rest of Alsace in 1697, Lorraine in 1766, and Corsica in 1768. To all of which was added New France, which Louis XIV established as a province of the kingdom in 1663.

Within the numerous fiefs that henceforth were part of the royal domain, the new subjects had to swear complete and total allegiance to the kings of France. To this end, the French monarchy imposed its own justice system; legislation, penal law, and civil law gradually fell under the control of the sovereign, notwithstanding resistances. Consequently, for the judicial system to be effective, the king and his subjects had to be able to understand each other. At the beginning of the sixteenth century, with the inclusion of regions with languages notably different from the idiom of Île-de-France, Francis I decided that linguistic normalization was necessary. Adopted in August 1539, the Ordinance of Villers-Cotterêts on the Administration of Justice established French, spoken mostly in the royal domain, as the kingdom's official language.

Ordinance of Villers-Cotterêts on the Administration of Justice
Villers-Cotterêts, France, August 1539

Francis, etc.: declares to all, present and future, that to provide for good justice, shorten proceedings, and relieve our subjects, we, through a perpetual and irrevocable edict decreed and ordered, do decree and order the following: ...

(110) And in order for there to be no reason to doubt the meaning of these judicial decisions, we desire and order that they be created and written so clearly that there can be no ambiguity or uncertainty [nor provide] reason to ask for an interpretation.

(111) And since these misunderstandings often occur because of the use of Latin words in judicial decisions, we henceforth want all the decisions, and all other procedures, be they originating in our sovereign courts or other lower and minor courts, be they registrations, inquiries, contracts, appointments, sentences, wills, and any other acts and explorations of justice, or whatever relies on them, be pronounced, recorded and delivered to parties in the French mother tongue and no other way.

> *Source:* "Ordonnance sur le fait de justice. Villers-Cotterêts, août 1539," *in* Recueil général des anciennes lois françaises depuis l'an 420 jusqu'à la Révolution de 1789, *ed. François-André Isambert et al.,* Troisième race, Ordonnances des Valois, Règne de François Ier, *Paris, Velin-Leprieur et Verdière, 1827, pp.600-01, 622-23.*

Even though there still was language diversity, French spread rapidly in the sixteenth century because it was the language of power and administration. Nobles, first of all, spoke the king's language in order to win his favour. Given the prestige of knowledge—the prestige of education—and of the written word, which was benefiting from the new printing technology, cultured people followed the trend: lawyers, notaries, tutors, medical doctors. In the cities, especially in Northern France, tradesmen and merchants increasingly communicated in French because to buy and sell and enter into an agreement, they had to understand each other. In the countryside, particularly in the south of the kingdom, the situation was different: dialects remained the means of expression in everyday life, except for those engaged in the world of the Church—who spoke Latin—and in temporal law— which required French. Even if by the end of the century Catholics and Protestants were fiercely tearing each other apart in the kingdom, language was not really an issue: they were killing each other in French.

During the era of colonization in the seventeenth and eighteenth centuries, New France had a certain linguistic unity. As highlighted in the works of the linguists Philippe Barbaud, Raymond Mougeon, and Jean-Claude Corbeil, several factors supported this extended knowledge of French among the settlers. Almost 90 per cent of them came from Northern France, where French was already widely spread. Some 70 per cent of the women—many of whom came from Île-de France—and 47 per cent of the men had lived in cities in France, and the majority of the settlers had received enough education to sign the various deeds that were of concern to them. Finally, almost a third of the settlers held a rank or practised a profession that required a good knowledge of the king's language. Still, not everybody mastered French, especially members of the first generation of settlers from Normandy, Poitou, Aunis, Perche, Saintonge, Picardy, Brittany, and Champagne. The linguist Adjutor Rivard reports, for example, on the minutes of a litigation that lasted from 1666 to 1669 between two settlers in the Lauzon seigneury. A witness in the case, recalling a conversation between the plaintiff and the defendant, ended his narration at a certain moment because the defendant was speaking "in his dialect," which the witness did not understand. However, if many people spoke in a dialect when they arrived, that tendency changed over time: the concentration of lands, proximity to the colonial administration, marriages between settlers from different provinces, and the role mothers played in the education of children led to the gradual disappearance of regional languages in favour of French.

The strengthening of linguistic unity in New France was notable in the speakers' accent. The linguist Jean-Denis Gendron found a whole series of contemporary testimonies, from those of Father Chrestien Leclercq to Pehr Kalm, through the Sieur Bacqueville de la Poterie to the Marquis de Montcalm, which refer to the "pure French" and the "accent-free pronunciation" of the inhabitants of the province. By the mid-eighteenth century, the speakers of French on either side of the Atlantic had adopted different accents. French as it was pronounced in Parisian colleges spread throughout the country during the French Revolution. The accent of the Versailles of Louis XIV lived on in the New World. When he visited Lower Canada at the beginning of the 1830s, Alexis de Tocqueville noticed the difference. Even though "the basis of the population and the great majority of people everywhere" were French and the cities had "a striking resemblance with our provincial cities," the lawyers in Quebec, he said, "particularly lack refinement" and "speak French with the Normand accent of the middle classes." [1]

With the French settlers consistently mastering their own language, any diversity in the spoken word in New France rested much more on the numerous Aboriginal peoples who lived in the immense territory, from the shores of the Atlantic Ocean to the Gulf of Mexico and the Rocky Mountains. To communicate and establish relations with these peoples, the newcomers needed first of all to understand them. The French colonial authorities realized that it was practically impossible to rapidly implement a language assimilation policy; if there was to be francization, it had to be through conversions to Catholicism. Indeed, the Act establishing the Compagnie des Cent-Associés in 1627 provided that, in converting, the indigenous peoples would become subjects of the king of France and would thereafter be submitted to his laws. Evangelization was then a means to impose the learning of French not just as a language, but also, and even more, as a culture. The Récollet fathers in 1620 and the Jesuits in 1634 sent Aboriginal children to France, although without any notable success. The French also introduced day schools and boarding schools, teaching a way of life that was remote from the indigenous peoples' own customs and experiences. Once again, success was not a given, even if Marie de l'Incarnation noticed some progress had been achieved by Huron and Algonquin boarders in 1668. Furthermore, taking a page from the Jesuits' book, missionaries were learning indigenous languages and translating missals, catechisms, and hymn books into Mi'kmaq, Abenaki, Attikamek, Algonquin, Innu, and Iroquois, among others. Finally, the French settlers sometimes borrowed from Aboriginal vocabularies to name the new reality surrounding them, from "*achigan*" (tilefish) to "*savoyane*" (goldthread), from "*carcajou*" (wolverine) to *caribou*, from "*babiche*" to "*ouaouarons*" (bullfrogs).

Admittedly, French policies towards the First Nations peoples were ambiguous, as historian Olive Dickason points out. At the international level, through their timely strategy of alliances with Aboriginal peoples the French implicitly recognized the principle of the sovereignty of the original inhabitants, which made it possible to deny any responsibility for these sometimes troublesome allies. In New France itself the situation differed slightly: the French did not necessarily know what course of action they should take in their negotiations with First Nations peoples. It was only when the colony became more solidly established that a consensus was reached on how to implement the French laws. In addition, at the heart of language relations was the "*truchement*," the interpreter, either Aboriginal or French, who translated the messages being communicated. The *truchements* also played a critical role in the fur trade. According to linguist George Lang, their great linguistic competence—the *coureurs de bois* were often polyglots—prevented the development of a pidgin or creole language so typical in the world of trade. Later, the Métis born from inter-ethnic marriages in the Prairies would adopt Michif, a singular language that combined Cree and Ojibwa grammar and verbs with French, English, and Gaelic grammar and names.

The language issue also had a particular dimension for the Aboriginal peoples themselves. Their political cultures greatly valued speech: they made decisions after engaging in collective discussions; the elders orally transmitted memory; the chief was the one who spoke the most eloquently to the members of his clan. The French had to take into account the importance of speech; for example, Samuel de Champlain dealt skilfully with the Huron-Wendat tribes; Jean de Brébeuf—who, as he was being martyred, forcefully delivered a sermon in Iroquois—gained the respect of some of the Aboriginal peoples. Keeping one's word was crucial in both cultures, and each in its own way gave honour a privileged place. The Great Peace of Montreal, concluded in 1701 between Governor Louis-Hector de Callière and the chiefs of thirty-nine indigenous tribes, was a case in point. For the French, who were part of a culture based on the written word, the document itself was officially binding because it was written in their language and affixed with the governor's signature and the ideograms of the chiefs. For the First Nations the peace was based on the symbolic gestures carried out during the ceremonies—planting the Tree of Peace, smoking the calumet, burying the war axe—and, especially, in the speeches. In this respect, Kondiaronk, chief of the Tionontati and main architect of the peace treaty, captivated the spirits with an eloquent speech that lasted two hours, before succumbing two days later to a fever.

In the events that unfolded during the War of Conquest, from the deportation of the Acadians in 1755 to the Royal Proclamation of 1763, the language issues as they existed in Great Britain itself played a part. From the end of the Middle Ages to the French Revolution and the beginning of the nineteenth century, the British Isles experienced a difficult process of political unification characterized by violent inter-denominational conflicts and the constant spectre of a foreign invasion. It was not so much the language or regional rifts as the particularly intense feelings of religious divisions between the Protestants and Catholics that marked the political identities of the time. The inter-denominational violence and the fear of a major invasion were important because they weighed heavily on the political concepts of those who became British during the eighteenth century.

Indeed, the unification of Great Britain started at the same time as the expansion of Protestantism. The Act of Union of England and Wales came only two years after the 1527 excommunication by Rome of King Henry VIII, and the Act of Supremacy of 1534 established the Protestantism of the Church of England as the religion of the state. During a time when threats of invasion were recurrent and the legitimacy of authority was contested, professing the Catholic faith meant swearing allegiance to a foreign and hostile sovereign: the pope. While the campaign against papists became very intense—the kingdom of Spain sent its Grand Armada in 1588 to conquer England—language mattered less than faith, and the repression of Catholics under the reign of Elizabeth I was firm. Although a relative appeasement occurred

43

L'Abenakis,

Quoy que ie parle des Derniers ie ne suis pas moins auiourd'huy
mon pere, vous sçauez que ie vous ay tousiours esté attaché
ie n'ay plus de haches vous l'auez mise dans vne fosse l'année
derniere et ie ne la reprendray que quand vous me l'ordonnerez

Les Gens Du Sault

Vous n'ignorez pas vous autres Iroquois que nous ne
soyons attachez a nostre pere nous qui demeurons auec luy
et qui sommes dans son sein, vous nous enuoyaste vn collier
il y a trois ans pour nous inuiter a vous procurer la paix
nous vous en enuoyasmes vn, en response, nous vous donnon
encore celuy cy pour vous dire que nous y auons trauaillé
nous ne demandons pas mieux qu'elle soit de durée faite
aussy devostre costé ce qu'il faut pour cela,

Les Gens dela Montagne

Vous auez faib assembler icy nostre pere toutes les
Nations pour faire vn amas de haches et les mettre
dans la terre, auec la vostre, pour moy qui n'en auoit pas
d'autre, ie me rejouy de ce que vous faites auiourd'huy, et
s'inuite Les Iroquois a nous regarder comme leurs freres &

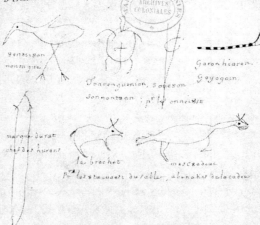

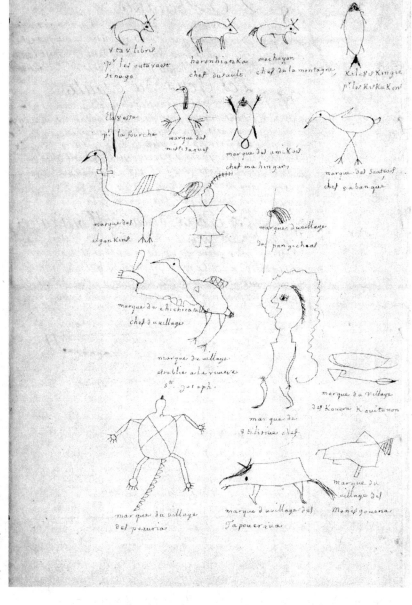

Copy of the ratification of the Great Peace of Montreal between the French and thirty-nine Aboriginal tribes, 1701 (detail).

under the reign of her successor, James I, the Stuart king who held the dual crown of England and Scotland as of 1603, the interdomina- tional violence resumed with renewed vigour in the mid-seventeenth century. From 1641 to 1659 the Civil War between the Royalists of Charles I—married to a French Catholic princess and suspected of being sympathetic to Rome—and Oliver Cromwell's Parliamentar- ians was devastating. Ireland was subjected to a systematic campaign of massacres and expropriations. Once the threat of Catholicism was eliminated with the Glorious Revolution of 1688 and the ascension to the throne of the Protestant William, Prince of Orange (the Nether- lands), the kingdom of Great Britain began to take shape with the Act of Union of England and Scotland in 1707. The union was strengthened under the sovereigns of the German Hanover dynasty, particularly dur- ing the reign of George III (1760–1820), the first king of the dynasty to speak English.

The management of the language issue was inscribed like filigree on the process of political and religious unification. As of 1487, English became the lingua franca of the kingdom, and particularly so following the dissemination of the English translation of the Bible, known as the King James Version, as of the beginning of the seventeenth century. After 1731 it was also the language of legislation and administration— that being the year when Parliament adopted an act referred to as "Use of English Language in the Law Courts Made Obligatory" (S.U.K., 4 George II, c.26), which imposed English in the courts of law in Eng- land, Wales, and Scotland, to the detriment of French and Latin. Still, a certain tolerance remained for other languages. The nobility conversed mostly in French, but also in German; the massive immigration of Huguenots in the seventeenth century and the prestige of French as the idiom of diplomacy through the following century influenced the popularity of using the language of Molière. In Wales, despite the lack of distinct institutions and a lengthier official connection to England, three-quarters of the population still spoke Welsh in the 1880s because of the transmission of that language through family networks. In Scot- land, given the persistence of the specific political and judicial institu- tions and the education system, the Presbyterian Scots conversed in Scottish Gaelic or broke into folkloric songs by the great poet Robert Burns. Although the Scots sustained a love-hate relation with their neighbours to the south, the English language spread among the Edinburgh and Glasgow elites who did business beyond Hadrian's Wall. A similar situation existed in the colony acquired on Manhattan Island in 1664. Although English was the lingua franca of business and politics in what became New York, the Dutch and (French-speaking) Huguenot descendants of the original colonists still spoke their native languages at the beginning of the eighteenth century, since, as the historian Joyce D. Goodfriend observes, women ensured the transmission of the mother tongue and their Protestant churches maintained a close relationship between faith and language. Another colony, Delaware—Nya Sverige or New Sweden until 1655—shared similar traits: at the beginning of the eighteenth century the Lutherans were still speaking the Swedish of their forebears. Better still, in their transactions with the indigenous peoples after 1638 the Swedish merchants developed a pidgin language, the Delaware jargon that William Penn mistook for the original language of the first inhabitants of the region.

The situation was significantly different in Ireland, where the Gaelic language did not benefit from the same latitude. The tenants who spoke Gaelic were Catholics, and therefore considered enemies of the Reformed faith. Beginning with the Tudor era, the royal authorities carried out a policy of anglicization, in particular through the implementation of an English justice system, the colonization of lands by English subjects, and conversions to Protestantism. Later, when Oliver Cromwell's troops sought to radically annihilate Catholics through carnage and deportations between 1649 and 1659, Gaelic went underground. Finally, following the Irish defeat at the Battle of the Boyne and the ratification of the Treaty of Limerick in 1691, the war against the supporters of the Catholic King James II ended with their exile into France. At that point a whole series of laws, referred to as Penal Laws, excluded Catholics from civil life, prohibiting them from entering into contracts and inheriting, marrying Protestants, voting and being elected to Parliament, and teaching and directing schools. This discriminatory regime lasted throughout the eighteenth century and at least until the Catholic Emancipation instituted by the Westminster Parliament in 1829. The conditions intensified the anglicization of the Irish, in particular members of the nobility and the inhabitants of cities such as Dublin.

To a certain extent the Irish experience would be mirrored in Acadia in 1755. After spending their first winter on Saint Croix Island in 1604, a French contingent sporadically resided on the shores of Fundy Bay. As of 1632, under Governor Isaac de Razilly, a settlement of several families from the southern Loire Valley, in particular Poitou, established a more permanent base around Port-Royal. Exposed to the English maritime attacks, the Acadian colony was tossed around according to the raids, to be finally ceded to London by the Treaty of Utrecht in 1713. Although they had become British subjects, the Acadians nevertheless preserved their Catholic missions and, because of their family-based education, continued to speak French. Furthermore, through the next forty years the Nova Scotia colony was a place of contrasting cultural and economic exchanges, for a number of reasons: the proximity to the French colony on Île Royale and the Fortress of Louisbourg, close relationships with the Mi'kmaq and Maliseet, the founding of Halifax with New England settlers, and the settlement of Germans at Lunenburg. However, English was the official language after 1749 with the adoption of Nova Scotia's colonial constitution and the instructions provided to Governor Edward Cornwallis that imposed the British Act of 1731 on the Use of English Language in the Law Courts Made Obligatory. The Seven Years War shattered the fragile balance. At the beginning of the conflict, in July 1755, the military governor Charles Lawrence summoned the Acadian leaders to Halifax to demand their complete allegiance to the Crown and force them to take an oath of allegiance to the Protestant king. Claiming neutrality, the Catholic leaders refused. The answer was not long in coming: Great Britain was at war, and the Acadians were considered rebels and de facto enemies. Subsequently British troops, applying methods well known in Ireland, deported two-thirds of the Acadians in Port-Royal, Grand-Pré, and their vicinities, separating families and confiscating their lands. Although some Acadians, such as Beausoleil Broussard, managed to take refuge in the woods to be in a better position to fight, others were dispersed to the thirteen American colonies and to Louisiana, the French colony of St. Domingue, Guyana, Canada, the Falkland Islands, and France. The Acadians who managed to remain, attempting to stay outside the scope of authority of the British king, faced an uncertain future until the end of the war. The clauses of the Capitulation of Montreal in 1760, drafted in French, as were those

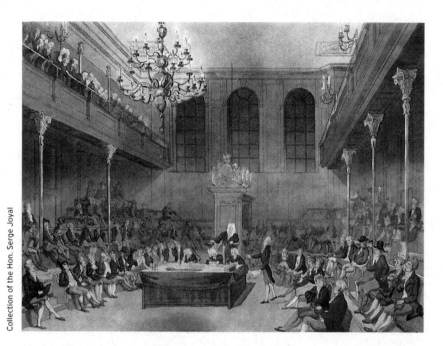

Collection of the Hon. Serge Joyal

The House of Commons, Westminster Palace, at the beginning of the nineteenth century. Engraving by J. Bluck based on a drawing by Pugin & Rowlandson, produced in London by R. Ackermann, 1808.

of the Capitulation of Quebec, bore witness to the rancour. The "Canadians"—as the occupants of the captured territory were called (later to be "French Canadians")—were immediately to become subjects of His Majesty of Great Britain based on the international laws of war; but that would not be the case for the Acadians who had taken refuge in Canada and remained rebellious subjects. They were allowed to come out of hiding and return to the Atlantic region only after the ratification of the peace treaty of 1763.

Emergence of a new language issue

The tragic episode of the Acadian deportation was a result of the beginning of the Seven Years War on American soil. The war would lead to the conquest of New France in 1760 and its cession to Great Britain by the Treaty of Paris in 1763.

The conquest took place at a key moment in Western political history. In the eighteenth century, Western political history was profoundly transformed by the development of modernity and the Age of Revolution, including the Industrial Revolution, American Revolution and French Revolution. Canada, which was redrawn within the new frontiers of the Province of Quebec in 1763, then within those of Lower Canada as of 1791, did not escape this intense movement of transformation. The context greatly influenced interlinguistic relations. By the end of this period, in 1848, new concepts not just of common interest and political communities, but also of the use of languages, would predominate.

One element of the transformation of the political culture rested on the issue of rights. In medieval political culture the king held most of the terrestrial sovereignty over his subjects, and granted privileges to them according to his whim and to the estate to which they belonged. The political community was, then, divided according to the requirements of the system of estates: those who fought, the nobility; those who prayed, the religious communities and the clergy; and those who worked, representing the vast majority of the subjects. Following the religious wars of the sixteenth and seventeenth centuries, which severely shook the foundations of the European kingdoms, the idea of having the political community become the depository of sovereignty was gaining force. According to such a concept, the individual would no longer receive benefits based on privileges arising from the arbitrary powers of the king; the individual would instead have rights and freedoms to which he or she was entitled by nature and in fact, irrespective of their status as noble, clergy, or tenants. The rights had to stem from a social consensus, and their definitions were bitterly debated, because they were linked to the maintenance of peace and public order. Therefore, the eighteenth century was the scene of numerous manifestations in the struggle for civil rights and freedoms, the very ones that ensured membership in a political community. For example, the freedoms of expression and religion and the right to private property became major issues and were often resolved only by force of arms, as in Ireland.

Mirroring transformations in Western political culture, the new regime that the British put in place in North America also faced battles to exercise rights: religious rights, and then language rights.

Although the Treaty of Paris was drafted in French, in keeping with diplomatic custom in the eighteenth century, its Article II already involved the use of English in the new colony of the British Empire. In establishing the Province of Quebec, the October 1763 Royal Proclamation diligently stated that the government had the power to adopt laws and statutes "as near as may be agreeable to the Laws of England and under such Regulations and Restrictions as are used in other Colonies." English and, especially, the Protestant faith therefore acquired their official character, with Catholic Canadians being excluded from decision-making positions. Conflicts were soon to break out between the supporters of a restrictive interpretation of the British laws and those who advocated a more liberal reading of them. Among those who favoured restrictions was a jurist of Huguenot descent, Francis Maseres, who in 1766, recalling the memory of James II in Ireland, deemed the Canadians to be "bigoted" in favour of "the Popist religion" and "unacquainted with, and hitherto prejudiced against, the laws and customs of England," while being "almost universally ignorant of the English language, so as to be absolutely incapable to debating in it."[2] Among the advocates of a more liberal approach were the ninety-four signatories of a petition sent to Governor James Murray in 1763. They asked, "What would become of the general good of the colony if those who make up the bulk of its population were to become useless members because of a difference in religion?"[3] Adopted at the dawn of the American Revolution, the Quebec Act of 1774 bought time by reinstating French civil law and liberalizing the practice of the Catholic religion, in particular by overturning the oath of allegiance, which had required Canadians to relinquish their allegiance to any foreign sovereign, who in this instance was the pope. Even though the measure greatly offended the American insurgents—who included it as one of their twenty-seven grievances in the declaration of the continental congress in Philadelphia justifying the independence of the Thirteen Colonies—the Quebec Act guaranteed the strong loyalty of the Canadian noblemen and members of the Catholic clergy during the war that unfolded in the following years.

Concluded in 1783, the Treaty of Versailles signalled both the end of the hostilities with the Thirteen Colonies and their independence as they went on to become a federal republic in 1789. Many inhabitants of the new United States spurned the verdict brought down by guns and diplomacy. Remaining loyal to the Crown, they took refuge in the British colonies to the north: Nova Scotia, New Brunswick, created in 1784, the territories immediately south of the Province of Quebec (which became known as the Eastern Townships), but mostly west of the Ottawa River in what would become Ontario. The Loyalists who ended up in the Province of Quebec did not want to be subjected to French customary law. Great pressure was also exercised to change the political regime. Following the recommendations of Governor Guy Carleton—then Lord Dorchester—and others, such as the postmaster, Hugh Finlay, Westminster adopted the Constitutional Act of 1791 (S.U.K., 31 George III, c. 31), which created two new provinces on each side of the Ottawa River: Upper Canada and Lower Canada. At the time of the tabling of the Act, the British prime minister William Pitt the Younger believed that "this division was hoped would put an end to the competition between the old French Inhabitants and the new settlers from Britain or British colonies."[4]

The international context greatly influenced the adoption of the Constitutional Act. Latent hostilities in the neighbouring American republic raised fear in the British colonial authorities and fostered the development of a garrison mentality, to reiterate the words of historian F. Murray Greenwood. But it was largely the European context that alarmed London and its colony. The French Revolution had just broken out, overthrowing the estates and proposing a model of citizens' rights that was triggering real sympathy throughout the West. In Great Britain, there were voices rejecting the French model; among them, Edmund Burke, author of *Reflections on the Revolution in France*, was the most eloquent. The member of Parliament from Dublin pitted the privilege of birthright against citizens' rights, which he considered abstract and dangerous; he believed that the exercise of freedom had necessary limitations and championed the idea of an inalienable heritage deriving from ancestors, intended to be transmitted to their descendants. His concept of heritage stemming from birthright ennobled the English in comparison to other nations. It became the ideological foundation of the British nationalism that emerged with the Industrial Revolution and blossomed throughout the famous Empire on which the sun would never set.

Edmund Burke (ca. 1730-97).
Engraving by Alonzo Chappel,
based on a portrait by Sir
Joshua Reynolds, produced
in New York by Johnson
and Wilson.

The conservative-leaning Whig Burke broke with his leader Charles Fox in May 1791, at the time of the parliamentary debates on the bill to create Upper and Lower Canada. The gesture, and especially the reasons invoked, had a huge repercussion throughout the Kingdom of Great Britain. Vigorously condemning "the horrible consequences flowing from the French idea of the rights of man,"[5] Burke believed that the British Protestants and Catholic Canadians could not be brought together under the same government: "an attempt to join people dissimilar in law, language, and manners" seemed to him "highly absurd."[6] Still, as he would later indicate to a young Irish colleague, religion no longer constituted a criterion of exclusion because, under the quasi-monarchic government of the Province of Quebec, "popish Canada was the only place which preserved its fidelity; the only place in which France got no footing; the only peopled colony which now remains to Great Britain."[7] Therefore, the Crown of Great Britain could have relative confidence in the Catholic nobles and their clergy. Remaining faithful to his doctrine on heritage and birthrights, the member from Dublin used a parliamentary debate to state the ethnic principle that would become the framework of political relations in Upper and Lower Canada: "Let the Canadians have a constitution formed upon the principles of Canadians, and Englishmen upon the principles of Englishmen."[8]

Adopted with the blessing of Edmund Burke, the Constitutional Act of 1791 (S.U.K., Geo. III, c.31), as historian Linda Colley notes, was part of a series of imperial reforms concerning India in 1784 and Ireland in 1800. The law aimed both to reinforce London's ascendency over its colonies and to appease the potential causes of discontent among subjects who might well be drawn to the revolutionary example—such people were numerous in Lower Canada, where most of the inhabitants were Catholics who spoke French. As a reflection of the dual movement of ascendency and appeasement, the Constitutional Act of 1791 renewed the Quebec Act inasmuch as it touched on seigneurial privileges and the rights of the Catholic Church in Lower Canada, while implementing an Elected Assembly with representatives of the population. Furthermore, it introduced a timid official recognition of French by factoring in an oath drawn up in both languages for the electors (Art. 24) and for the members of the Legislative Assembly and Council (Art. 29). Following the example of the other colonies populated by people from the British Isles, Upper Canada adopted English as the language of its political institutions. The political recognition of French applied only in Lower Canada.

Yet many loyal British subjects challenged this recognition: the principle of allegiance to the Crown could not allow any discrimination. For example, a debate surrounding the regulation on the statutory language of the House of Assembly in January 1793 both demonstrated the long-term stability of the norms of the estates in Lower Canada and raised the question of how Britain should deal with the language issue. In the debate two groups clashed: the members of British origin who could not envisage why a linguistic dispensation should be allowed in Lower Canada's parliamentary jurisdiction; and the Canadian members—mostly nobles—who were advocating the preservation of their language prerogatives in the context of loyalty expressed for the place of the sovereign. The partisan *Quebec Gazette* reported:

> The reasoners on the English side threw down a fair challenge to the others
> to show that such a claim as to enact laws in a foreign language was ever

granted by the British Nation to any other colony or province of the empire; or that other nations proceeded upon such a maxim as that claimed; they asserted that our laws here since the conquest have been uniformly made in English with a French translation, and that no petition to the Throne or Parliament from this Country have ever complained of it as a grievance.[9]

Obviously influenced by his readings of Burke, the member from Montreal West, John Richardson, even specified that "to be governed by laws made in the English Language is the birthright of every British subject; and no power on earth, but the British Parliament, can disfranchise him of that inherent privilege."[10]

The reply for the other camp was prompt. The member from York, the nobleman Michel-Eustache-Gaspard-Alain Chartier de Lotbinière, countered by recalling the privilege granted by the sovereign:

The greatest number of our electors having been placed in a unique position, we are obliged to push aside regular rules and compelled to request the use of a language that is not the language of the empire; but, to be as fair towards the others, as we hope they will be towards us, we would not wish that our language would come to banish that of the other subjects of Our Majesty; but we ask that both be allowed.

Invoking his own loyalty, he added:

We are convinced that the new subjects [the Canadians] are as dear [to George III] as the others. ... When a part of our constituents [the Canadian subjects] will be capable of understanding the language of the empire, then the time will have come to pass *all* our laws in the English enactment, but doing so before would be a cruel act that the best of kings, or his Parliament, would never want to allow.

Another nobleman, the member for Dorchester, Gabriel-Elzéar Taschereau, went even further by emphasizing that the Constitutional Act of 1791, "which makes us free ... decrees that the two principal legislative authorities [the executive and legislative councils] must join us" in using both languages, "in order to meet the caring intentions of His Majesty and His Parliament."[11] Following the debates, a compromise

The debate on language. A painting by Charles Huot (ca. 1910) commemorating the sitting of the Lower Canada Legislative Assembly, Jan. 21, 1793. Photo by Francesco Bellomo, Éditions Stromboli.

was reached to guarantee everyone's privileges: the House of Assembly of Lower Canada accepted the use of both French and English, but only the English version of laws had official status. In the end, as jurist Henri Brun and historian John Hare note, although French could not be used to express the current legislation, the language was not being deprived of a legal status—an initial ambiguity in the bilingualism entrenched in the laws of Lower Canada.

Nationalizing language

As the nineteenth century evolved, the political culture underwent a transformation: the values of the estates and the allegiance to a sovereign based on a religious denomination gradually faded; the ideals of nation and democracy blossomed; parliamentarism expanded; the modern state became solidly implanted. Even if it remained colonial, the state was capable of establishing its discipline through legal and bureaucratic rationality and an order based on individual rights and freedoms and scientific thinking. Within a liberal movement of the acknowledgement of rights, the battle slipped specifically towards the domain of political rights and freedoms that governed participation in the activities of the political community. The rights to vote and to run as a candidate in an election were at the heart of the debates. From 1807 to 1811, for example, under the government of James Henry Craig in Lower Canada, intense disputes took place concerning the eligibility of judges and of Ezekiel Hart, a Jew elected to the Legislative Assembly for the constituency of Trois-Rivières.

The issue of the relation between language and politics in British North America took on a new dimension. Edmund Burke's ideas gained special attention among the British established in the various provinces, whether they were Loyalists who had fled the Thirteen Colonies or immigrants who arrived after the Napoleonic Wars. His ideas created a bond between those who were worried about the French threat in Europe and the war against the United States waged from 1812 to 1815. They also used the Empire's victories and its expansion throughout the world as a pretext to emphasize the outstanding character of the British nationality, understood as the ethnic concept of the Anglo-Saxon *race*, a pseudo-scientific category with biological overtones, which gained great popularity as of the 1830s. For many loyal subjects, birthright had become the rationale that above all else justified the existing relations of domination, including the most violent manifestations. In 1849, in typically fiery prose, the Montreal *Gazette* editor James Moir Ferres goaded the Orange rioters to burn the building housing the Parliament of the United Canada in Montreal.[12] By the first half of the nineteenth century the English language had gained even more value in ethnic relations; it became the tongue that could presumably transmit the inalienable heritage of the Crown's subjects. From then on, the growth of a nationalist feeling among various ethnic groups in the British Empire required the nationalization of the English language; through this language were conveyed the relations of dominance, rights, and freedoms, according to their Burkean meaning, as well as the sense of belonging to the political regime.

The ethnic concept of political community was not without its competition. Another competing vision was in place—that of the republican ideal. Historian Louis-Georges Harvey mentions that this ideal—showing up, among other places, in the discourse of the Patriotes in Lower Canada—proposed a representation of the national collectivity in its territorial dimension, in its civic rather than ethnic incarnation, and was greatly inspired by the U.S. model, in particular by the model of democracy advocated by Thomas Jefferson and Andrew Jackson. Indeed, for the Louis-Joseph Papineau Patriotes, but also, to a certain extent, for the William Lyon Mackenzie Reformists in Upper Canada, the republican plan was the ultimate outcome of the journey of colonial history—that is to say, independence from the home country, like other republics in the New World. For the Patriotes, the sources of conflict were not so much to be found in the aspects of ethnic belonging, such as language, but rather in the ancient system of privileges, which led to the corruption of colonial institutions.

The quarrel surrounding the plan to unite the two Canadas clearly underlined the tensions between the ethnic and republican concepts. As put forward by James Stuart and other English merchants in Montreal, the plan aimed to promote the commercial development of the two colonies by uniting them under the same government and a single justice system, that of common law. The advocates of the law made no attempt to hide the goal of assimilation—the merchants believed that the homogenization of the population based on ethnic criteria would remove the obstacles to economic progress—and it was tabled in Westminster by Edward Ellice in June 1822. In particular, Article 24 of the bill foresaw that the official documents of the House of Assembly would be in English only, and that the parliamentary debates would be carried out only in that language for the next fifteen years.

As soon as the people of Upper and Lower Canada got wind of the unification plan, a storm broke out, and it revealed the divisions within the political community. A total of 68,739 voters in the two provinces—60,642 east of the Ottawa River, and 8,097 to the west—signed petitions against the bill on the Union. Their reasons for opposition differed. In Lower Canada the criticisms had republican undertones, with spokespersons insisting on common interests and the protection of rights. The petitioners—with Louis-Joseph Papineau and John Neilson as leaders—pointed out that the union would rekindle the disputes over language, laws, religion, and local interests, which would harm the objectives of having enlightened and beneficial legislation for all. Even worse, the prohibition of French in the House of Assembly would disqualify a great number of voters who did not speak English and deprive those loyal subjects of His

Majesty of their rights. In Upper Canada ethnic motivations prevailed. The petitioners from the counties of Stormont and Wentworth raised another element against the union: they did not have the same origin, religion, customs, or even the same institutions or language as the people of the neighbouring colony. They did not believe in the union of two bodies so heterogeneous and discordant, and had no commitment to the neighbouring province. Faced with such an imposing opposition, Westminster retreated in 1823.

Nonetheless, the consequences of the unification plan ran deep. Some Patriotes, such as Louis-Victor Sicotte in 1832, implicitly accepted the accuracy of Burke's conception of Lower Canada, seeing it as "a bad mix of interests, customs, language and religion that were deemed to collide sooner or later."[13] Yet, before the insurrections of 1837–38 most Patriotes still supported Papineau's republican ideal. The 92 Resolutions of 1834 clearly expressed the Patriotes' concept of the language issue: language was neither a transcendental characteristic of an ethnic group nor a reason for exclusion or subordination; its public use guaranteed citizens the fullness of their rights and freedoms, in particular in the resolution of disputes; in the exercise of the functions of the state, to not know or to ignore the language of the majority not only deprived certain individuals of their rights and freedoms, but was also greatly detrimental to the common interests because it violated laws and unduly favoured individual interests.

_ _ _ _ _ _ _ _ _ _ _ _ _ _ _

The 92 Resolutions (1834)

52. Resolved, – That since a circumstance, which did not depend upon the choice of the majority of the people, their French origin and their use of the French language, has been made by the colonial authorities a pretext for abuse, for exclusion, for political inferiority, for a separation of rights and interests, this House now appeals to the justice of His Majesty's Government and of Parliament, and to the honour of the people of England; that the majority of the inhabitants of this country are in nowise disposed to repudiate any one of the advantages they derive from their origin and from their descent from the French nation, which, with regard to the progress of which it has been the cause of civilization, in the sciences, in letters, and the arts, has never been behind the British nation, and is now the worthy

rival of the latter in the advancement of the cause of liberty and of the science of Government; from which this country derives the greatest portion of its civil and ecclesiastical law, and of its scholastic and charitable institutions, and of the religion, language, habits, manners and customs of the great majority of its inhabitants. ...

76. Resolved, – That this partial and abusive practice of bestowing the great majority of official places in the province on those only who are the least connected with its permanent interests, and with the mass of its inhabitants, has been most especially remarkable in the judicial department, the judges for the three great districts having, with the exception of one only in each, been systematically chosen from that class of persons, who, being born out of the country, are the least versed in its laws, and in the language and usages of the majority of its inhabitants; ... the majority of the said judges have introduced great irregularity into the general system of our jurisprudence, by neglecting to ground their decisions on its recognized principles; and that the claim laid by the said judges to the power of regulating the forms of legal proceedings in a manner contrary to the laws, and without interference of the legislature, has frequently been extended to the fundamental rules of the law and of practice; and that in consequence of the same system, the administration of the criminal law is partial and uncertain, and such as to afford but little protection to the subject, and has failed to inspire that confidence which ought to be its inseparable companion.

77. Resolved, – That in consequence of their connexion with the members of the Provincial Administrations, and of their antipathy to the country, some of the said judges have, in violation of the laws, attempted to abolish the use in the courts of law of the language spoken by the majority of the inhabitants of the country, which is necessary to the free action of the laws, and forms a portion of the usages guaranteed to them in the most solemn manner by the law of the nations and by statutes of the British Parliament.

Source: Quoted in Théophile-Pierre Bédard, Histoire de cinquante ans (1791-1841): Annales parlementaires et politiques du Bas-Canada depuis la Constitution jusqu'à l'union, *Quebec, Léger-Brousseau, 1869, pp.349-77. English translation from "Statutes, Treaties and Documents of the Canadian Constitution, 1713-1929,"* Early Canadiana Online, *http://www.canadiana.org/view/9_03428/300/650/0.*

A few days before the battles of 1837, the republican discourse on the language issue remained firmly in place. Drafted by Wolfred Nelson, Amaury Girod, and others, the address of the Confederation of the Six Counties called to mind that "God did not create any artificial distinctions between man" and the people remained "the only legitimate source of all power"; it called upon citizens "of all origins, languages and religions" to prepare to defend their principles.[14] Written by Robert Nelson in February 1838, the Declaration of Independence of Lower Canada represented the last stand of the republican ideal. It was steadfast in its faithfulness to civic values, recognizing the use of both languages in all public matters.

The relation between language and politics was not confined solely to the issue of the recognition of French or English in the political community. With the Industrial Revolution underway, and with the development of the era of nations and the rise of the "Springtime of the Peoples" (the European Revolutions of 1848), this relation also raised the question of how language would be transmitted to the younger generations. It seemed crucial that the political community—whether in the form of a full or partial nation, an ethnic group, or a republic—be capable of renewing itself, being part of a historical continuity, developing itself socially and expanding economically. From the beginning of the nineteenth century, political leaders in the British North American colonies were preoccupied with the establishment of a modern and efficient school system capable of making sure children learned to read and write and were prepared to face the industrial labour market. In this endeavour language was of crucial importance: mastering it through education would make it possible for citizens not only to participate in political life and transmit the values inherent to their national culture and heritage, but also acquire wealth through commerce or industry. The trilingual clerks in the Jersey fishing companies in the Gaspé and elsewhere around the Gulf of St. Lawrence were trained in Anglo-Norman schools, for instance, and they gladly used their mother tongue to speak to each other so that their English and French fishing clients could not understand what they were saying.

In a colonial society split by ethno-linguistic divisions, where one group has better access to the political institutions of the home country, the linguistic conditions had a material basis, that of the relation between capital and labour. Consequently, the political debates surrounding the education system became focused on the inequality in the sharing of capital, a situation increasingly rooted in language.

The experience of the Acadians at the beginning of the nineteenth century clearly demonstrated the importance of the language of instruction within the education system. Following the Deportation of 1755, the Acadians had gradually returned to the Maritime Provinces. As of 1780 in Nova Scotia, 1802 in New Brunswick, and 1825 in Prince Edward Island these colonies adopted education laws creating local schools—the grammar schools—and setting out the rules for the qualification of teachers. Initially the networks of schools were financed by parent contributions, and in most cases the schools were compelled to propagate the values of the Anglican Church. Confined to the poorest lands and the less lucrative fishing activities, the Acadians often practised a subsistence economy in which the participation of all the members of the family was crucial. For these families, financing a school proved to be a difficult goal, and as a result it was frequently French missionaries, such as Father Jean-Mandé Sigogne, or Canadian missionaries, such the fathers André-Toussaint Lagarde and Jean-Louis Beaubien, who taught children to read and write. After the War of 1812, and especially during the 1820s, the various Maritime Provinces subsidized the networks of primary schools, including the Acadian schools. Nova Scotia even created a uniform school system in 1841, in which the teaching of German, Gaelic, and French was tolerated. However, because of fiscal constraints, access to higher education was limited for French-speaking Acadians. Created in Memramcook in 1854, the Séminaire Saint-Thomas, the first college offering education in French, had to close down in 1862 because of a lack of funds. It was followed by the founding of the Collège Saint-Joseph in 1864, under the aegis of Father Camille Lefebvre. From 1789 to 1855, no less than ten colleges and universities, all denominational, were established in the Maritimes. Although some institutions, such as St. Mary's and St. Francis Xavier in Nova Scotia, were Catholic, none of them provided courses in French.

In Lower Canada the question of the linguistic relations between capital and labour was raised early in the nineteenth century. The key indicator of this power struggle was the knowledge and quality of the language spoken at work. For example, during his stay in Lower Canada from 1807 to 1809, John Lambert had rather unkind words regarding the ignorance of the Canadians when it came to the English language. He attributed this failing to the Catholic clergy and its refusal to teach English in schools. He also observed a strange "jargon" used in the marketplaces, some turns of phrases filled with anglicisms, used between French- and English-speaking people who did not understand each other. As the linguist Chantal Bouchard indicates, at the beginning of the 1830s Michel Bibaud and Alexis de Tocqueville each reported separately that French among Canadians had been contaminated by English, especially among those whose work or profession had led them to deal with the British on a daily basis.

And so, in this instance also, the relation between capital and labour had an impact on the issue of education. Following the Conquest in 1760, many schools were closed. Having become impoverished, the Catholic clergy could no longer provide for the maintenance of schools and, after the death of the last Jesuit in 1800, the Province of Lower Canada claimed the goods of this religious order, which had been dissolved by Pope Clement XIV in 1773. Faced with the new requirements of the economy, and bent on assimilation, the colonial authorities, spurred by Governor Robert Shore Milnes, set up a public school network in 1801, known as the Royal Institution for the Advancement of Learning. Its goal, as the *Quebec Gazette* of January 15, 1801, stated, was "the establishing of a competent number of free schools for the instruction of their children in the first rudiments of useful learning, and in the English tongue." [15] The measure was a failure; only about thirty schools were opened in the following fifteen years, most of them among the British population, because the Catholic clergy refused to collaborate with a system that it found too favourable to Protestantism. Consequently, the House of Assembly adopted the Loi des écoles de Fabrique [Fabrique schools act] (S.B.C., 4 George IV, c. 31) in 1824, to spread the principles of a moral education and, in so doing, contribute to the growth of industry and agriculture. In this case also, notwithstanding the opening of some sixty parish schools, the success was mixed, because financing was not constant. With the adoption of the Loi pour encourager l'éducation élémentaire [Act to encourage elementary education], called "*loi des écoles de syndics*" [schools under public trustees act] (S.B.C., 9 George IV, c. 46), promoted by the Parti Patriote, the colonial state intervened to "spread the benefits of education to all the classes of His Majesty's subjects in the Province." Based on this very republican ideal, schools now received provincial subsidies managed by representatives elected by taxpayers. This time the approach proved successful: by 1836 no less than 1,600 schools under public trustees were in place, offering instruction in the language used by the majority of the local population. In that same year Governor Archibald Acheson, Count of Gosford, raised the ire of the Patriotes when he ordered an end to the subsidies. For a few tumultuous years the schools were financially suffocated.

The insurrections of 1837–38 demonstrated the state's need to restore order as the basis of social progress and economic prosperity. With the repression of the Patriotes the republican ideal—that of a strong state capable of guaranteeing rights and freedoms for all citizens, whatever their condition and origin—was at least for a long while removed from the political horizon. Clearly, if the modern state was going to achieve maximum legitimacy and efficiency in the colonies, those in authority would have to push for the homogenization of the political community. The favoured criteria now became based on ethnicity: origin, religion, and customs would mobilize the institutions of civil society. To implement the homogenization, several political leaders proposed a series of measures: the creation of stable political structures through the union of the two provinces and ministerial responsibility, the reform of the previous regime through the abolition of the seigneurial system, and the overhaul of civil law. Some, going even further, promoted a single means of communication between individuals—a single language—rooted in the education system, an approach that would presumably obliterate ethnic differences through assimilation.

The 1839 report by John George Lambton, Lord Durham, summed up this vast program. Mirroring the prejudices of the conquering Anglo-Saxon bourgeoisie, the Durham Report clearly represented what is called "the Whig interpretation of history" with its focus on the principles of past progress to produce a narrative of ratification and glorification of the present. According to this interpretation, the dominant position of the United Kingdom in the global capitalist system was the product of a remarkable economic growth, an equally exceptional social mobility, and a flawless progression in political freedoms. The supporters of the Whig interpretation ranked historical actors and peoples according to the contribution those actors or peoples made to the progress of liberalism and democracy, or the reverse—how those features were delayed—with liberalism and democracy being understood in terms of the British model. In drafting the report, Lord Durham—who earned the nickname of "Radical Jack" because of his total adherence to Whig liberalism—did a historical analysis of the relations between the two ethno-linguistic groups. He believed that the French institutions during the colonization of North America were "perhaps, more than those of other European nations, calculated to repress the intelligence and freedom of the great mass of the people." [16] Therefore, French settlers would have experienced the same centralizing and incompetent despotism as the one imposed on the other French subjects in the home country. Durham condescendingly believed that the French colonists were an ignorant, apathetic, and reactionary people controlled by the Church. Given that two peoples initially hostile and dissimilar were being brought together under a common government, but with different institutions, "each was taught to cherish its own language, laws, and habits." [17] The governor concluded that the conflict rested in "the vain endeavour to preserve a French-Canadian nationality in the midst of Anglo-American colonies and states." [18] He believed that assimilation was the solution to ensuring both social and economic progress and civil peace. Inspired by the case of Louisiana, where "the Union is never disturbed by the quarrels of these races; and the French language and manners bid fair, in no long time, to follow their laws, and pass away like the Dutch peculiarities of New York," Lord Durham proposed that the same treatment—that is, "a popular government, in which the English majority shall permanently predominate"—would provide, if promptly applied, a remedy to the disorders and a way of ensuring peace in Lower Canada. [19]

Lord Durham's push for assimilation was not limited to the union of the two Canadas. It also applied to the field of education, where the logic was also shared by several political leaders. Arthur William Buller, one of Lord Durham's investigators and a member of the Special Council of Lower Canada in 1838, became the champion of a single public system based on the model implemented in Ireland.

The language of the school system was to be English, and the system was to be based in the Christian religion in general (rather than Catholicism or any other particular Christian denomination) and financed by local communities. Buller presented his goals in plain language to the Quebec bishop, Mgr. Joseph Signay. Given the distinctions in race and religion prevalent in Lower Canada, each institution, he said, must necessarily be designed "with a view of uniting and nationalizing its entire population." In so doing, "the children that are brought up together in the same schools and play together and are punished together become friends."[20] Buller's naive optimism met with strong opposition from the clerics of various religious denominations who wanted to preserve their exclusive hold on education in the classroom, as well as from French-speaking members who were concerned by both the harshness of the proposed measures and the harmful consequences of assimilation.

Buller's project rapidly died a natural death. Having decided to abandon setting up a new school system, in 1842 the provincial leaders created the position of superintendent of public instruction for both the West and East parts of the United Canada. As historian Lucia Ferretti points out, this step avoided the anglicization goals of Buller's project. Following the "*guerre des éteignoirs*" in 1846—a controversy over the payment of property taxes for all the schools—the province had to finance part of the construction and maintenance of the educational institutions.

From then on, the churches took the initiative in matters concerning education, including the Catholic Church under the leadership of the energetic bishop of Montreal, Mgr. Ignace Bourget. In the wake of the Ultramontane revival flourishing in Europe, Mgr. Bourget attributed the recent insurrections to the disorders caused by modern liberalism and anticlericalism. He believed that French Canada needed to be rechristianized through the revival of religious practices, guidance of the faithful by clerics and the various Catholic congregations, and the use of the religious press as managed by laypersons. Furthermore, as sociologist Fernand Dumont and historian Roberto Perin note, rechristianization in a United Canada took place because of an ethnic church, comprising mostly French Canadians who were also heading its hierarchy.

Finally, since the creation of confessional school boards in Montreal and Quebec City in 1845, the Catholic revival came under the control of the educational institutions, from primary school through classical colleges to university, with the involvement of an increasing number of personnel from various teaching orders from France—the Clerics of St. Viateur, Jesuits and Oblates of Marie-Immaculée—or new congregations. From Eastern Canada, the operation of control expanded west of the Ottawa River. Mgr. Joseph-Eugène-Bruno Guigues, the new bishop of Bytown (Ottawa), founded Collège Saint-Joseph in 1848 to provide Catholic Ontarians with classical education in both languages. The Collège became the University of Ottawa in 1866, a few years after the creation of Université Laval in Quebec City.

In what was now French Canada, the nationalization of the French language—one of the consequences of the assimilation policy during the Union—went together with the dominance of Catholicism. With the control of Catholics over educational institutions, among others, the link between language and religion became secured during the 1840s. As a space of autonomous power vis-à-vis the state, entrenched in its community, offering a universal dimension, the Catholic Church took on a leading responsibility in the definition of the French-Canadian nation, as Fernand Dumont observes. The link between language and faith was to remain solid until the dawn of the Quiet Revolution in Quebec.

— — — — —

The Durham Report, combined with the Act of Union of 1840, whose Article 41 established English as the exclusive official language, provoked a major shock wave in the British North American colonies. For the Canadians (who were then becoming French Canadian), it sent a strong signal that the state would no longer be the only guarantor of their collective existence. It would be the role of the nation to guarantee henceforth the conditions of survival by relentlessly fighting for "our language, our institutions, our laws," as Étienne Parent put it. French was no longer a simple mode of communication, or a code on which to base social distinctiveness. Like a canary in a mine, French indicated either the strength of the fighting nation or its humiliations in facing the threatening breakthroughs of assimilation. Its use in

Louis-Hippolyte La Fontaine around 1840.

public became a manifestation of the strategies of the French-speaking population against the disciplinary order that sought to push it to the margins of the political space. The time had finally come for French to be nationalized, as English had been, but in a context of domination in which it was clearly at a disadvantage. From then on, the fight for the recognition of French was to be combined with the struggle for the political recognition of the French-Canadian nation.

This shift explains the symbolic importance of the debates surrounding French within the parliamentary chambers during the period of United Canada. In 1842, in response to the member from Toronto City, John Henry Dunn, who was commanding him to speak in English because "the honourable gentleman could speak English very well," Louis-Hippolyte La Fontaine asserted his right to use French in the House of Commons, given his ethnic roots. "Has he [J.H. Dunn] already forgotten that I belong to an origin so horribly mistreated by the Act of Union?"[21] shot back the member from York-Fourth-Riding:

I must inform the honourable member, and the other honourable members, and the public that, daringly appealing to a sense of justice, and regardless if my knowledge of the English language is as familiar to me as that of the French language, I will nonetheless give my first speech in the language of my French-Canadians compatriots, if only to protest against the cruel injustice of this part of the Act of Union that aims to ban the mother tongue of half the population of Canada. I owe it to my compatriots; I owe it to myself.[22]

As of that moment, in this united regime in which the bourgeoisie would gain power and ministerial responsibility in 1848, the political issue of language appeared to be taking on a new shape, a modern form.

CHAPTER 2

THE FIRST LANGUAGE TREMORS

- -

The school crises in Canada, 1848-1927

For he might have been a Roosian,
A French, or Turk, or Proosian,
Or perhaps Itali-an! . . .
But in spite of all temptations
To belong to other nations,
He remains an Englishman!
He remains an Englishman!
  - William S. Gilbert and Arthur Sullivan,
    For He Is an Englishman (H.M.S. Pinafore)

Ô notre Histoire! écrin de perles ignorées!
Je baise avec amour tes pages vénérées.
Registre immortel, poème éblouissant
Que la France écrivit du plus pur de son sang!
  - Louis Fréchette, *La Légende d'un peuple*

During the period of 1848 to 1927 the new political culture conveyed the values of the conquering bourgeoisie, characterized by state activism in language-planning policies. In 1848 the members of the United Province of Canada Assembly restored French as a language of use, eliminating one of the irritants in the Act of Union of 1841. In 1927 the government of George Howard Ferguson in Ontario amended school regulations that had limited the use of French as a language of instruction. Between these two pivotal years, the language issue was dominated by the question of its place in schools.

The issue symbolized the tension between the state's decision to homogenize the population within a given territory and the citizens' *will to live collectively* and participate in the political community through the exercise of rights and liberties—which was a key dimension of the new liberal order that came into being in the Age of Revolution and the rise of the bourgeoisie to positions of power. The school issue was also at the core of the transmission of community values because it was through schools that the nation would ensure its own permanence. The issue also had much to do with the relations between capital and labour because the mastering of the language of work and a resultant engagement in the economy would ensure better access to resources. As a result, the major school conflicts revolved around the right of French-Canadian and Acadian minorities to use their own language as they went about their everyday lives.

The conflicts, experienced in several provinces, reverberated throughout Canada. Section 133 of the Constitution Act of 1867 entrenched French and English as official languages in the country, but the reach of that law was limited to parliamentary institutions and federal and Quebec courts. In Section 93 of the act the designers of the federal pact granted responsibility for education to the provinces, while protecting the rights of the religious minorities in Quebec and Ontario to their own schools. Throughout the following years, various provincial governments took action that demonstrated the limits of the rights granted to Catholics, namely by putting an end to the financing of denominational schools: this was the case in Nova Scotia in 1864, before it entered Confederation, New Brunswick in 1871, and Manitoba in 1890. Subsequently the legislatures of the Northwest Territories (1892), Ontario (1912), Manitoba (1916), and Saskatchewan (1931) established English as the sole language of instruction.

These conflicts crystallized opinions and gave rise, among other things, to a continuing debate on the French-Canadian minority's

The Parliament of United Canada in Quebec in 1852. Lithography by Sarony and Major, New York.

enshrined rights. They challenged in particular the nature of the political compromise that had created the Canadian Confederation in 1867. The conflicts also reflected the passionate promotion of a model for a unified political community, a national model based on ethnic characteristics—origin, religion, language, and memory—that would provide in Canada, and the British Empire in general, a prominent position to a specific group: the Anglo-Saxon community. As a result, the period between 1848 and 1927 witnessed critical transformations in the relations between language and politics. Although religious denominations were at the heart of the conflicts at the outset, language gradually gained ground to become the main issue of nationalist struggles. A mastery of the language became essential not only in the encouragement of socio-economic development, but also in the manifestation of a sense of belonging to a national community, and to its memory. In the first decades of the twentieth century, the language issue became a central question within the federation.

Prohibiting in a context of fear

Outside Quebec, Acadian and French-Canadian communities faced language and school policies that promoted linguistic assimilation. For them, the state had become an instrument of oppression in the hands of the Anglo-Saxon community, which represented the majority in Canada but was nevertheless troubled by the arrival of more than three million immigrants between 1896 and 1914. Unlike the migratory waves at the beginning of the nineteenth century, when newcomers arrived mostly from the British Isles, those at the beginning of the twentieth century came from Eastern Europe and, to a lesser extent, Asia. Even so, to reassure the citizens of British Columbia, some of whom were downright hostile to the presence of Asians, the federal government passed discriminatory regulatory measures aimed at limiting substantially the entry of those immigrants in particular.

Influenced by the theories of social Darwinism and the belief that Canada should be shaped in the image of the Anglo-Saxon race, members of the dominant community, imbued with the tradition of defending Protestantism, chose the policy of assimilation as a key response to the challenge of managing cultural diversity. Immigrants from population pools outside of Great Britain or the United States had to abandon cultures and beliefs that would prevent integration into the Anglo-Canadian community. In taking up this task of wiping out immigrants' strongly held cultural references, the school system emphasized socialization and valorization of the Empire and its symbols, but its most effective tool was the imposition of English as the common language. If the newcomers learned to master the language of Shakespeare, the theory went, they could become better integrated into society, respectful of public order, and able to advance themselves economically.

For First Nations and Inuit peoples the case was rather different. The new political culture of 1840–50 destroyed the old system of alliances with the Aboriginal tribes and established a justice system based on the values of the conquering bourgeoisie, including, as one of those values, the principle of private property. From then on, an inconsistent logic guided relations with Aboriginal peoples: to become enfranchised and gain full membership and participation rights in the political community they had to abandon their traditional values and assimilate with the developing civilization. As of 1850 in Canada East, and 1857 in Canada West, Canadian authorities adopted laws "for the Gradual Civilization of the Indian Tribes in the Canadas." In accordance with these laws, whose spirit was carried into the Indian Act of 1876, every male adult who demonstrated a good moral behaviour, who was free of debt and able to read and write—especially English—could become enfranchised. In the meantime, First Nations peoples and Inuit were granted only the status of minors in the eyes of the state and confined to reserves, where they could presumably become gradually "civilized" and assimilated. Since the Canadian Prairies and the Rockies were, according to the Dominion of Canada, a *terra nullius* (land belonging to no one), the state took possession of those lands through a series of treaties in which the Aboriginal peoples gave up their rights of ownership. Furthermore, the implementation of the sadly famous residential schools everywhere in Canada after 1883 removed Aboriginal children from their homes and cultures and even more forcibly pushed for language assimilation. As Elders increasingly became the only ones to retain the various First Nations and Inuit languages, the original voices went through difficult times; the first Aboriginal language-teaching programs in reserves appeared only a century later, in the 1980s.

In managing the difficulties of cultural diversity and the assimilation policy, the Anglo-Saxon community faced another more complex case: that of the French Canadians. Some French-Canadian communities outside Quebec—for example, in the Winnipeg and Windsor regions—had established themselves early on as settlers under the French regime. Spokespersons in the Anglo-Saxon community now likened them to ethnic groups participating in the effort of populating the country and pressured the provincial governments to deliver a clear message to everybody who refused to comply with the Protestant Anglo-Saxon model. The linguistic, cultural, and religious assimilation of non-Christian ethnic groups was a given, but for intellectuals such as George Monro Grant, George Parkin, and Sir Andrew Macphail, who were supporters of the British Empire, French Canada was inexorably destined to be based in a British North America; they deemed the battle of French-Canadian militants like political leader and publisher Henri Bourassa to be harmful because such a battle was contrary to the march of history. The Anglo-Saxon majority tolerated the French presence in Quebec, as long as it accepted the Anglo-Saxon's vision of the world. As soon as French Canadians left Quebec to settle elsewhere in the country, they had to accept that they would from then on be living in a territory dominated by a community of English-language speakers and culture.

When the provinces enacted laws to preserve and promote the Anglo-Saxon character of their territories, they received indirect support from the Vatican. Conflicts over schooling demonstrated that Rome's objectives were often incompatible with French-Canadian and Acadian communities that were attempting to preserve schools in which French was the language of instruction. While the Catholic hierarchy in Quebec was controlled by French Canadians, in the Maritime provinces the Church leadership, after separating from the Diocese of Quebec in 1818, was dominated by the Irish. The Acadian clergy struggled to carve a place for itself within this hierarchy. Indeed, the Acadians did gradually improve their situation. Their clergy managed to lead part of the Catholic hierarchy in the twentieth century, at least in New Brunswick, after the appointment of Mgr. Édouard-Alfred Le Blanc as bishop of the Diocese of Saint John. Moreover, priests such as Mgr. Marcel-François Richard were among those spearheading the national project in Acadia, which took shape during the congresses in Memramcook in 1881, Miscouche in 1884, and Pointe-de-l'Église in 1890.

In Western Canada the situation was reversed; French Canadians solidly held the reins of the Catholic hierarchy. However, according to the authorities in Rome, in the missions of Western Canada English would become the dominant language. In their respective reports drafted in 1903 and 1913 after touring Western Canada, the apostolic delegates from Rome, Mgr. Donato Sbarretti and Mgr. Francesco Pellegrino Stagni, indicated that the new dioceses to be created should be led by "English-speaking bishops."[1] The arrival of large numbers of immigrants meant that the francophone bishops had to struggle to retain control. It proved to be a losing battle because, as had been the case for francophone Catholics in the Maritimes, the Vatican promoted the assimilation of North America Catholics into the anglophone majority. Gradually the domination of the francophone bishops in the West crumbled, despite the efforts of the archbishop of Saint-Boniface, Mgr. Louis-Philippe-Adélard Langevin, to contain the German, Polish, Irish, and Flemish Catholics by attracting bilingual[2] and sometimes multilingual priests to be in charge of education and pastoral work—in response to pressure from these groups. In 1912 the archbishop of Saint-Boniface lost his battle for the appointment of a French Canadian as head of the Diocese of Calgary. In 1914 and 1915 Irish Catholics in the Diocese of

BANQ, centre d'archives de Quebec, P1000, S4, D83, PB90-2

Henri Bourassa, member of the
Quebec Legislative Assembly
from 1908 to 1912.

Saint-Boniface approached the Vatican to propose the division of the
diocese and to request that one of their own be appointed head of the
future bishopric of Winnipeg; their petition was granted. In 1921 the
new archbishop of Edmonton spoke only English. From the Vatican's
point of view, Catholics had to opt for what was essential in the school
conflicts, which meant the preservation of their faith and not their
language. When Mgr. Francis Bourne, the archbishop of Westminster
in England, bluntly reminded participants of this principle at the 1910
International Eucharistic Congress, he drew a fierce reply from Henri
Bourassa, who demanded the same rights for his fellow countrymen as
those held by the Irish: "to pray to God in the language of their race and
country, the blessed language of their fathers and mothers." [3]

In the Maritime provinces, given the state's intervention in education, the question of denominational schools caused major upheavals
that had an impact on the language issue. In 1864, under the aegis of
Charles Tupper, the Nova Scotia Assembly enacted a law establishing
a non-denominational educational system: it imposed English as the
language of instruction, to the detriment of French and Gaelic, even
though those other languages had been officially recognized since
1841. After 1902 in Nova Scotia, the Liberal government of George

H. Murray allowed the use of French as the language of instruction during the first three years of primary school. The province of Prince Edward Island had taken this step in 1877. However, a similar measure taken in New Brunswick in 1871 set off a Canada-wide political crisis. Confronted with a bill proposed by Attorney General George E. King stipulating that schools would be non-denominational, the Catholics in the province, Acadians as well as Irish, requested that the Dominion of Canada intervene to restore their schools. Their request was fruitless because the motion, tabled by Member of Parliament John Costigan, was rejected by the majority in the House of Commons. The behaviour of the federal caucus, particularly of George-Étienne Cartier, leader of the Quebec Conservatives, raised the ire of the bishop of Montreal, Mgr. Ignace Bourget, who stated his firm belief that the duty of the Dominion was to "do and sacrifice everything it could to protect the weak against the strong."[4] The duty of the Catholic members of Parliament, he said, was to ask themselves if they could vote for non-denominational schools. As the study of Ignace Bourget by historian Roberto Perin reveals, the bishop of Montreal put pressure on the Catholic newspaper Le Nouveau Monde to denounce the leader of the Quebec Conservatives. This gesture created uneasiness among the clergy: on the eve of the 1872 federal elections, some of its members feared that the defeat of Cartier would harm their capacity to influence the Conservative government to adopt the objectives of the Catholic Church. The John A. Macdonald Conservatives were re-elected, but without Cartier, who was defeated in his riding of Montreal East— though he was elected a few months later in the riding of Provencher, in Manitoba. The Canadian Pacific Railway scandal caused the fall of the Conservatives a year later.

Mgr. Bourget did not throw in the towel on the arrival of the Liberals, because he believed that the cause of the Catholics and their right to denominational schools were legitimate, though the turn of events made him bitter. Court decisions confirmed the constitutionality of the law and, with civil disobedience encouraged by the Catholic clergy, among others—a refusal to pay school taxes, the creation of alternative schools—tension heightened. In 1875 in Caraquet, N.B., a riot led to the deaths of two people, one of whom was Louis Mailloux, who immediately became a symbol of the Acadian resistance.

Following this crisis, members of Parliament once again reached a decision on the New Brunswick school issue. On the one hand, they rejected a motion that would have amended the Canadian Constitution to protect the rights of Catholics in the province. On the other, they asked the prime minister to encourage the New Brunswick government to respect the school rights of its Catholic population. The premier of New Brunswick, George E. King, gained time by proposing a compromise to the Catholics that would allow teaching by religious communities and religious teaching after school hours.

The battle for French rights raged on in Manitoba, a province created in 1870 after the Métis uprisings led by Louis Riel in 1869 and 1870. Riel and the Métis opposed the move by federal authorities to take possession of the Prairie region without considering the inhabitants' land-holding rights and requests regarding language rights. Admittedly, by sending in militia, the Dominion of Canada intended to quell what it defined as a rebellion. Nevertheless, it was obliged to negotiate with representatives of a provisional government established by the Métis. The 1870 Manitoba constitution, at least with regard to school and language rights, drew on the situation in Quebec. Section 22 guaranteed the existence of denominational schools, and Section 23 recognized French as one of the two official languages in the province.

With the Dominion pushing for settlement of the West, Canadians and immigrants arrived in the new province, changing the religious and linguistic balance within its territory. The proportion of Catholics and French Canadians was reduced, as reflected in decennial census figures. While in 1871 Catholics formed 45 per cent of Manitoba's population, ten years later they represented only 18.56 per cent. During the same period, the numbers of French Canadians and Métis were similarly reduced as a proportion of the population, to 25 per cent and 15 per cent respectively.

Given these demographic changes, the position of Manitoban activists in favour of cultural homogenization prevailed in 1890. Eager to turn the school system into a tool of cultural assimilation, Attorney General Joseph Martin, a member of the government led by Thomas Greenway since 1888, introduced a law to eliminate the financing of denominational schools. He also spearheaded the adoption of the Act

LAC, C-062552, Canadian Illustrated News, Feb. 13, 1875

The 1875 riot in Caraquet according to *Canadian Illustrated News*. The magazine illustrated the death of Constable Gifford, turning a blind eye on that of Louis Mailloux.

to Provide That the English Language Shall Be the Official Language of the Province of Manitoba, which, as its title indicated, abolished French as an official language.

The abolition of French and the lack of financial support for denominational schools drastically transformed the symbolic capital of the province, particularly with regard to how Manitoba defined itself and projected itself outward. This was the province's response to the challenge of managing ethnic diversity. By the same token, the gestures compelled the Manitoba House of Assembly to allocate administrative resources for the enforcement of this major reframing of the social contract linking Manitobans to their province. Admittedly, the Manitoba House of Assembly had the power to legislate and regulate. Yet in implementing laws and regulations, and especially in tracking their enforcement, the province relied on various agents, and some of those were not necessarily civil servants.

The state's action raised concern among Catholics—especially the Métis and French Canadians, because the vast majority of them shared this faith. In 1892 and 1909 the courts ruled against the law abolishing French as an official language, but the governments of Thomas Greenway and Rodmont Palen Roblin disregarded the judgments. Moreover, the province relied on municipalities to enforce its new education law, adopted in 1890. As Perin found in his research on the Vatican and the school crises in Canada, whenever francophone Catholics within a sector represented the majority of a municipal council, they expected to be able to mitigate the effects of the provincial law. Such councils sought to reserve part of the municipal taxes intended for the so-called "neutral" schools, which, though they were not called denominational schools, were indeed of that nature because Catholics attended them and the teaching staff was Catholic. The situation was different in municipalities in which the francophone Catholics were a minority, particularly in urban centres such as Winnipeg and Brandon. There, Catholics were faced with a kind of double taxation. Not only did they have to pay municipal taxes to finance schools that their children did not attend, but they also necessarily had to pick up the costs of a private school if they chose to send their children to one.

The reality of double taxation drove parents, often with the support of the clergy, to attempt to steer the action of the Province of Manitoba in a different direction, but the steps they took were in vain. This provincial crisis reverberated in other parts of the country. It became a conflict between a province and the Dominion of Canada and, above all, obliged the federal government to assume its responsibilities as defined in Section 93 of the Constitution Act of 1867.

In 1893 Mgr. Louis-Philippe-Adélard Langevin arrived in Winnipeg, and in 1895 he became the successor of Mgr. Alexandre-Antonin Taché. The new bishop was a fierce opponent of the so-called "neutral" or non-denominational schools of the Greenway government. He pressured federal authorities to meet their constitutional obligations and disallow the Manitoban law. In the meantime he pressured Catholics to financially support private denominational schools until the provincial government amended its law.

Mgr. Langevin could count on the unwavering support of Mgr. Louis-François Laflèche, bishop of Trois-Rivières and a famous Ultramontane, who became a pillar in the mobilization of French-Canadian bishops in Quebec. Mgr. Laflèche wanted to maintain denominational schools, put an end to state intervention in education, and preserve the nationalist mission of the denominational school system.

Mgr. Laflèche pressured the Conservative government of John A. Macdonald to disallow the Manitoban law. In a letter sent to the Conservative minister Joseph-Adolphe Chapleau, he wrote:

It is in the name of a federal compact that the minority in Manitoba is requesting your protection against an unjust law that violates this federal compact, because the compact guarantees them the usage of French as an official language equal to English, and the preservation of separate schools, without which the Catholic and francophone population in Manitoba would never have agreed to enter Confederation. However, without even the slightest pretext, the [Manitoban] law rode roughshod over these guarantees to strip the minority unjustly of the most precious right of a people, which is the right to preserve the language and faith of their forefathers.[5]

The federal government refused to disallow the Manitoban law, preferring to leave it to the courts to intervene. Tactical factors were at play here. Court interventions had the advantage of helping Ottawa gain time. Furthermore, courts became a useful way out because they allowed the Macdonald government to hail the soundness of the judges' action if they ruled in favour of the Catholics or, conversely, to justify its inability to act due to an unfavourable ruling. The government also feared the recurrence of a national crisis, as at the time of the trial and death of Riel in 1885. Given the circumstances, court interventions were preferable to political action, as Chapleau told Mgr. Laflèche in a letter of May 23, 1890.

If the courts of justice were to rule that this measure was illegal, they would put an end to the question without giving rise to the political unrest that an official act of the federal government would definitely cause. Just imagine a veto of the Governor in Council published against the [Manitoban] law; [the government of that province] would surely stir up unrest that, even if limited to the province of Manitoba, would definitely lead to a dissolution of the legislature and an election being called linked undoubtedly to this issue. The new legislature would enact the same law, making it even more prominent, since it would be supported throughout the country by an element as strong as it would be violent. ...

On the other hand, a court decision would not give rise to popular unrest. Sanctioned by the lawful authorities of the Empire, it would impose itself even on the most rowdy, their political passion having nothing to go on.[6]

The first legal defeat spread turmoil among francophone Catholics. In its July 1892 ruling, the British Judicial Committee of the Privy Council, which was Canada's final court of appeal, declared that Part 1, Section 22 of the Manitoba law did not guarantee the existence of denominational schools. Some three years later, however, in the *Brophy* case, the same court ruled that Catholics had suffered a prejudice. Consequently, they were authorized to ask the Dominion of Canada to intervene pursuant to Section 93 of the Constitution Act of 1867. Furthermore, as Perin points out, the judges also indicated that the 1890 laws did not need to be disallowed. It was a precarious victory because the fate of the Manitoban Catholic minority depended on the good will of the Government of the Dominion. Ottawa, led by Mackenzie Bowell, tabled a remedial bill on February 11, 1896, but the bill died on the order paper of the House of Commons.

At the end of the 1896 federal elections, the Liberals, led by Wilfrid Laurier, formed the government and the new prime minister undertook negotiations with Greenway. Known as the "Laurier-Greenway compromise," the agreement reached in November 1896 did not reinstate denominational schools, but it did guarantee support for Catholic parents by authorizing religious instruction for one hour a day. On the strength of this victory, the Greenway government pursued its homogenization policy by making English the only language of instruction as of 1916. Not until 1947 would French once again be tolerated as a language of instruction, at the rate of one hour a day.

At a time when Manitoba was mobilizing the attention of political leaders, courts of law, the Catholic clergy, and all the citizens, the Legislative Council of the Northwest Territories, which became the Legislative Assembly in 1888, also took action regarding the language issue. In 1875 the lieutenant governor of Manitoba lost administrative

control over the Northwest Territories—a vast territory corresponding to a portion of the actual provinces of Manitoba, Saskatchewan, and
Alberta—when the Dominion of Canada granted the territories their
own administration. Two years later the federal Parliament recognized
French and English as official languages of the courts and of debates
in the Legislative Assembly, which had been established to support
the lieutenant governor in the administration of the territories. However, pressure for English unilingualism and cultural homogenization
mounted within the legislature. Controlled essentially by Anglo-Saxons
from Ontario, the Assembly could rely on allies among the federal
members of Parliament. Consequently, in 1890, D'Alton McCarthy, a
Conservative member of Parliament from Ontario, supporter of the
"One Nation, One Language" principle and head of the Equal Rights
Association, proposed the abolition of bilingualism in the Northwest
Territories. McCarthy was in fact voicing the request expressed in the
Legislative Assembly of the Northwest Territories. The Macdonald gov-
ernment proposed a compromise when the minister of justice, John
Thompson, tabled a bill authorizing the Assembly to determine the
language of use in its legislative affairs.

It took little time for the Legislative Assembly of the Northwest Territories to exercise its new powers. As of 1892, the Assembly
recognized English as the only language of use in its law-making.
Furthermore, all the legal and administrative documents were to be
published in English only from then on. During the debate, the intervenors claimed that putting an end to the printing in both languages of
reports and other documents related to the business of the Assembly
would lead to budgetary savings—although, of course, they were not
able to quantify the exact magnitude of the amounts that would be
saved. The issue of savings was in fact a pretext to imitate Manitoba
and the transformation of its symbolic order. By instituting English as
the language of use, the government wanted to send a clear message
to all its residents about its objectives, the promotion of unilingualism and homogenization. Furthermore, the intervenors did not shy
away from reminding people that French was a foreign language and
was not widely used in any case, given that the proportion of French
Canadians was decreasing in the Northwest Territories. While in the
1870s the French-speaking residents, including the Métis, represented

LAC, Topley Studios fonds, PA-025698

D'Alton McCarthy (1836-98),
Conservative member of
Parliament and leader of the
Equal Rights Association.

85 per cent of the population of the Territories, the proportion had fallen to only 17 per cent in 1885.[7]

The attack continued at the end of 1882 with the enactment of an ordinance proclaiming English as the only language of instruction. As Edmund A. Aunger mentions in his study on the issue of bilingualism in the Northwest Territories, the ordinance nevertheless authorized school commissioners to allow the use of French in primary schools.

The creation of the provinces of Alberta and Saskatchewan in 1905, out of the Northwest Territories, brought to the forefront the issue of school rights. It obliged legislators to ask themselves how to protect these rights, given that English-Canadian opinion leaders wanted the program of "Canadianization" or cultural homogenization of immigrants to apply also to the Métis and French Canadians. As historian Réal Bélanger points out in his biography of Wilfrid Laurier, the prime minister wanted to guarantee the Catholic minority's right to have denominational schools. However, following petitions and protests in the English-Canadian press, including the *Globe*, and opposition within his cabinet—particularly from Clifford Sifton, who resigned to prevent the recognition of denominational schools—Laurier retreated, to the great displeasure of the Quebec members of Parliament, in particular Henri Bourassa. Given the general outcry, the issue of the status of the French language was set aside.

As of 1918, on the strength of its new powers in the field of education, the province of Saskatchewan limited the use of French as a language of instruction to the first year of primary school and to one hour a day in all the other grades. Furthermore, as sociologist Wilfrid B. Denis notes, any kind of religious uniform or symbol was forbidden in public schools in 1930. A year later the use of French as a language of instruction was forbidden, except if schools requested an exemption. If an exemption was granted, the use of French was limited to one hour a day. In Alberta a 1905 law limited teaching of the Catholic religion to a half-hour a day in separate schools, while the use of French as a language of instruction was to be allowed only during the first years of primary school. After that, the use of French was to be allowed only in classes in which the language was being taught.[8]

Preoccupied with the survival of English culture and language in Ontario, the supporters of the English Only movement helped the Conservatives take power in the 1905 provincial elections. In 1912, based on a report by Dr. F.A. Merchant citing the weak qualifications of French-Canadian teachers and inadequate teaching in bilingual schools, the James Whitney government enacted Regulation 17, limiting the use of French as a language of instruction. Ontario did not go so far as to abolish denominational schools as Manitoba had done in 1890—a gesture that was in part the result of the efforts of the Catholic bishop in the diocese of London, Mgr. Michael Francis Fallon, who worked to counter the pressure of English Canadians.

- -

Regulation 17: Circular of Instruction No. 17 for Ontario Separate Schools for the School Year 1912–1913

Section 1: There are only two classes of Primary Schools in Ontario—Public Schools and Separate Schools; but, for convenience of reference, the term English-French is applied to those schools of each class which shall be designated as such by the Minister whenever requested so to do by the Board or the Boards having jurisdiction in the matter, for inspection as provided in 5 below and in which French is the Language of instruction and communication as limited in 3 (1) below. ...

Section 3: The following modifications shall be made in the Course of Study of the Public and Separate Schools.

The Use of French for Instruction and Communication

1) In the case of French-speaking pupils, French may be used as the language of Instruction and communication but such use of French shall not be continued for the Study of English beyond Form I, excepting that, on the approval of the Inspector, it may also be used as the language of instruction and communication for the study of English in the case of pupils beyond Form I who are unable to speak and understand the English Language.

Special Course in English for French-speaking pupils

2) In the case of French-speaking pupils who are unable to speak and understand the English language well enough for the purposes of instruction and communication, the following provision is hereby made:

(a) As soon as the pupil enters the school he shall begin the study and the use of the English language.

(b) As soon as the pupil has acquired sufficient facility in the use of the English language he shall take up in that language the study of English.

> Source: http://www.salic-slmc.ca/showpage.asp?file=legislations_ling/ documents_hist/1912_reglement_17&language=en&updatemenu= false& noprevnext.

— — — — — — — —

The government's decision mobilized Ontario's French-Canadian community, whose members were in despair when the courts sided with the provincial government. Indeed, in November 1916 the British Judicial Committee of the Privy Council determined that Regulation 17 was legal because it complied with Section 93 of the Constitution Act of 1867, which protected the right of minorities to denominational schools. Contrary to what the leaders of the Association canadienne-française d'éducation d'Ontario (ACFÉO) believed, the right to be educated in one's mother tongue was not guaranteed by Section 93. As a result, the resolution of the school crisis became strictly political. Until 1916 the ACFÉO implemented a strategy of mobilization and confrontation in the hope of getting the Conservative governments of James Whitney and

University of Ottawa, CRCCF, Fonds Association canadienne-française de l'Ontario (C2), Ph2-142a

Demonstration by the teachers and students of École Brébeuf during the era of Regulation 17, Ottawa, February 1916.

William Hearst to back down, but it gained nothing of any significance. While the mobilization of citizens in the francophone community of Ontario was huge, Quebec also demonstrated solidarity on the issue, particularly in 1915 by tabling a motion in its Legislative Assembly with regard to minority rights, and in 1916 with a law authorizing Quebec school boards to contribute funds to the campaign against Regulation 17. In 1916, at the federal level, Wilfrid Laurier and Ernest Lapointe tabled a motion in Parliament that, while claiming respect for provincial autonomy in the area of education, encouraged the Ontario government to take steps to avoid infringing minority rights. The ruling government led by Robert Borden refused to support the motion. The great orator Henri Bourassa lent his voice to the combatants, but in vain. For its part, the Standing Committee of the first Congrès de la langue française organized two fundraisers in support of the French Canadians in Ontario.[9] The controversy surrounding Regulation 17, which greatly intensified the polarization between the two nations in Canada, peaked during the conscription crisis of 1917.

According to historian Pierre Savard, the arrival of Senator Napoléon-Antoine Belcourt at the helm of the ACFÉO in 1921 brought about a change in strategy. From then on the organization concentrated on gaining allies for the Franco-Ontarian cause among English-speaking citizens, a task that would be supported by the Unity League, an organization founded by sympathetic English Canadians with the support of Belcourt, and which took aim at the repeal of Regulation 17. The weaknesses of the so-called bilingual schools as noted in the 1912 Merchant report also had to be corrected. To help youth improve their knowledge of English, teachers would have to receive the appropriate educational training. To that end, in 1923 the University of Ottawa established its École de pédagogie, but by that time, too, the public mobilization of citizens was wearing thin and the Franco-Ontarian leaders focused on discreetly lobbying provincial authorities. The Quebec premier Louis-Alexandre Taschereau assisted by pressuring his Ontario counterparts.

These initiatives were successful. George Howard Ferguson, who had been Ontario's education minister at the time of Regulation 17, became premier of Ontario in 1923. From his point of view the school crisis had already lasted too long. He wanted to find a solution. The school conflict ended in 1927 when the Ministry of Education issued new guidelines allowing the teaching of particular subjects in French, which would at the same time not prevent learning in English. During the following years the challenge for the ACFÉO would be to increase the proportion of French used as a language of instruction.

School inspection became an important issue. The province relied on school inspectors to ensure that schools complied with the guidelines and instructional objectives of the Ministry, and French Canadians in Ontario recognized the importance of exercising some control in this regard. They could not as a matter of course determine the objectives of the Ministry, but they could expect support from inspectors who were sympathetic to the objectives of the ACFÉO and especially to its goal of gaining control over schools attended by francophone Catholics. To achieve a certain autonomy the choice of inspectors was crucial. The ACFÉO won a victory when it was decided that the so-called bilingual schools would no longer be subjected to a double (English and French) inspection. From that time on, inspections carried out by French Canadians would be sufficient. The Ministry also recognized the École de pédagogie and its teacher-training degree at the University of Ottawa.

The school crisis had a major impact on French Canadians in Ontario. With a noticeable lack of unanimity among them, the community was displaying its divisions. In the regions of Ottawa, Pembroke, and Eastern Ontario, many francophones waged fierce battles, particularly at the Ottawa School Board; but in the Windsor region, most French-speaking communities did not contest Regulation 17. Parents in the Windsor area were happy that they no longer had to pay additional amounts of money to send their children to school, and, moreover, they appreciated that learning English would help their youth find jobs in the emerging auto industry. These contrasting reactions created tensions between French-Canadian leaders in the East and South. The conflicts also stemmed from class relations and how each social class perceived the importance of educating their children—an effect notable in the Prescott region of Eastern Ontario. A study of the school crisis carried out by historian Chad Gaffield reveals that French-Canadian parents in agricultural communities were not preoccupied with educational issues as long as their youth could find work that contributed to family income. But when their economic situation changed and their children's work was no longer necessary, parents objected if the province stopped them from sending their children to French-language schools.

Quebec: denouncing and enacting

The period from 1848 to 1927 was characterized by activism within civil society, and it was an activism based on an elitist idea of language and the role of members of the elite in the battle for the preservation of French. Through newspaper campaigns, petitions, and other means, activists sought to heighten the awareness of French Canadians regarding their duty to demand services in their language from governments and the private sector. And so, in 1908, more than 435,000 individuals signed the petition of the Association catholique de la jeunesse canadienne-française requesting bilingual public services.

Preservation of the language was based on a strategy relying on individual and collective measures. First of all, members of the elite assigned to the French-Canadian mother the duty of teaching the rudiments of the French language. The mother's work was to keep a close watch on the family. Then the school network would take over. The French-Canadian associations also played a role in the preservation of the language. As for the state, it was not perceived as being part of the strategy, except when it was called upon to support schools controlled by French Canadians. Whenever measures taken by the state hindered the institutional network and associations qualified as essential to the preservation of French, the French Canadians mobilized.

In spite of regular criticisms expressed by school inspectors on the incompetence of teachers, and in particular the weakness of their training, the school system contributed to increasing the level of literacy throughout the nineteenth century. During the decade of 1890 to 1899 the rate of literacy reached 74.4 per cent. The percentage was slightly lower among men—at 69.3 per cent—and higher among women—at 79.4 per cent.[10]

The disparity between the language abilities of men and women stemmed from the relation between capital and labour. It highlighted in particular the differences in how working-class, lower-middle-class, and middle-class environments valued education and a mastery of the French language. While the literacy rate within the French-Canadian bourgeoisie and business and professional circles was almost 100 per cent, it varied among shopkeepers, skilled tradespeople, and day labourers. The literacy rates for the period of 1890–99 in those three categories were 87.5 per cent, 88.9 per cent, and 70.4 per cent respectively.[11]

Working-class families, especially those led by day labourers and skilled tradespersons, did not encourage their children to go to school, especially when the youth were old enough to get a job. This trend was particularly noticeable during the period of massive immigration of French Canadians to the United States, a major phenomenon in the history of Quebec in the nineteenth century. As historians Bruno Ramirez, Yves Roby, and François Weil point out, from 1840 to 1929 the misery of economic deprivations in the countryside drove almost 900,000 individuals to depart for New England's industrial cities. During much of that time, as part of the economic survival strategies of immigrant families, ten- or eleven-year-old children routinely held factory jobs. To face the economic challenges of urban industrial life, families encouraged their children to work rather than go to school. In working-class families the father often held an insecure or badly paid job, making the economic survival of the whole family equally precarious. When one or two teenagers in a family had a paid job, their financial contribution allowed their parents to make ends meet. In many cases, work in U.S. industrial cities provided the first contact with the English language. Although they remained attached to their mother tongue, French-Canadian emigrants rapidly understood that a knowledge of English could bring economic returns, and all the more so because members of the second generation often married a person from another ethnic group. Critics who denounced the very poor quality of French-language usage and the lack of interest of some parents, in particular those from the working class, in instilling into their children the proper mastery of the French language were not aware that those conditions were dictated by economic needs.

At the same time those critics continued to emphasize the fragility of the language, not hesitating to declare that it was in a pitiful state, and worked to impose standards on the spoken language to improve its quality, which would in turn indicate a certain social distinction on the part of the speakers. Many language activists sought to organize popular education campaigns to spread the standards of proper language—the standards of the cultural elites. As a result, in 1895, the École littéraire de Montréal and, seven years later, the Société du parler français au Canada—on the initiative of Father Stanislas Lortie and Adjutor Rivard—were launched. Based in Quebec City, the Société opted for a normative approach, hoping to improve the quality of the spoken language and attempting to purify it by hunting down anglicisms. At first it published the *Bulletin du parler français au Canada*, which was then replaced by *Le Canada français*. In addition to its *Glossaire du parler français au Canada*, by the 1930s the Quebec organization was publishing columns called "*Corrigeons-nous*." The writing not only appeared in reprints in French dailies in Quebec and elsewhere in French America, but was also put to use in educational institutions. At the beginning of the 1920s another organization, the Association catholique de la jeunesse canadienne-française, also took up the issue of the presence of anglicisms in the French language, launching a francization campaign, as political scientists Guy Bouthillier and Jean Meynaud relate.

In addition to the work of these organizations, individuals used their symbolic capital and positions of authority to raise the awareness of French Canadians about their own language. Journalists Arthur Buies and Jules-Paul Tardivel and writer Edmond de Nevers denounced the use of anglicisms, proposing to ban them from the vocabulary. In 1880 Tardivel published a brochure with a catchy title: "*L'anglicisme, voilà l'ennemi*" [Anglicism: there lies the enemy]. According to the fiery journalist, a battle needed to be waged against anglicisms so "that our language can remain really French."[12] For his part, throughout his career Buies collaborated with several dailies to attack, sometimes vehemently, the anglicisms polluting the French language and proliferating in print media. In an article published in *L'Électeur* on January 14, 1888, he wrote, "Anglicisms are swarming us, flooding us, distorting us, altering us."[13] The Jesuit Louis-Joseph-Papin Archambault published several articles in the daily newspaper *Le Devoir*, before and after the Congrès de la langue française in 1912, addressing the sad fate of French in commercial advertising and in the corporate names of businesses and corporations. In 1913, supported by Anatole Vanier and Joseph Gauvreau, he launched the Ligue des droits du français, which would become the Ligue d'action française in 1921 and then the Ligue d'action canadienne-française before disappearing in 1928. The action undertaken by the Ligue was at first educational and aimed at spreading the use of proper terms in French by publishing lists of appropriate technical words and expressions. The Ligue also became an advocacy organization; it channelled the complaints of the population in an attempt to compel corporations and governments to francize themselves or the commercial landscape. Father Archambault pursued his action in the journal *L'Action française*, which joined the effort to raise awareness by urging citizens to become vigilant agents of the proper use of French.[14]

The actions generated further debates on language quality and especially on what was characterized as French patois. While some critics deplored the use of patois and launched attacks on people who were careless with language, others found it difficult to conceal their discomfort regarding denunciations of what they considered to be the peculiarities of Quebec French. In 1892 the former member of the Legislative Assembly, Narcisse-Henri-Édouard Faucher de Saint-

Maurice, author of *Honni soit qui mal y pense: Notes sur la formation du Franco-Normand et de l'Anglo-Saxon*, pointed out that it should not be said that French Canadians and Acadians were speaking a patois rather than, as proper, the French language.[15] Although journalist Jules-Paul Tardivel criticized the use of anglicisms, he encouraged people to be proud of their patois and Canadianisms. He warned people not to share "the negative opinion of the language that we speak."[16]

The Province of Quebec intervened in many ways in the issue of language. At first the political leaders were concerned about the migration towards New England cities because population movement was threatening the very survival of the French-Canadian nation, especially given the added insidious danger of assimilation. Their first reaction was one of condemnation, as evidenced by the scornful words attributed to George-Étienne Cartier: "Let them go. It's the rogues who are leaving."[17] Yet any such scorn, as Yves Roby notes, was short-lived. After attempting to encourage migrants to return through new land-granting policies implemented from 1873 to 1879, the members of the Quebec elite realized the inevitability of the migratory movement to the south and, as in the case of former premier Pierre-Joseph-Olivier Chauveau in 1880, took a different approach. A new discourse then took shape. French Canadians became endowed with the providential mission of establishing the French language and Catholic faith in North America. Quebec would be their fortress; the Franco-Americans in New England or French Canadians in other provinces the outposts.

On the Canadian front as a whole, political leaders in Quebec were not indifferent to the fate of the French Canadians in Manitoba and Ontario who were denouncing their respective governments following the enactment of laws prohibiting or limiting the use of French as a language of instruction. In many cases, members of the Legislative Assembly in Quebec adopted motions in support of the battles waged by French Canadians elsewhere, and, as in the case of Ontario, they encouraged the government of the provinces concerned to demonstrate an understanding of and respect for this community. From time to time, members evoked the notion of the founding compact to justify federal action on language matters. In 1907 the member for Montmagny, Armand LaVergne, tabled a motion stating:

Quebec National Assembly, mosaic, 1912

Armand LaVergne (1880-1935), member of the Legislative Assembly in Quebec, 1908-16. Photo by M.-A. Montminy.

It is in the interest and for the good of Confederation that, in the spirit of the federal compact of 1867, French language, official by virtue of the Constitution, be integrated in public business on an equal basis with the English language, particularly in minting and postal management.[18]

On rare occasions politicians asserted that the federal and provincial governments had the right to promote and protect the French language. On LaVergne's initiative in 1910, the Province of Quebec intervened in the area of language planning by enacting a law of only a few paragraphs aimed at railway, telephone, telegraph, electric power, transport, and express delivery businesses, urging them to offer their services and publish their documentation in French. A fine of no more than $20 was to be imposed on offending companies. However, the state's means of intervention were limited. The law did not anticipate the allocation of administrative resources to oblige businesses to present their clients with an active offer of French services. If clients were dissatisfied, they could initiate proceedings in a court.

The LaVergne Law (1910)—An Act to amend the Civil Code, respecting contracts made with public utility companies (1 George V, c. 40)

Section 1: The following articles are added after article 1682b of the Civil Code as enacted by the act 5 Edward VII, chapter 28, section 1:

1682c. The following shall be printed in French and in English: passenger tickets, baggage-checks, waybills, bills of lading, printed telegraph forms, and contract forms, made, furnished or delivered by a railway, navigation, telegraph, telephone, transportation, express or electric power company, as well as all notices or regulations posted up in its stations, carriages, boats, offices, factories or workshops.

1682d. Every contravention, by a railway, navigation, telegraph, telephone, transportation, express or electric power company, doing business in this Province, of any of the provisions of the foregoing article shall be punished by a fine net exceeding twenty dollars, without prejudice to recourse for damages.

Article 2: This act shall come into force on the first day of January, 1911.

Source: University of Ottawa, Site for Language Management in Canada, http://www.slmc.uottawa.ca/?q=leg_lavergne_law.

Showing solidarity to improve action

The Manitoba school battle and the battle waged for schools in the provinces of Alberta and Saskatchewan revealed to the French-Canadian clergy and political circles the existence of forces hostile to linguistic diversity and eager to shape the West—acquired in 1869—along the lines of Anglo-British civilizing ideals. These events influenced how the elites would fashion relations between French and English Canadians. To make sense of what was happening they permeated their representations with images oriented around the goals of assimilation and a kind of fanaticism that would promote the English-Canadian nation. On another level, the construction of an important political myth was also taking shape: the compact between the two founding peoples. Henri Bourassa, a member of Parliament at the turn of the twentieth century and later a member of the Quebec Legislative Assembly, was the most active propagandist of this myth, but was even more so a leading figure of Canadian and French-Canadian nationalist thinking. For example, at the 1912 Congrès de la langue française au Canada, in a memorable speech Bourassa used the forum to spread his constitutional and nationalist vision.

In conjunction with the development of this theory of a compact between two founding nations, which was meant to represent the true nature of Confederation, French-Canadian communities became the custodians of a mission of salvation not just for French Canada, but for all of Canada. Their presence in provinces outside Quebec became an essential element in ensuring the transformation of the representation of the country among English Canadians. Canada would therefore be judged according to its respect for the rights of these communities. Until this theoretical concept of Canada was accepted, daily life in the nation was to be made up of a series of battles for the survival of French-speaking people, and of sacrifices for the preservation of the francophone minority groups outside of Quebec.[19]

The daily battle of French-Canadian communities gave life to the French-Canadian nation. The presence of these various communities was viewed as essential to the entire nation because each one of them constituted an outpost of French Canada. Based on this defensive concept of the relations between French Canadians and English Canadians—influenced by the interpretation of the school crises as offering proof of the hostility of the other nation towards French-speaking communities—the image of an outpost came to symbolize the French-Canadian communities. As noted by the bishop of Regina, Mgr. Olivier-Elzéar Mathieu, Quebec was the "fortress" of the nation, and "everything that contributed to the greatness of Quebec contributed to the strength and the greatness of the French groups on the outside. . . . Everything that strengthened the outposts was transformed into the glory and strength of Quebec."[20]

For Acadians and French Canadians outside Quebec, the battle was vital because it ensured the preservation of acquired rights. As Senator Napoléon-Antoine Belcourt told the delegates at the Quebec Congress in 1912, "The survival of French in Ontario will be won through constant vigilance, through a battle waged every moment of the day, requiring great sacrifices in time and money, and an absolute and unwavering determination to speak French and make your children speak it."[21]

At the end of the Congress the hopes of the delegates were founded on the creation of a French-Canadian and Acadian institutional network. The standing committee of the first Congrès de la langue française was given the mandate to defend the "culture" and promote "the development of the French language and literature in Canada and in general among the Acadians and French Canadians within North America."[22] The committee was to be short-lived; it ended its activities in the 1920s.

– – – – –

For the Acadian and French-Canadian communities involved in the various school and language crises after 1848, the 1920s ended with a harsh acknowledgement: that of their minority condition. The management of language diversity meant that French-language minorities in English provinces had to blend into the Anglo-Saxon cultural and linguistic homogeneity. Whether they were members of the clergy or politicians, professionals, farmers, or labourers, Acadians and French Canadians were becoming aware of the precariousness of their rights. In all of this they came to a compelling conclusion: Canada was dominated by a majority determined to give its own rights precedence to the detriment of those who spoke French. Given the circumstances, anyone who hoped to regain the right to use French as a language of instruction, as in Manitoba and Ontario, would have to build strategies of resistance and accommodation. This dilemma posed a problem: for want of a legal solution, to ensure the survival of the French-Canadian nation throughout Canada a political solution had to be found. Otherwise, the spectre of assimilation would descend on the nation, as in the Franco-American outposts in which French was being abandoned at the onset of the Great Depression. The crises also became founding myths of the francophone minority communities, whose people were to integrate the memory of these events into their cultural identity references.

At the federal level any control exercised by French Canadians in state jurisdictions was the result of constant negotiations with the representatives of the majority. Within the dynamics of the relation between a majority and a minority, the Acadians and French Canadians knew that they had somehow to fashion political solutions around the issues of language diversity and their own collective rights in the country. They put their faith in constitutional guarantees, in particular Section 133 of the Constitution Act of 1867, and especially in the spirit of the Constitution. In establishing its ideal of peace, order, and good government, the English-Canadian nation would be compelled to adhere to a different vision of Confederation: that of a compact between two founding peoples.

Based on the experience of the Acadian and French-Canadian minorities, a conception of the relations between the two language groups in Canada evolved, and called for action. The struggle for survival became something that French Canadians—especially those living outside Quebec—waged every moment of their lives. They fought for their land; they fought to preserve their faith and language. They also fought to strengthen the institutional framework that was so indispensable to their continued existence. Finally, they fought against the unequal relations of domination that so heavily constricted French-Canadian and Acadian workers at the turn of the twentieth century. Barriers of language had economic repercussions. They blocked growth by preventing a fair allocation of resources; those who spoke the language of business held a definite advantage over the others.

In this context English Canadians became seen as champions of assimilation and bosses who were covetously protecting their assets, especially when it came to the cultural war against the francophone minority—as, for instance, at the peak of the school issue in Ontario. After 1927 this representation would slowly change as years went by. Within the realm of the *bonne entente* promoted by members of the francophone elite, English Canadians—at least those who supported the theory of a compact between the two founding peoples—would become allies.

CHAPTER 3

ALL QUIET ON THE FRONT

From the repeal of Regulation 17 to the
Laurendeau-Dunton Commission, 1927-63

Il en est qui n'ont pas voulu partir
Qui ont voulu ne pas partir, mais demeurer
On les regarde on ne sait pas
Nous ne sommes pas de la même race . . .
On n'a rien à dire et l'on n'entend pas la voix d'un compagnon.
 - Hector de Saint-Denys Garneau, *Il nous est arrivé des aventures*

Although it faded away, the Regulation 17 crisis left deep scars that cut across the entire public sphere in Canada. The original notion of homogenizing all of Canada under a British national order was now obsolete because, given the political confrontation and strong resistance of French Canadians, civil peace between the "two solitudes"—an expression coined by novelist Hugh MacLennan in 1945—was no longer possible without an armistice or a major compromise. From 1927 to 1963, while the central characters momentarily withdrew from their duelling grounds, the dust of battle surrounding the language issue subsided. Yet the echo of the conflicts continued to reverberate.

Questions of identity and language

At the outset of the Great Depression in the 1930s, Canada was what the Dutch political scientist Arendt Lijphart defined as a "consociational" democracy. The term refers to a political system that has major social and ethnic divisions, but a stable democracy. Within such a political system, each social group is relatively distinct from the other, with its own ideologies and institutions. The sense of national unity is all the more weak because the various groups carry on minimal social communications with each other. Their communication is basically filtered through the community elites who establish relationships of mutual accommodation, cordial proximity, or common understanding. Therefore, consociational democracy implies an expression of indifference towards the political problems encountered by the other group, as long as those problems have minimal to no influence on one's own group. The insensitivity is even more manifest when the problems result from unequal relations of domination that seem "natural," and when the dominant group retains its favourable position with regard to the other. As political scientist Kenneth McRae notes, the New Brunswick of Loyalist Maritimers and of Acadians was in this regard a case in point. Given how it manifested itself in English and French Canada between 1927 and 1963, the language issue was a sensitive gauge of consociational democracy in all the force of its inertia and the weight of its indifference.

Increasingly, the seeds of new questions of identity were planted in English Canada. The old attachment to the British Empire weakened after the First World War and the Conscription Crisis of 1917. Social and political phenomena played their part in the transformation. Immigrants from Eastern Europe, Italy, Greece, and Portugal did not share the same Anglo-conformity criteria. The assimilation of these groups—who were so vastly different on ethnic, linguistic, and religious levels and less sensitive to English-Canadian national ideals—would require more time. Also, the postwar context was different; now ethnic discrimination against immigrants, once they had entered the country, contravened the evolving international justice system. Moreover, following the signing of the Statute of Westminster in 1931 Canada gained official independence from the United Kingdom. Given the economic crisis of the Depression, followed by the Second World War and subsequent peace, many English Canadians who were concerned about the survival of their nation now found it important to emphasize differences from the United States, especially given that the urban, industrial, and social realities in both nations were increasingly similar. After 1945, as historian José Igartua argues, English Canada experienced its own Quiet Revolution. From the introduction of Canadian citizenship in 1946 to the enactment of a policy of multiculturalism in 1971, a new consensus slowly emerged. To ensure the homogeneity of the population within Canadian borders—which was seen as being essential in differentiating the country from its U.S. neighbour and integrating immigrants—it became necessary to redefine the collective identity of the nation and revise the agreed-upon ethnic boundaries that shaped the Canadian consociational democracy. As historian Ramsay Cook, political scientist Philip Resnick, and anthropologist Eva Mackey point out, the redefinition and revision would impose a new symbolic order in which the language issue would take on a different meaning altogether in the 1960s.

In 1936 even a staunch imperialist such as Stephen Leacock, expressing concern about the weakening of the link with the motherland, was raising the issue of language differences. He argued that English was being spoken differently in Canada than in Great Britain. The McGill University sexagenarian said that when he had left his native Hampshire in England at six years of age, "I spoke English. But I've lost it, and it might be too late to pick it up again." [1] Still, the renowned humorist granted only condescending consideration to French, the other language in Canada. "A little group of our French people," he stated haughtily in 1939, "like to talk to a sort of dream republic called Laurentia. It is a lovely place: there are no English there, and no capitalists or power companies, and there are no soldiers and armies. ... In this dream world, the government is all by orators—young orators—and they talk and talk, and write newspapers and pamphlets, and fall asleep and wake up and talk." [2] However comic his intention, his disdain effectively conveyed the lack of attention granted to the unequal relations between the two ethno-linguistic groups. It also demonstrated the persistence of a hegemonic representation within English Canada at the time, which aimed, to use the analysis of historian Daniel Francis, at the infantilization of French Canada.

From the perspectives of those in French Canada and Acadia, the language situation presented itself differently because the relations of domination were not experienced in the same way in the two areas. The school crises during the previous years had led to the harsh acknowledgement that the francophone minority in Canada as a whole was losing ground. The Great Depression had hit French-speaking communities hard; misery, poverty, and unemployment were rampant in both the countryside and cities. After the Second World War the resumption of immigration seriously raised the question of integration of newcomers. Furthermore, confronted with these phenomena, the manifestations of civil society in French Canada and Acadia—because they continued to intensely mistrust states, which they perceived as potential assimilators—were facing even greater social demands than were similar bodies in English Canada.

Consequently, the interpretation of the language issue varied. The diagnosis reached by numerous stakeholders in French Canada and Acadia was that the French language was suffering from anaemia and required a strong prescription. Conferences on the issue of the French language took place in 1937 and 1952 in Quebec City, and another on refrancization was held in 1957. They were organized by representatives of religious and nationalist circles, and followed the tradition of giving pre-eminence to the Catholic clergy, political representatives, and members of the middle-class elite. Businessmen and workers were largely absent from these gatherings, at least among the organizers and speakers. The conferences provided an opportunity to provide an update on the vitality of the French language in North America. Speakers had a forum in which they could call attention to the negligence or leniency that many social groups were demonstrating with regard to French because, after all, they did not seem overly concerned with mastering the language. The speakers harangued fellow citizens about the seriousness of their negligence, stating that their presumed insensitivity and lack of attention were harming the quality and vitality of the language.

The conferences on the French language also provided French minority groups from other Canadian provinces or the United States with the opportunity of bearing witness to their difficulties and to the ravages caused by linguistic and cultural assimilation, even though the

BANQ, centre d'archives de Québec, P600, S6, D2, P37

Elites and language accommodation. Mgr. Jean-Marie-Rodrigue Villeneuve, Cardinal of Quebec, and the Lieutenant Governor of the Province, Ésioff-Léon Patenaude, at the Second Congress on the French language in Quebec City, June 1937.

ravages were not empirically quantified. Some speakers from Quebec took advantage of being part of the forum to denounce the inhabitants of their province for their lack of vigilance towards French usage. Several among them portrayed the French-speaking communities as models for Quebecers, despite the difficulties they faced. The speakers often concluded by emphasizing the importance of maintaining relations between Quebec and French-speaking minority groups outside the province. The latter had to rely on the indispensable solidarity between the various French-speaking communities in order to make sure that the demographic weight of francophones in Canada remained significant. These communities also became the prism through which English-Canadian society was judged when confronted with the ideals of respecting French-Canadian rights. On this point, the English-Canadian provinces provided numerous examples of intolerance and negation of rights. Therefore, several speakers reflected on the meaning of the 1867 compact between the two founding nations and questioned it. They insisted on how Quebec, contrary to other provinces, did respect the compact.

Despite the grievances regarding the lack of respect for the rights of French Canadians to receive education in their language, the conferences allowed participants to renew their faith in the nationalist vision conveyed by a man of Henri Bourassa's stature. And so the French-Canadian and Acadian communities outside Quebec, though clearly outposts in the battle being waged to prevent assimilation, were above all essential components of the strategy of solidarity that needed to be the driving force of French Canada as a national space seeking political and constitutional recognition. At the same time, the plight of French-speaking minority groups, notwithstanding their demographic weight and the level of vitality of their language, proved to be a useful reminder of how French Canadians could be overwhelmed if they refused to preserve their language.

Defined as outposts, French-Canadian and Acadian communities had an indispensable role, which was to fight not just for themselves and Quebec, but also for Canada. In the case of Canada, the aim was that the compact forged between two founding nations not be relegated to wishful thinking, but reflected in the country's constitutional framework and symbols of belonging. In their response to the invitation to the Second Congress on the French Language in Canada in 1937, the institutional spokespersons from the francophone community of Ontario evoked the meaning of the battled waged against Regulation 17 from 1912 to 1927.

We managed to break the wave of anglicization that, intermittently, if not as a constant flow, threatened to unfurl over Quebec and, following the example of the heroes of Verdun, we are rightfully proud to be able to confirm that our common invaders did not cross the interprovincial line that separates us; however, we feel a strong need for help in building on our decisive victory.[3]

During the conferences on the French language in Canada, speakers reminded participants that the struggles of the French-Canadian and Acadian communities had generated new life. At the 1937 Congress Mgr. Émile Yelle reiterated the meaning of the battles led by francophones. Speaking of the French Canadians in the West, the bishop of Saint Boniface stated that they "had preserved their French heritage because they had defended it; and they intend to continue to defend themselves, with no illusions on the difficulties in store, in order to preserve their French heritage."[4]

The struggle for survival brought to the forefront once again the need to build an institutional network as complete and diversified as possible, not just in each province but also at the national level. To do so, parishes, schools, cultural organizations, mutual companies, economic co-operatives, and other financial institutions, as well as provincial associations, became components of the institutional network under construction. Speakers took advantage of the opportunity to remind political and religious leaders that they should encourage interprovincial migration of French Canadians. The success of such an incentive would strengthen the French-speaking groups outside of Quebec. It would also make it possible to correct the deficiencies in the institutional network regarding its capacity to integrate the mainly European immigrants who chose Canada as their new home following the Second World War.

The conferences were not the only place in which representatives of the clergy and the education and cultural circles expressed themselves on the substandard quality of language use and the indifference of people towards the situation. Victor Barbeau, a professor of French at the École des hautes études commerciales and one of the founders of the Société des écrivains canadiens, made resounding statements on the subject. For example, in a 1935 speech to members of the Société d'étude et de conférences, he declared that people were not really speaking French because their pronunciation was flawed and their language was filled with anglicisms. In 1952, on Radio-Canada, he brashly denounced the school system—characterizing it as disastrous—because youth were leaving school with serious gaps in their mastery of the spoken and written language.[5] A little less harsh than Barbeau, columnist Pierre Daviault encouraged people to worry about the state of the French language and recognize the existence of what he called "Canadian French." Still, he insisted on the necessity of speaking French properly, arguing that language gave people access to culture. If the understanding and use of language were flawed, cultural experience would suffer.[6]

These judgments worked as a kind of social control exercised by the Quebec bourgeoisie, who transformed their concerns for proper language into a social problem. In so doing, they were seeking to impose their own notion of language norms and their view of the right way to speak the language. However, they paid no attention to the socio-economic realities of the time, one of which was that English was the language of work for many people. In addition, they did not rejoice in the progress made in literacy. Indeed, in 1931 the literacy rate in Quebec was 93.9 per cent among men and 96.7 per cent among women. Nevertheless, comparisons with other ethnic groups and other provinces did cast a shadow over the apparent successes of the school system. For example, in Ontario the literacy rates were 97.3 per cent for men and 98.1 per cent for women. Furthermore, the performance in Quebec related to the entire population, notwithstanding ethnic origin. Although the proportion of illiterates was just over 1 per cent among individuals of English origin, it was 5.2 per cent among those of French origin. Finally, the provincial law enacted by the Liberal government of Adélard Godbout in 1943, which made attending school compulsory for children from six to fourteen years of age, concealed the low proportion of students pursuing their education beyond primary school. That proportion was only 34 per cent in 1954.[7]

A knowledge of English—given that it was the language of work in Quebec—understandably appealed to both the francophone population and to immigrants. As historian Jean-Pierre Charland observes, countless francophone parents sent their children to a school in which English was the language of instruction. The situation was different in immigrant communities.[8] As a place of immigration, Quebec welcomed many expatriates at the end of the Second World War. Whether they were from Western Europe or "refugees from communism"—a term used by the religious and conservative elites to designate the wave of immigrants following the 1956 Soviet repression in Hungary—they forced Quebec society and its state to face the challenge of managing cultural diversity. Most of these immigrants chose English-speaking educational institutions, in particular if these schools were Anglo-Catholic; this was the case among Italians, Ukrainians, and Portuguese. Their choice was made with the complicity of leaders in the French Catholic school system, who believed that the newcomers were far removed from French-Canadian cultural touchstones and, therefore, could not be integrated in the majority community. The schooling of immigrants in English facilitated their integration into the anglophone community. The socio-economic reality also dictated the choice of English-speaking schools, given that English was not only the language of work in Quebec, but also the language of socio-economic mobility.

Such a situation raised concerns among French-Canadian activists from 1948 to 1960. Of course, some gains were made with regard to improving the control of the social integration of immigrants. For example, the Mackenzie King government issued order-in-council P.C. 4186 on September 16, 1948, granting French immigrants the same privileges as those held by British and U.S. immigrants. However, this step was not really sufficient. Other initiatives were brought forward, such as the one by the Montreal Catholic School Commission (MCSC), which led to the creation of the Neo-Canadian Committee in 1947. At that time, as historian Miguel Simão Andrade notes, almost 65 per cent of the Neo-Canadians were sending their children to English Catholic schools. The Committee's objective was to francize immigrants by creating various French-language training

Sainte-Catherine Street, facing east, Montreal, October 1937.

programs. In the 1950s the Committee provided French evening courses and bilingual courses on Saturdays, although the programs were discontinued in 1969. The MCSC's programs for immigrants ran into major problems. The poor qualification of teachers assigned to the courses harmed the francization program. Although francization was not very successful, the integration of the new immigrants' children into Catholic schools was different. Under pressure from the Anglo-Catholic commissioners, the MCSC redirected its efforts to attracting the children of immigrants to its anglophone sector. The situation enraged some neo-nationalists, in particular Jean-Marc Léger and André Laurendeau.

For some activists, the education issue demonstrated the urgency of intervention by the Province of Quebec with respect to the integration of immigrants into the francophone majority. From the beginning of the 1950s, *Relations*, with René Gauthier, *L'Action nationale*, with Camille L'Heureux, Pierre Laporte, and Jean-Marc Léger, and *Le Devoir*, with Gérard Fillion and Laurendeau, pleaded for the province to take action. To guarantee French immigration, René Chaloult, an independent member of the Quebec legislature, tabled a motion in

1952 advocating the creation of a welcoming body for immigrants and a subsidy program for the existing organizations. His motion died on the order paper. At the time of the hearings of the Royal Commission of Inquiry on Constitutional Problems—known as the Tremblay Commission—the Société d'assistance aux immigrants and the District of Montreal Chamber of Commerce pleaded in favour of having the Province of Quebec control the selection of immigrants, and thereby favour the entry of French people. Even though the Tremblay Commission adopted the solution advocated in the memoranda from organizations in 1956, the time was not yet ripe for provincial intervention because sufficient pressure had not been exercised on rather indifferent political representatives.

Where were governments through all of this?

Wherever francophones did exercise effective control, as in Quebec, the civil society was not particularly intent on transforming the state into a tool aimed at establishing language standards and promoting French as the language of communications and work. The French-speaking activists often pleaded for incentives, but nothing more. At other times, they begged for a basic respect of the rights of the French-Canadian people.

Elsewhere in the country, French-speaking activists pinpointed areas of intervention for the Canadian state because the capacity of French-speaking minority groups to influence provinces was limited based on their relatively low population numbers and their varied capacities for political mobilization. Divisions also sometimes undermined the action of francophone minority groups. The need to sustain a lobby required major financial and human mobilization, which also caused difficulties, as evident in the school crises in New Brunswick, Manitoba, Alberta, Saskatchewan, and Ontario at the end of the nineteenth and beginning of the twentieth centuries. By focusing on Ottawa, these communities were leaning on the entire group of francophone parliamentarians, in particular the strong contingent from Quebec. They hoped that any gesture supporting the implementation of a language-planning policy based on the compact between the two founding nations would have a spillover effect on the provinces.

Organizations promoting the rights of French Canadians and Acadians included Ordre de Jacques-Cartier, Sociétés Saint-Jean-Baptiste, Conseil de la vie française en Amérique, and school associations in most English-speaking provinces. They lobbied the provincial governments, but mainly the Government of Canada. Their aim was to pressure governments into providing French services by sending them letters, petitions, and memoranda, or by holding private and public meetings with politicians. The lobbying efforts met with limited success, as the work of the Royal Commission on Bilingualism and Biculturalism, better known as the Laurendeau-Dunton Commission, would reveal during the 1960s.

The actions undertaken by members of the French-Canadian institutional network and aimed at the federal government were numerous, but rather sporadic, and they did not necessarily follow a strategy for the promotion of a comprehensive language-planning policy. For lack of drawing up a list of demands, the French-Canadian activists proceeded piece by piece, usually after a policy had been announced or when an event was taking place. These occasions became a pretext to remind the Canadian state of its obligations, at least morally, keeping in mind that the courts had not been generous in their interpretations when they had become involved in the earlier school crises.

The members of the institutional network, some members of provincial legislatures or Parliament, and some figureheads in intellectual circles, such as André Laurendeau, focused on specific matters. They tackled, among other issues, the issue of provision of services in the French language, which in itself indicated a change in conceptions regarding the role of the state and the exercise of rights. Leaving aside the question of whether the Canadian state should actively and systematically provide services in both languages, the activists demanded the hiring of francophone civil servants capable of providing services in French. At the time the job of translating laws was less subject than it had been in the past to the vagaries of recruiting contract employees, as linguist Alain Otis indicates. Indeed, in 1936 the Canadian Parliament had created the Translation Bureau, in which a small expert team of civil servant lawyers was busily translating English legal material into French. Still, the situation remained clearly unfavourable for French Canadians, who continued to be underrepresented within the federal civil service. While in 1918 22 per cent of federal civil servants were French Canadians, that number had dropped to only 13 per cent in 1946. The French-speaking activists mobilized to place pressure on this situation. Working alone or in concentrated groups, they took advantage of the departure of a senior civil servant or a deputy minister—as at the Canada Employment Insurance Commission at the beginning of the 1940s—to request the hiring of a bilingual replacement. In 1947 the issue even landed in the Quebec Legislative Assembly, where the independent member René Chaloult tabled a motion of censure. The Quebec members of the Assembly unanimously protested "to the government in Ottawa against the injustice suffered by the French-Canadian minority in this country," an injustice that was "contrary to the spirit of the Constitution."[9] Finally, during the 1950s, the activists also suggested that francophone deputy ministers be hired to ensure a "just representation" of French-speaking citizens.

At other times the activists congratulated politicians for taking steps to establish a policy promoting the hiring of francophones. They were delighted by a bill tabled by Wilfrid Lacroix and enacted by the federal Parliament in 1938. By virtue of this Act to Amend the Civil Service Act (S.C., 2 Geo.VI, c. 7), civil servants could no longer be transferred to another province if they did not speak the language of the majority in that province. The hope was that this ruling would lead to the hiring of civil servants fluent in French. However, as political scientist Daniel Bourgeois indicates, policy-makers, both elected and members of the civil service, were in no rush to ensure follow-up. Moreover, in 1964 the Royal Commission on Bilingualism and Biculturalism drew attention to the persistence of the underrepresentation of francophones within the federal public administration.

An Act to amend the Civil Service Act
(S.C., 2 Geo. VI, c. 7), a.k.a. the Lacroix Bill (1938)

This bill was adopted by the Parliament of Canada in April 1938. ...

No appointment to a local position in a province shall be made on a permanent or part-time basis, and no employee, permanent or part-time, shall be transferred from a position in a province to a local position in the same province or another province, until the candidate or employee has qualified, by examination, in the knowledge and use of the language of the majority of the persons with whom he is required to do business; provided that such language shall be the French or the English language. ...

Each examination prescribed under this Act shall be conducted in English or French, at the option of the candidate; notice of each examination shall be published in English and French in the *Canada Gazette*, and the notice shall indicate the number of positions to be filled, the positions actually vacant and, in each case, the qualifications required for these positions.[10]

Source: S.C., 2 Geo. VI, c. 7, s.1 and 2.

A second area of intervention focused on the symbolic order. One goal was to encourage the Government of Canada to work everywhere in both official languages, a step that countered those who confined the French-language question to Quebec and refused to recognize the presence of French-speaking Canadians in the rest of the country. An example came when the Conseil de la vie française en Amérique, known in 1939 as the Comité permanent de la survivance française en Amérique, denounced the noticeable lack of French to be found in the Canada Pavilion at the New York World Exposition. Then, a year later, as a follow-up to the National Resources Mobilization Act, enacted in June 1940 as part of the war effort, Ottawa ordered the enlistment of all Canadians over the age of sixteen for the defence of Canada. Federal civil servants distributed English-only enlistment forms outside of Quebec, raising protests from organizations for the defence of French-Canadian rights. At the end of the 1950s, the Conseil de la vie française en Amérique pressured the Canadian government to publish the new geographic atlas of the country simultaneously in both languages.[11]

Federal voting events provided another opportunity for reminding Ottawa of its obligation to distribute all of its documentation in both official languages, everywhere in Canada. When a plebiscite on conscription took place in 1942, the Comité permanent de la survivance française en Amérique requested that the Canadian government print and distribute bilingual ballots in all the polling stations. Ottawa decided otherwise. It distributed French ballots only in jurisdictions in which at least fifteen French-speaking voters lived.[12]

These battles ended up focusing on a major symbol of the state's sovereignty, which was the right to mint coins. After a victory won in 1927 to have stamps printed in both languages, in the 1930s the battle for a bilingual Canadian currency mobilized associations and *Le Devoir*, where the journalist Omer Héroux actively engaged in favour of the cause. The pressures gradually had an effect. As a result, in 1934 the Conservative government of Richard Bennett allowed for the printing of a double series of unilingual banknotes, so that the money could be English or French, as required. Some two years later the Liberal government of William Lyon Mackenzie King passed the Act to Amend the Bank of Canada Act (S.R.C. 1936, 1 Edward VIII, c. 22), imposing bilingualism permanently on Canadian currency, therefore avoiding the abusive duplication of currency.

As a sign of the times, another battle started brewing—this one too involving the symbolic function of the state, in this case the welfare state—with an intervention aimed at reducing inequalities and ensuring that every citizen had the financial means to exercise his or her socio-economic rights. Following the publication of the Leonard Marsh Report in 1942, Ottawa began to design a social safety net, which would eventually be implemented after the Second World War. Various federal income-support programs led to government cheques being issued to citizens entitled to receive them across the country. At that point the language issue once again came sharply into focus—it became apparent that, given the language used on the cheques (English), Canadian citizens were not all equals within the state. The supporters of French-Canadian associations—waging a battle aimed at changing in a lasting way the Canadian symbolic order—constantly reminded the state of its obligation to issue and distribute cheques in both languages. It was a cause that would mobilize the institutional network over a long period of time. When the first old-age pension cheques were sent out in 1952, the activists pressured Ottawa to take action. For them, the state's solution—to send bilingual cheques only in Quebec—was but a first step. They were pleased by the gesture, but they renewed their demand that bilingual old-age pension cheques be sent everywhere in Canada. If Ottawa accepted this approach for pensions, the move would set a precedent for all the cheques issued for other social programs. The activists within the institutional network started their campaign of pressure by sending letters to political leaders. Then members of the Quebec institutional network and francophone minority groups created delegations to lobby federal authorities. In addition, private member bills were tabled in Parliament, such as the one by the independent MP for Beauce, Raoul Poulin, and, as of 1958, those tabled by Louis-Joseph Pigeon and Samuel Boulanger, which all died on the order paper. The publication of articles in dailies by journalists sympathetic to the cause provided weight to the lobby and, especially, helped to support this long battle, which ended in February 1962 when the government of John Diefenbaker announced that it would thereafter print all its cheques in both languages.[13]

The length of this battle can be explained by the obstacles that the activists had to overcome. Even after the victory around the distribution of bilingual cheques, they continued to face the active and passive opposition of members of Parliament, especially those in unilingual English ridings, who feared for their seats. The cheques were an important symbol for citizens—a dimension that escaped neither French-speaking Canadians nor politicians, much less English-speaking Canadians.

The result of almost ten years of lobbying, the victory for bilingual cheques was nonetheless followed by disillusionment. At the beginning of the 1960s, for the Quebec nationalists this lengthy battle clearly demonstrated a lack of leadership on the part of the members of Parliament who were failing to support the creation of a language-planning policy based on the concept of two founding nations. The activists believed that Canadian symbols and the Canadian state's administrative practices should reflect the linguistic and cultural duality throughout the country. Actually, the battle for bilingual cheques foreshadowed even fiercer and more fruitless battles. For example, members of the French-Canadian institutional network had little confidence that they would make significant gains on the issue of language use in the delivery of services, which would oblige the Canadian state to communicate with its citizens in both official languages, or on the language of work, which aimed to provide federal civil servants with the right to work in either of the official languages.

These actions to transform the symbols of the Canadian state did not push the school issue into the background; on the contrary, that issue remained important for the French-speaking minority groups. Although the liberalization of policies on French as a language of instruction came about because of decisions taken by provincial politicians and bureaucrats, the representatives of minority groups believed that Ottawa nevertheless had responsibilities in this area under Section 93 of the Constitution Act of 1867. Therefore, they took advantage of forums provided by a series of federal royal commissions—such as the Royal Commission on Dominion-Provincial Relations (1937–40) chaired by Newton W. Rowell and Joseph Sirois; the Royal Commission on National Development in the Arts, Letters and Sciences (1949–51), chaired by Vincent Massey and Father Georges-Henri Lévesque; and the Royal Commission on Broadcasting (1955–57), chaired by Robert Fowler—to present their requests. Even though the commissions were not dealing specifically with education, community leaders used them to stress the need to solve the school issue and guarantee the use of French in the provinces. At the Rowell-Sirois Commission hearings in 1938, Acadians declared: "How crazy the 'Fathers' [of Confederation] would have been to decree the use of French in Parliament and in federal courts if they had not intended for its use to be possible everywhere in Canada." They believed the solution was to amend Sections 93 and 133 of the Constitution Act of 1867 "in a way that would make it possible for French minorities in the Maritime Provinces to enjoy the same rights and privileges as the Province of Quebec actually provides its English and Protestant minorities." [14] The French Canadians from Alberta demanded that "the Catholic religion and French language be officially recognized in schools in every province in Canada and ... that the French language be made official in every Parliament and every court in the country." [15]

The news media were the activists' final area of intervention. With the arrival of radio, French Canadians in Quebec and French-speaking minority groups turned their attention to the Canadian Broadcasting Corporation (CBC). Until 1958 this Crown corporation had been both a regulatory body for the development of the broadcasting industry—providing broadcasting licences—and a broadcasting undertaking. Community leaders asked the CBC board of governors to create French radio and television stations with the future development of the new media in 1952.

At the beginning of the 1930s, only two radio stations were in operation in Montreal: CFCF, broadcasting in English, and CKAC, a bilingual radio station. When the Canadian Radio Broadcasting Commission (CRBC) was created in 1932, and replaced by the CBC in 1936, the issue of the French language on air and the responsibilities of the federal level of government with regard to bilingualism dominated the development of this new technology. The CRBC created radio stations in Quebec City and Chicoutimi. Outside of Quebec, the Commission's intervention raised strong hostile reactions.

Historian Mary Vipond recalls that when new radio stations began broadcasting in Ottawa, Toronto, Vancouver, and Windsor, complaints poured into the Canadian Radio Broadcasting Commission concerning the portion of time allocated to French-language programming. Many Canadians absolutely rejected the presence of French on air. The battle for bilingualism was thus transferred to on-air radio, raising major questions about the role of the state in this field. Supporters of private enterprise became restless and opposed the intervention of the state in an area that was supposedly a matter for the private sector. They believed that Ottawa should not have any responsibility in the area of broadcasting. Private enterprise and the law of supply and demand were to determine the presence of French on-air. Other opponents, particularly Orange lodges and Ku Klux Klan activists, expressed their opinion violently at the opening of radio stations that broadcasted programs in French outside the boundaries of Quebec. They wrote to the CRBC to manifest their hostility. They put pressure directly on the prime minister for him to go over the head of the Commission, and especially made sure that members of Parliament were well aware of the power of the opposition to the presence of French on radio. These radicals believed that the Canadian Radio Broadcasting Commission was forcing people to listen to bilingual or French programs—although less than 5 per cent of the programming was either in French or in both languages in 1934. In Quebec, 80 per cent of radio programming was broadcast in English. For those opponents who harboured prejudices against French Canadians and were at times intensely hostile to the French language and culture, the broadcasting of programs in French had to be limited to the boundaries of Quebec. Outside of this province, English was to occupy the entire broadcasting space. The radicals wanted to prevent the development of bilingualism in the country and the effective fulfilment of the compact between the two founding nations, which in essence meant respecting collective rights throughout the country, even if they related to demographically minority people.

For the supporters of bilingualism, the issue of its implementation caused a dilemma. Should there be stations offering bilingual programming or, instead, two radio networks, one French and one English? Economic and political requirements dictated the choices made by the CRBC and later, as of 1936, by the Canadian Broadcasting Corporation. Ultimately, the costs of developing a French-language radio network, the weakness of the French markets outside of Quebec, and the competition with private interests in obtaining the available broadcasting licences marked the development of radio in Canada. These factors became major obstacles for francophones and their desire to listen to radio in French.

Faced with how slowly the CBC was extending its French network outside of Quebec, some community members mobilized. When French radio promoters presented a request to establish a station, English-speaking and ethno-cultural groups opposed the application on the grounds that the CBC would be favouring one ethnic group at the expense of the others. The Canadian Broadcasting Corporation's refusal to make French radio one of the priorities in its development plans forced members of French communities in Alberta, Saskatchewan, and Manitoba to rely upon the generosity of their respective communities and collect the money needed to open four radio stations. To cover the major costs of such a project, local leaders helped to organize a fund-raising campaign in Quebec in 1945, as the Acadians had done in 1943 to launch *L'Évangéline*, a daily newspaper in New Brunswick. The campaign led to four radio stations being launched in the 1940s and 1950s, although the high operating costs of these stations later led the CBC to acquire them.

Wherever there were radio stations, the potential of this new means of communication did not escape those concerned with proper language use. During the Third Congress on the French Language, held in Quebec City in 1952, the delegates adopted a number of resolutions:

> Be it resolved that our radio stations become increasingly involved in using
> proper French in order to be themselves guardians and propagators of
> French culture in Canada, from the Atlantic to the Pacific;
> Be it resolved that the television of tomorrow, through its respect for moral
> laws, become also a school of good taste and proper language;
> Be it resolved that the producers and promoters of Canadian films be
> imbued with the same concern for French culture.[16]

Language activism was also aimed at English-speaking provinces. In 1959 the Fédération des Sociétés Saint-Jean-Baptiste de l'Ontario asked the province's Ministry of Roads to print in both languages its pamphlets explaining road safety regulations.[17] Two years later the Association canadienne-française d'éducation d'Ontario convinced the premier not to prohibit the use of bilingual road signs, especially the compulsory stop signs.[18]

In 1957 the Congrès de la refrancisation advocated for a greater respect for French, although for the most part the speakers avoided mentioning the intervention of Ottawa and the provinces as tools for promoting the French language. That intervention would be limited to the creation of an organization intended to advise companies in how to adopt a French corporate name, and another to be in charge of promoting French culture. The promotion of the proper use of language was entrusted instead to the civil society and its bodies, such as literary societies and the business community. In short, a language-planning policy aimed at "influencing or having the effect of influencing the behaviour of others regarding the acquisition, structure and functional distribution of their linguistic codes" was not yet on the agenda.[19]

Turmoil and new questioning

During the 1950s the quality of French-language usage became, once again, a hot subject of public debate. Not only did language seem to have become a social problem, but some stakeholders identified the state as an institutional actor capable of correcting the situation. At the same time the number of French speakers became a matter of concern. The Jesuit Richard Arès—a former member of the Royal Commission of Inquiry on Constitutional Problems, chaired by Mr.

Justice Thomas Tremblay, and editor of the journal *Relations* from 1959 to 1969—sounded the alarm in articles published during the 1950s and 1960s. After reading his articles on French-speaking minority groups, nationalists in Quebec felt they had reason to be worried.

After spending time teaching at the Collège de Saint-Boniface in Manitoba at the beginning of the 1940s, Father Arès was well aware of the reality faced by French-speaking minority groups. The experience had raised his concern for their survival, and he decided to measure their ethno-linguistic strength using so-called objective data found in decennial censuses. Based on his calculations of the difference between the number of speakers whose mother tongue was French and the number of speakers of French-Canadian ethnic origin, Arès believed that he could measure the vitality of the French-speaking minority group in the country. The demographic data had been gathered in a questionable manner. Beyond the problems relating to the wording of the questions, the enumerators were the ones entering the answers and not the respondents themselves.[20] This factor led to repeated criticism, which representatives of the institutional network in French-speaking minority communities passed on to the Dominion Bureau of Statistics, an agency that often failed in its task of hiring bilingual enumerators.

Contrary to the vague and generalized estimates that activists had presented at the conferences on the French language, the information provided by Father Richard Arès was precise and considered to be scientific because it was based on quantifiable data. Despite shortcomings in the method used to collect data, and in the gathered census information as a whole, Father Arès used the collected data to reveal the results of his research in a series of articles published in *Relations* in 1954.

Arès noticed a regression of French usage everywhere in the country. For example, in the Maritime provinces (with the exception of New Brunswick), Ontario, and the Prairie provinces, the shifts in usage to the English language were undermining the well-being of the French-speaking minorities. Arès had trouble hiding his pessimism concerning the communities in the Prairies in particular. He pleaded for concrete measures, though he did not specify which ones, in order to avoid having "the results of the 1961 census reveal even more brutal losses."[21]

The Jesuit writer/researcher was the first to measure language shifts and their impact on socio-linguistic vitality. Arès found that a

French-speaking vitality endured in the region that demographer Richard J. Joy called the "bilingual belt," which ran between Sault Ste. Marie, Ont., and Moncton, N.B. Francophone communities living within this territory, which included, to the west, the cities of Ottawa and Cornwall as well as Sault Ste. Marie in Ontario, and, to the east, Edmundston and Moncton in New Brunswick, had high language vitality rates. Outside this corridor, language use shifted in favour of English as people moved further away from the belt.

The decline in French-speaking minorities outside of Quebec and, to a lesser extent, in Quebec itself led to a reframing of the idea of the nation and its objectives. Some commentators concluded that Arès's data demonstrated the failure of the strategy of calling on the Canadian state to implement an institutionalized bilingualism policy bit by bit. Others believed that the decline in ethno-linguistic vitality created a need to review the territorial boundaries of French Canada and to refocus national action on a state that would be controlled by francophones—and that meant the Province of Quebec. Although the reframing of the thinking and objectives of nationalists had not yet led to the disappearance of the two founding nations theory, it transformed ideas about the boundaries of the territory of one of the founding peoples. As a result, the vision of a French Canada was redesigned to become, essentially, one centred on Quebec.

Historians Maurice Séguin, Guy Frégault, and Michel Brunet played a major role in reframing the nationalist thinking that became identified under the term "neo-nationalism." From then on, the prisms of social representations changed. At the turn of the 1960s, Brunet and the Quebec independentists judged harshly the battles waged in English-speaking provinces in support of the francophone minorities, those passionate battles in the days of the ideology of survival. They reckoned that the time had come to sever ties with the French-Canadian past and redesign the future by using the Quebec state as the guarantor of the future of French-speaking people in the country.

Supporters of independence such as Marcel Chaput, André d'Allemagne, and Raymond Barbeau offered to participate in the accelerated march of history during the final years of the 1950s: the march of peoples shaking off colonialism and opting for national independence. They believed that the battles of the past gave cause to be saddened rather than to rejoice. As it stood, Canada was preventing the realization of a French-Canadian nation, which would need a state of its own to guarantee its well-being. As for the French-Canadian and Acadian minorities in the rest of the country, they would become proof of the fate awaiting French Canadians if they did not support the strategy of making Quebec a nation-state. Attaining independence would be the new means of ensuring the development of the French-Canadian nation. In the end, according to Chaput, d'Allemagne, and Barbeau, Quebec would certainly not be abandoning the minority groups. As Father Arès's research revealed, these communities would be disappearing in any case because of the language shifts in favour of English.

At the time of the decolonization movement, and in the days when adherence to the ideal of an independent Quebec was constantly increasing, francophone citizens were also voicing their interest in what could become the vehicle of independence: the French language itself. According to the first independentists, whether they were from the literary world, like Hubert Aquin and Jacques Ferron, or the socio-political world, like Chaput, d'Allemagne, Andrée Ferretti, and Barbeau, the lack of mastery of the French language and the weakness of the vocabulary were rooted in the process of linguistic colonization.

The first leaders of the independence movement considered the state to be a major actor in the implementation of a language-planning policy aimed at making French the only official language in Quebec. Barbeau, of the Alliance laurentienne, and d'Allemagne, of the Rassemblement pour l'indépendance nationale, saw the accession of Quebec to political independence as the first step in a process that would lead towards French becoming the only official language. They rejected bilingualism in favour of French unilingualism. For the first independentists, the language issue took on a new political meaning: the weakness of the language was due to the political weakness of Quebec. They believed that the French Canadians' position of socio-economic inferiority was the result of their political subordination. Their language and its deficiencies were simply mirroring this situation.

Influenced by the theories of decolonization—articulated in particular by Frantz Fanon in *The Wretched of the Earth* and Albert Memmi in *The Colonizer and the Colonized*—the first independentists explained the precarious state of French language through the reality of colonization. They believed that the socio-economic inferiority of the French Canadians was a logical consequence of the British Conquest in 1760. This colonized condition was seemingly still present in French Canada, and no radical change regarding the future of French would be possible without putting an end to this irrefutable fact. A harmonious co-existence between the English and French languages was impossible. On the contrary, the former dominated the latter. Furthermore, the French-language users, they believed, had internalized a demeaning notion of the language, which caused the proliferation of anglicisms and the vocabulary weaknesses that many individuals had denounced in recent decades.

For the supporters of an independent Quebec and followers of the theories of decolonization, bilingualism was a manifestation of cultural colonization and inferiority, which required not only political intervention, but also—or especially—a change in the political status of Quebec. Nobody among the French-Canadian and Acadian minority groups could remain indifferent to these discourses. Evidently, the independence option scared many people, and leaders within the institutional network reassured themselves at the end of the 1950s that only a small minority embraced this ideological option. As for the notion that bilingualism "killed," as the brochure of the Rassemblement pour l'indépendance nationale proclaimed,[22] members of French-Canadian and Acadian minority groups understood that this concept did not apply to them because bilingualism was a necessity of their economic life.

The supporters of the theories of decolonization understood that the presence of two languages demonstrated the impossibility of co-existing within the same territory. Their presence revealed in particular how one of the languages was a tool of cultural assimilation. Faced with this dilemma, other militants of the French cause, such as Jean-Marie Laurence, columnist and member of the French-speaking CBC's linguistic committee, argued in favour of recognizing the existence of various levels of language practice. These activists believed that it was important to take this factor into account in efforts to encourage citizens to correct themselves. At the turn of the 1960s, a controversy broke out over this issue, more specifically over the notion that the French-Canadian patois was a hybrid language called *joual*.

The controversy over *joual* started with the publication of a vignette by Laurendeau in *Le Devoir*, on October 21, 1959, in which the author argued that young people were speaking *joual*. This claim prompted the Marist Brother Pierre-Jérôme—whose real name was Jean-Paul Desbiens—to support the analysis of the Montreal daily's editor-in-chief. Laurendeau published Desbiens's letter under the pseudonym of "Frère Untel" [Brother anonymous]. *Le Devoir* published several other letters from this Brother Anonymous in 1959 and 1960. Assembled in a book, *Les Insolences du frère Untel* [*The impertinences of Brother Anonymous*], the letters raised a media storm and a public debate on the quality of the French language. With the wit, if not the spiteful anger reminiscent of Léon Bloy's pamphlets, Desbiens launched an attack against *joual*, which he considered a sign of a great poverty of language and of a problem of civilization.

The Impertinences of Brother Anonymous (1959)

The language of defeat. ...

Our pupils talk joual, write joual and don't want to talk or write any other way. Joual is their language. Things have gone so far that they can't even tell a mistake when it is shown them at pencil point. ...

Joual, this absence of language, is a symptom of our non-existence as French Canadians. No one can ever study language enough, for it is the home of all meanings. Our inability to assert ourselves, our refusal to accept the future, our obsession with the past, are all reflected in joual, our real language. ...

Of course joual-speakers [the students] understand each other. But do you want to live your life among joual-speakers? As long as you want merely to chat about sports and the weather, as long as you talk only such crap, joual does very well. For primitives, a primitive language is good enough; animals get along with a few grunts. But if you want to attain to human speech, joual is not sufficient. ...

Now we approach the heart of the problem, which is a problem of civilization. Our pupils speak joual because they think joual, and they think joual because they live joual, like everybody around here. Living joual means rock'n'roll, hot dogs, parties, running around in cars. All our civilization is joual. Efforts on the level of language don't accomplish anything, these competitions, campaigns for better French, congresses, all that stuff. We must act on the level of civilization. ... What can we do? What can a teacher, buried in his school, do to halt the decay? His efforts are ridiculous. Whatever he accomplishes is lost an hour later. From four o'clock on, he is in the wrong. The whole culture contradicts him, contradicts what he defends, tramples on what he preaches. ...

EDUCATION FOR HEAVEN.

We talk joual, we live joual, we think joual. The smart guys will find a thousand explanations for that, the nice people will say it's better not to talk about it, the little female souls will say we mustn't hurt mama's feelings. Nevertheless the only possible explanation for this lamentable failure is that the system of education is a flop. ...

Let's give all the officials all the medals there are, not forgetting the one for Agricultural Merit. Let's create some special ones, such as one for Solemn Mediocrity. Let's give them all a comfortable and well-paid retirement and send them home to their mamas. That would be a lot cheaper than paying them to complicate our lives the way they do now. For there's one sure thing, the Department has given evidence of its incompetence and irresponsibility a hundred times over.

Source: [Jean-Paul Desbiens], The Impertinences of Brother Anonymous, Pref. by André Laurendeau, translation by Miriam Chapin. Montreal, Harvest House, 1966, c1962, pp.27-29, 37, 47.

— —

Contrary to those who for some time had been holding the individual accountable for this sad situation, Desbiens denounced the francization campaigns and the other strategies developed in the past to enhance language proficiency and promote proper language and the enrichment of vocabulary. The fiery Brother Anonymous estimated that these means were outdated and inadequate for correcting the situation. The time had come to consider other solutions. His call was for the intervention of the state.

There is talk of a provincial language agency. I'm all for it. LANGUAGE IS A COMMON GOOD, and it is the State itself that should protect it. The State protects moose, partridges and trout. Some say it even protects cranes.

The State protects national parks, and it does it well: these are common goods. Language is also a common good, and the State should protect it rigorously. A expression is well worth a moose; a word is well worth a trout.[23]

While denouncing the use of *joual*, Desbiens inserted two key elements in the public debate; the first was the idea that language is a common good. The second was to request an energetic intervention by the provincial state.

How did this controversy over *joual* and the poor quality of French echo among French-speaking minority groups? Was there the equivalent of a Brother Anonymous among the Acadians or franco-phones in Manitoba, for example? The debate in Quebec led the Con-seil de la vie française en Amérique to finance at least one research study on the quality of French spoken by French-Canadians. Gaston Dulong, a professor at Université Laval's Faculty of Arts, interviewed youth, professors, teachers, and members of the clergy to assess the quality and vitality of French in Manitoba in 1963. His findings turned out to be a shocking account: "This Francophone minority is already deeply involved in the process of rapid and massive anglicization and, if the school situation is not changed rapidly and radically, French will disappear totally in the near future."[24] The situation, he argued, was the result of deficiencies in the school system. It prepared the young to master the language of the majority, though provincial law allowed the use of French as a language of instruction, one hour a day, from the fourth year of primary school. Dulong's investigation revealed that, in some schools, the use of French could even start in the first grade, as long it was for no more than one hour a day. As for the quality of the language, the Université Laval expert noted the presence of num-erous anglicisms. His account was anything but reassuring because, even though the socio-linguistic vitality of francophone residents in rural communities was better, the situation in urban areas gave rise to concern. Called to the bedside of the ailing Franco-Manitoban, Dulong proposed some strong remedies, including several based on the need for French to become the language of instruction in schools. In addition, he indicated that the teaching personnel had to receive appropriate training. The specialist from Quebec even proposed that

LAC, PA-133218

Christmas shopping in Montreal, December 1961. Photo by Gar Lunney,
National Film Board.

to enhance language vitality the province should attempt to group
French populations together.[25]

All of these debates on the quality of language and the urgency
of state action were not simply about wishing things to happen. On
the contrary, they were meant to stimulate action. Georges-Émile
Lapalme, the former leader of the provincial Liberal Party and author
of the party's 1960 platform, understood the need very accurately. In
a document, "*Pour une politique*," distributed to the party pundits,
Lapalme devoted two chapters to the issue of culture. He believed
that the context was ripe for state intervention in this field. He proposed the creation of a government agency to be called "Office de
la linguistique," which would address the poor quality of French-
language usage. The agency would come under the authority of a
future "Ministère des Affaires culturelles" that would in turn head all
the interventions in the area of culture; it would be in charge, among
other things, of language use, relations with French-speaking minority
groups, urban planning, and historic monuments. Lapalme later wrote

in his memoirs that the time "had come to conceive of the Provincial state as a cultural phenomenon."[26]

These suggestions became part of the Liberal Party's electoral platform, presented to citizens during the 1960 elections. The party promised to create a ministry of cultural affairs that would include a bureau, to be called Office de la langue française, dedicated to the French language. Its rationale for these measures stated:

Within the Quebec context, the most universal element is the French fact, which we must develop even further. It is through our culture, more than by people, that we will impose ourselves. Aware of our responsibilities with regard to the French language, we will provide it with an agency that will be both protective and creative; aware of our responsibilities with regard to the three or four million French Canadians and Acadians who live beyond our borders, in Ontario, the Maritimes, the West, New England, and Louisiana, Quebec will become the motherland for all of them. In the domain of the arts, although we will participate in what is happening in the world, we will attempt to build a culture that will be our own, and at the same time, through urban planning, we will celebrate what is left of our French profile. It is through our French language and culture that we can assert our French presence on the North American continent.[27]

Elected in 1960, the Liberals followed through on their electoral promises by creating the Ministère des affaires culturelles a year later. Its founder, Georges-Émile Lapalme, masterminded the setting up of the Office de la langue française, whose first director was to be Jean-Marc Léger. Under Section 14 of the law establishing the ministry, the Office was responsible for advising the government on any action "involving public notices in order to make sure that the French language is given precedence."[28] Léger interceded with companies to facilitate the use of French, and he promoted correctness in the language. To that effect, the agency published a newsletter entitled *Mieux dire* [Saying it better].

Driven by the energetic minister Paul Gérin-Lajoie, the state action also focused on education and the school system. The creation in April 1961 of a royal commission on education in the province of Quebec, called the Parent Commission, stimulated thinking around the purpose of education, the socio-economic barriers to receiving an education, and the role of the state. Encouraged by the Commission's work, the provincial government undertook to reform its educational structures and proceeded in particular to regroup school boards and create secondary schools called "*polyvalentes*" (multi-purpose, for both general and vocational programs), colleges called CEGEPs (Collège d'enseignement général et professionnel, literally college of general and vocational education), and the Université du Québec network. In addition, it examined the content of programs and promoted the democratization of access to education by investing major amounts in infrastructures and teacher-training. Efforts were, then, obviously being made to enhance the quality and proficiency of French through the reform of primary and secondary school programs. Still, the Commission noted that education was only one aspect of the immense mobilization task required to enhance the standing of the French language. Indeed, the commissioners acknowledged that the learning of French was an integral part of the promotion of the mother tongue as the language of work and communications in Quebec—and only the Quebec government could intervene in both of these areas.

> Schools can only do so much; the erosion and extinction of French in Quebec will remain a constant threat if teaching is not supported by strong and profound socio-economic motivations.... The Ministry of Education is not the only body involved in this issue. The entire Government of Quebec must be watchful not to let the province become isolated in a ghetto; it must implement very strict measures to protect French, not only in schools and universities, but in every aspect of public life. The need is particularly urgent in Montreal.[29]

In the world of education, a nerve centre in which public opinion played such a large role, the Parent Commission produced a genuine mobilization around the issue. It also stimulated discussions on what was needed to increase the quality of language learning as a means of ensuring that young people were capable of meeting the challenges of an economy requiring a more specialized workforce.

– – – – –

While in English Canada the reaction to the language issue was a somewhat disdainful indifference, in Quebec and French Canada the question remained a matter of concern within the public sphere. The conferences on the French language held in 1937 and 1952, and on refrancization in 1957, are proof of this concern. Through these decades, contrary to the previous period, government decisions restricting or prohibiting the use of French in school did not cause major crises. Those were the years of an apparent *bonne entente*, typical of a consociational democracy in which each social group pursued its own interests. Everything seemed calm on the language front, except for the debates on the quality of the spoken language and the strategies to be put in place to raise awareness, and especially to make francophones accountable for their own language usage; they were expected to pay constant attention so that they could both speak and write it properly. When the language issue reappeared, nationalist spokespersons in Quebec and leaders of the French-Canadian minority groups' institutional network were no longer content with demanding respect for their rights. Some activists did not hesitate to declare that they were not interested in begging for rights, in pleading for the majority to demonstrate generosity towards its largest linguistic minority. Meanwhile, those in charge of policy in the Canadian state, clearly wanting to avoid provoking a backlash among members of the other nation, were in no rush to respond to the demands of the French-speaking activists.

Nevertheless, one should always be wary of still waters. The seeming tranquility around the question of language was concealing warning signs of turmoil. Indeed, important debates on French as a language of use took shape at the end of the 1950s. The weakness of the language was proof of the headway made in language assimilation, and Father Richard Arès's research spread concern among some people. His findings prompted various voices to request state intervention to increase the use of French in education. Furthermore, the integration of immigrants into the dominant culture was raising more and more questions. For some critics the prevailing signs simply confirmed the impossibility of living in French outside of Quebec, where francophone communities were being assimilated into the majority. While Brother Anonymous's "*impertinences*" made waves in previously calm waters, others linked the patois or *joual* to the colonization of minds.

The cohabitation of both languages might not be possible, because the English language dominated while the French language suffered. The French-speaking activists established a link between the socio-economic situation of francophones, particularly in Quebec, and the level of French vitality. The economic condition could not be separated from the cultural. These debates foreshadowed the emergence of language as a social problem requiring the intervention of the state.

The solution proposing that the state be placed in charge of creating an overall language-planning policy came from various individuals of different ideological backgrounds, but, as it turned out, it was the Quebec government that had the means needed to implement a language policy. Although many onlookers agreed with the solution, the challenge was to extend the consensus in order to create new symbolic orders—and that would come about through commissions of inquiry, including one set up by the Government of Canada in 1963.

CHAPTER 4

ACTION-REACTION

Commissions of inquiry and agitation, 1963-69

Un jour j'aurai dit oui à ma naissance.
- Gaston Miron, *Pour mon rapatriement* (*L'Homme rapaillé*)

— Don't go! Get him to speak more!
— Patience, citoyen, the Revolution has begun.
- Leonard Cohen, *Beautiful Losers*

Throughout the world the 1960s were a critical period of political, social, and cultural protests. The decade is also associated with flower power, counterculture movements, Black Power and Red Power, student activism on campuses, issues of sexual equality, and opposition to the Vietnam War. With an increase in individualism and various manifestations of the mass-consumption society linked to the emergence in the public sphere of new partners from international migration movements and greater access to education, the 1960s witnessed the erosion of the political culture of informality and accommodation. As members of various communities were becoming publicly vocal while freeing themselves—sometimes in an unruly manner—from power or authority figures, they abandoned the slogans and definitions extolled by these same elites.

For francophones, in the continuing debate around French usage, language—an identifying feature and cultural reality—took on a new, crucial meaning. In Quebec specifically, it came to represent a key element in the definition of the nation-state because it represented the common interest of a community seeking not just to survive, but also to reduce socio-economic inequalities, conditions that in themselves caused public unrest. The need to promote and reassert the value of French became front and centre. In view of the potentially explosive situations—highlighted by 1967–68 disturbances over the language to be used in education in Saint-Léonard and in the Opération McGill français campaign, aimed, among other things, at bringing the rightful use of the French language to the attention of the university—the status quo was no longer an option. Community elites were obliged to request the intervention of the federal and provincial states.

Before that time, federal and provincial leaders, including those in Quebec, had hesitated to adopt measures to promote the French language. Under the former regime of consociational democracy, the issues were addressed by civil authorities. During the 1960s, as citizens began speaking out, debates on the status and future of French led to a questioning of the moral and intellectual authority of community leaders and their inability to singlehandedly determine how citizens should express themselves. From then on, these citizens obliged governments to intervene to meet or defer demands expressed by social actors, and especially to set the groundwork for the implementation of language-planning policies. At the same time, new experts from the fields of social science—demography, in particular—started influencing public debates and government structures. In so doing, they managed to drive discussion of the language issue and propose solutions that they believed could conclusively resolve problems.

Speaking out

The transformation of language into a social problem requiring a political solution came about in combination with an enlargement of the public sphere. The expansion was due in part to postwar demographics, which in turn related to the birth of the cohort known as the baby boomers. It was also due to the cultural diversity emerging from new immigration to the country, which increased when the federal state abandoned certain racial criteria and introduced a point system for newcomers based on their education and technical capital. New communications technologies also contributed to the change. From then on, given that the public space was no longer the exclusive pre-serve of community elites, more and more intervenors spoke up to express their various concerns, which now tended to be rooted in the private sphere and sprang forth from the feminist protest movement or other domains, such as that of cultural identity issues, that tended to be neglected by political leaders.

The expression of concerns took on various forms, including the poor quality of the spoken language, which Brother Anonymous had denounced in his writings. From 1959 to 1975, more than "2,523 articles and works by 1,303 different authors" were published on the subject,[1] numbers revealing the prominence of the issue.

Some authors and poets came to the defence of *joual*. For example, poet Gérald Godin signed several articles in the journal *Parti pris* in which he denounced those who criticized and condemned *joual* as being a sign of the great poverty of the language. He seemed to believe (without expressing this point explicitly) that, on the contrary, the attacks on *joual* were symptomatic of the value judgment of edu-cated elites. The poet also attacked the Office de la langue française and its director Jean-Marc Léger, as well as the implementation of a new specific language standard. According to Godin, the Office was disregarding some of the French Canadians' historical realities, such as their economic, political, and cultural colonization. The use of English and the assimilation of some French-Canadians in Quebec provided proof of how "the *lingua del pane*, in Quebec, was English. It's the language of work; it's the language of money; it's the language of busi-ness."[2] To end this state of colonization, the language issue had to be constructed as a political problem: any enduring solution to the prob-lem would involve actions by the state. According to Godin, the lan-guage problem was a "perfect replica of the decadence of our national culture" and presented a "replica of the economic and political reality in Quebec."[3]

In his defence of *joual*, the poet argued that the literary world should adopt this scorned language to better reflect the reality of the poor and working classes. The people from these classes would stop being ashamed of their language if they heard it on stage or read it in literary works. Various creators, including stand-up comedian Yvon Deschamps, rock singer Robert Charlebois, and playwright Michel Tremblay, started using *joual*. Some of these efforts provoked intense reactions, as indicated by a storm that arose surrounding the production of Tremblay's play *Les Belles-Soeurs* in 1968. The literary, theatrical, and intellectual worlds erupted, which did not prevent the play from becoming a popular success. Although Tremblay made it clear that *joual* as a means of literary communication was mostly suitable for the theatre, he did not shy away from taking a swipe at some of the monuments of Quebec's theatrical world. In an interview with *Le Devoir* in 1969, he stated that "he considered *joual* as a reaction against the theatre of compromise, like [Marcel] Dubé's, which is neither totally French nor totally *joual*, hovering between both."[4]

Tremblay denied that he was promoting *joual*, yet the controversy was rekindled in 1972. Some decisions by the Ministère des affaires culturelles concerning the financing of the production of *Les Belles-Soeurs* in Paris and the refusal to grant a subsidy to Tremblay revived the dispute over the use of *joual* within the creative and cultural milieu. Indeed, government department officials opposed its use and led a fierce battle against it. The criticism—including attacks by *La Presse's* language columnist Pierre Beaudry, writer Claude Jasmin, former minister of cultural affairs Georges-Émile Lapalme, and Yvette Mérat, author of a manifest against *joual*—irked Tremblay. He hardened his tone when responding to his critics. Passionately recalling the reality of economic dominance, he flayed those who still believed in the virtues of campaigns aimed at correcting language. "Let's start by feeding people. It's none of our business to tell them how to speak. The proper language campaigns are the most stupid things on earth. To speak properly is to respect ourselves? That is not true. To eat well, that is to respect ourselves! You have to be colonized to come up with slogans like that."[5]

Another writer, Victor-Lévy Beaulieu, also came to the defence of *joual*, as Karim Larose points out in his study of the language debate. Beaulieu denounced those who took part in campaigns to correct language and who sought to impose specific standards. He believed that the project was an attempt to exercise social control, a move orchestrated by the bourgeoisie to impose its value judgments and assert its own language standards, the ones associated with proper French language.

The controversy over *joual* raised the issue of the quality of language and the standards to be used to achieve that quality. For many specialists, the Parisian standard was the proper point of reference. For linguists, other language experts, and learned people, international French was the standard. In taking this stand, they were subscribing to the efforts of individuals who, like Jean-Marc Léger, envisaged the creation of a community of states with French as the common language.

In New Brunswick, Acadian student activists and their demands caused several people to point out that the young protesters were expressing themselves in awful French. But according to the young people being confronted by academicians and members of the elite, the "bad language" problem of Acadians was the sign of a much greater problem: the condition of a minority group deprived of its rights. These young people believed that Acadians were alienated—even worse, they were "intellectual bastards."[6] In the 1969 documentary *Éloge du chiac*, director Michel Brault demonstrated, through conversations between a young teacher in a French school in Moncton and her Acadian students, the gaps between international standards and the spoken language in Acadia, in a context in which English dominated.

The voice of protest was expressed through massive participation in the renewal of political parties, as in the creation of the Parti Québécois in 1968. Furthermore, associations and unions became democratized and secularized. The expression of citizens' will also demonstrated that citizens' awareness was being raised through various means of mobilizing the public. The subject of wide media coverage, demonstrations, sit-ins, and various expressions of civil disobedience influenced by the counterculture movement replaced backroom lobbying, which many considered to be lacking in transparency and efficiency.

The public protests expressed in these debates resulted in greater social mobilization, based as they were on firm convictions aimed at restoring the value of using French in the public sphere as a means of social and economic promotion. Consequently, between 1963 and 1965 the Société Saint-Jean-Baptiste de Montréal organized a huge awareness campaign called Opération visage français. The goal was "for Montreal to become the natural metropolis of French-Canadians, a city where the language and culture would be French."[7] The Montreal organization adopted unilingualism as the solution to the French-language problem and its practical absence from the commercial landscape, in particular in the metropolis.

Throughout this period, individuals such as Léger, Raymond Barbeau, Marcel Chaput, Jacques-Yvan Morin, and Paul Toupin shared the opinions of the Société Saint-Jean-Baptiste. They were joined in this by organizations such as the Société des écrivains canadiens-français, Fédération des étudiants libéraux du Québec, Presse étudiante nationale, Fédération des jeunes chambres de commerce du Québec, and Fédération des travailleurs du Québec, journals such as *L'Action nationale* and *Parti pris*, and political parties such as the Rassemblement pour l'indépendance nationale (RIN). They all demanded that the state implement a language policy based on the principle of unilingualism. They believed that, in doing so, the province would become engaged in a salutary action of cultural recovery.[8]

Delegates at a meeting of the États généraux du Canada français, held in November 1967, joined in debating the language issue. While some of them wanted French to be the only official language in Quebec, others, especially people from Quebec and Acadia, supported a proposal encouraging the Quebec Legislative Assembly to adopt measures that would be "radical and concrete in order to impose, in actions, the widespread use of French." The proposal called for restrictions on the learning of English in high schools and demanded that schools attended by ethnic minorities not fall under the control of anglophone school boards. The proposal recommended French and English as the two official languages of New Brunswick and indicated that the other provinces should enact laws encouraging the "blossoming" of French. Several segments of the proposal related to the Quebec state, which, the writers said, should encourage the use of French in the workplace, decree French as the only official language of agencies that it controlled directly or indirectly, and promote the use of French in outdoor signage. Other languages could be used "on condition that French is dominant."[9] Finally, the proposal requested that the federal government use both official languages in its public service.

Clash between francophones and members of the Italian community, September 1969.

The public protests led to even greater radicalization of the controversies. In 1967, in Pierrefonds, the RIN staged a demonstration to request the opening of a French school in the municipality. The protest required the intervention of an anti-riot squad to separate the nationalist demonstrators from the anglophone counter-demonstrators. That same year, tensions heightened in Saint-Léonard, a suburb of Montreal. Pitted against each other were the Association des parents de Saint-Léonard (APSL), which included Italian-speaking members demanding English schooling for their children, and the Mouvement pour l'intégration scolaire (MIS), made up of French-speaking parents demanding that the Saint Léonard-de-Port-Maurice school board establish a French primary school system. The two groups opposed each other during the school elections. After the MIS's victory and a resolution it passed in June 1968 on unilingual teaching, the APSL shot back in October with the creation of clandestine English classes. Challenged by an outburst in fall 1968, when several militant groups came to blows, the Quebec political leaders had to step in to restore social peace.[10] The Saint-Léonard case raised the question of schooling for children from allophone communities and the parents' tendency to favour English education, something that exasperated a growing number of francophones.

Given how slowly the Province of Quebec was moving in the area of language, the battle for French unilingualism focused on a prominent institution of the Montreal English-speaking world, McGill University. In 1969 Opération McGill français led a campaign to restore the French language to its rightful place in a setting that predominately and traditionally looked the other way—on one March 1969 day thousands of protesters marched to the gates of the university with radical demands, including the idea of transforming the institution into a francophone institution.

The polarization surrounding language issues did not remain within the borders of Quebec. During the winter of 1968, in protest against an increase in tuition fees, the student association at the Université de Moncton condemned a policy on the distribution of grants to universities in New Brunswick, which they believed discriminated against their French-speaking establishment. The protest movement provoked famous demonstrations at the Legislative Assembly in Fredericton and at the municipal council in Moncton, where student spokespersons heckled the anti-French Leonard Jones, mayor of Moncton from 1963 to 1974. The university sit-ins were nevertheless the swan song of these Acadian militants. They were expelled by the Université de Moncton administration shortly after, at the same time as the school shut down its sociology department.[11]

Among so many other events, the symbolic actions linked to Saint-Léonard, Opération McGill français, and Moncton provided examples of citizens speaking out and questioning the hegemony of traditional positions on the language issue. They also echoed the fears of the community elites who were faced with these movements challenging social order. With the view of channelling the voice of citizens, some bearers of scientific knowledge—experts in demography and sociology—tried to find a rational explanation for the problems rooted in the language situation. Their studies aimed to reduce the potential for violence by raising the discussion to the level of dialogue and seeking for a resolution of the social conflicts with the help of the state.

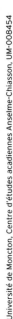

New Brunswick premier Louis Joseph Robichaud meeting a delegation of Acadian students on strike, 1968, Université de Moncton.

Their diagnoses revealed the precariousness of the French language. The publication of their studies also revealed sombre prognoses on the preservation of a dynamic Francophonie, or French-speaking world, in Canada and even in Quebec. From then on, given the recognition they received within the civil society and the state, these scientific experts took centre stage.

Once again Father Richard Arès led this campaign. His findings from the previous decade were not reassuring; based on federal census data, they pointed to a spiralling assimilation of francophone communities. In 1963 Arès became much more pessimistic when he based the rationale for his findings on the 1961 Census data. In the wake of his catchy title, "*La grande pitié de nos minorités françaises*" [Our pitiful French minorities], he argued that Confederation had been "very costly for the French language: not only did it lose many of its members, but it was also showing a loss of more than 400,000 people who should normally be speaking it." [12] He noted the lack of any significant progress in reversing the trend in language shifts towards English. The rates of assimilation of French-speaking minority groups remained high, with the phenomenon continuing to increase as they became further removed from Quebec borders.

Convinced that his approach was scientific, Arès estimated that more than half a million individuals were no longer speaking French. He figured that assimilation was also undermining the Acadian population in New Brunswick. Faced with these conditions, he came to a sombre conclusion: "The tragedy of the French-speaking minorities in Canada is also that of the entire Canadian Confederation; its destiny is linked to theirs. If the former were to die, the latter would also be heading to its tomb." [13] Even though he remained silent on the preferred means of reducing language shifts, from then on Father Arès linked the fate of French-speaking minority groups to the future of Confederation. He knew that, due to a transformation in strategy after the Liberals gained power in the province in 1960, constitutional reform was now on the agenda of federal-provincial meetings. The provincial Liberals wanted to increase the powers and financial means of the Quebec state. Given the context, Arès was hoping that the French-speaking minority groups would not become the great forgotten in Canadian constitutional reform. He turned language assimilation into a political problem whose solution would require state intervention.

On November 4, 1969, three demographers from the Université de Montréal, Hubert Charbonneau, Jacques Légaré, and Jacques Henripin, sent Le Devoir the preliminary pages of their study on the future of French-speaking people in Quebec. [14] These researchers proposed a series of demographic scenarios based on the evolution of migratory movements and birth rates. Known in the past for their purportedly high birth rates, the francophones in Quebec had entered a period of low birth rates in the 1960s. The three demographers were careful to warn readers that their hypothetical scenarios should not be interpreted as certainties, but, despite this caution, they noted that all of their scenarios showed a reduction in the relative proportion of francophones in Quebec (from 82.3 per cent in 1961 to 80.4 per cent or 76 per cent in 1986). In the case of Montreal, various scenarios set the proportion of francophones at 63.2 per cent and 58.2 per cent in 1986.

According to the demographers, a major problem—the francization of immigrants—needed to be resolved, and they saw the Quebec state as the best hope for undertaking the task (see Table 1). The scientific nature of the data they presented impressed various participants in the language debate, who gave little consideration to the ideological and nationalist motivations of the experts.

Table 1

Language chosen by immigrants to Quebec, by periods

Years	French language	English Language
Before 1960	21 per cent	79 per cent
1960-70	36 per cent	64 per cent
1971-75	47 per cent	53 per cent
1976-80	61 per cent	39 per cent
1981-86	54 per cent	46 per cent

Source: Quebec Bureau of Statistics, *Quebec Official Publisher, 1987,* Tables 9-2, p.322.

Sociologist Paul Cappon joined in by analysing the language preferences of immigrants. Using statistical data, he noted that, no matter which "ethnic group" was being considered, "an economic bias ... worked against the assimilation of immigrants into the francophone community." This factor explained the trend of "assimilation into the group that economically dominates Quebec society": the anglophone group.[15]

The research and publications of language-learning specialists supported the position of the individuals and groups promoting French unilingualism. They wondered when would be the best moment to undertake the learning of a second language. Many argued that bilingualism harmed the acquisition of the mother tongue, and, consequently, francophones should delay learning English as long as possible.[16]

The scientific experts had a strong influence on political leaders. As civil servants, they took part in the development of public policies in the federal and provincial states. As independent experts, they were often called upon to work on commissions of inquiry. What they said also influenced the debate unfolding in the public sphere. Occasionally they spread concerns about the vitality of the French language. They helped to broaden the debate to include the issue of language shifts, the role of French as a tool of social mobility, and the place of French in the workplace and in other economic activity.

Channelling the citizens' voices

The proposals being put forward for unilingualism as a policy of language planning in Quebec raised certain apprehensions. To channel the expression of public opinion, the federal and Quebec states opted for the creation of commissions of inquiry.

As major exercises in public consultation set up by state leaders, these commissions of inquiry provided an accumulation of knowledge prior to the making of political decisions. On two occasions scientific experts were mobilized around the language issue: during the Royal Commission on Bilingualism and Biculturalism (Laurendeau-Dunton Commission), set up by the federal government; and the Commission of Inquiry on the Situation of the French Language and Linguistic Rights in Quebec (Gendron Commission), set up by Quebec.

The Liberal government of Lester B. Pearson established the Laurendeau-Dunton Commission in 1963, following incendiary comments made by Donald Gordon, president of the Canadian National Railways, to the effect that French Canadians were not suitably qualified for management positions in his business. The Pearson government was inspired by a suggestion made by André Laurendeau, who, writing in *Le Devoir* in January 1962, did little to hide his disappointment at the announcement that henceforth all the cheques issued by the federal government would now be printed in both languages—he believed that bilingual postage stamps and cheques were mere "crumbs" for French Canada.[17] According to the Montreal intellectual, the time had come for Ottawa to meet the aspirations of French Canadians and take into consideration their expectations for full participation within Confederation—which meant full acceptance of their language rights.

The Laurendeau-Dunton Commission began in a climate of nationalist effervescence in Quebec and a profound transformation in ethnic relations in Canada. From the start, as co-chair Laurendeau was aware of the Commission's historic mission: to seek to understand the present state of relations between the two "founding peoples," a term still in use at the time.

Royal Commission on Bilingualism and Biculturalism (1963)

Mandate: "To inquire into and report upon the existing state of bilingualism and biculturalism in Canada and to recommend what steps should be taken to develop the Canadian Confederation on the basis of an equal partnership between the two founding races, taking into account the contribution made by the other ethnic groups to the cultural enrichment of Canada and the measures that should be taken to safeguard that contribution."

Source: Order in Council of the Privy Council 1963-1106,
Part I of the Inquiries Act (S.R.C. 1952, ch. 154), July 19, 1963.

Anxious to enable the participation of citizens for the first time in the history of commissions of inquiry, the Laurendeau-Dunton investigation, as Paul Lacoste explains, departed from the traditional procedures of public hearings to reach out directly to Canadians through regional meetings held across the country. The voices heard were impressive: 104 ethnic and cultural associations; 169 professional associations, organizations, and companies of all sorts; 12 churches and religious organizations; and 114 individuals—4 of whom remained anonymous—sent briefs to the Commission prior to July 1, 1964. The twenty-three regional meetings with the commissioners were even more popular: from March 18 to June 16, 1964, more than 3,600 individuals attended the day sessions and 8,200 the evening ones. The public forum allowed less-well-known groups to put forward their points of view and, in some cases, to see their opinions prevail because of the very quality of their arguments.

To prepare minds for radical solutions, Laurendeau presented a disturbing diagnosis in the preliminary report, published in 1965. He declared, "Canada is in the most critical period of its history since Confederation." [18] At the time, even though it was categorically rejected by the future leader of the federal Liberal Party, Pierre Elliott Trudeau, the statement raised concerns within the political microcosm.

After several years of patient lobbying, the leaders of French-speaking minority groups interpreted the creation of the Laurendeau-Dunton Commission as a victory. The commotion that the preliminary report raised in political and intellectual circles prompted community leaders to take advantage of the wave of sympathy that they thought they were seeing among anglophone policy-makers. They believed the time was ripe for settling their grievances, in particular regarding education. But there was a fly in the ointment. In keeping with the interpretation of its mandate, the Commission had to take the role of ethnic groups into consideration. The leaders of French-speaking minority groups feared the impact of other ethnic groups and reiterated in their briefs that Canada was a country created by two founding people, a country in which two languages and two cultures co-existed. Consequently, governments should recognize those realities.[19]

What position did these leaders ascribe to the other ethnic groups? And, in particular, should the demands of those groups be taken into account? A brief submitted by the Conseil de la vie française en Amérique provides an example of the response:

We are pleased by the presence in Canada of thousands of fellow citizens whose cultural ancestry is different from ours and enriches us. However, we believe that an English-Canadian culture and a French-Canadian culture exist in Canada, and that these cultures are distinct from those of France and England; but we do not believe that it is possible to claim that there is a German- or Italian- or Ukrainian- or Israeli-Canadian culture here, to name but a few.[20]

A key brief submitted by the Montreal section of the Sociétés Saint-Jean-Baptiste rejected the notion of institutional bilingualism: "It is impossible for a French Canadian in 1964, aware of the real problems facing the nation to which he belongs, to recall the history of bilingualism in the federal administration without a feeling of weariness or revolt." The Montreal organization proposed a constitutional reform based on the recognition of two founding nation-states: Quebec and Canada. Each state would choose its national language. In

Quebec that language would be French unilingualism. The two states would create a federal structure whose common bodies and capital would be bilingual.[21]

Other citizens did not believe that the diagnosis of the crisis as articulated by the Laurendeau-Dunton Commission in its preliminary report reflected their own understanding of the situation. Indeed, they argued, the remedy envisaged by the commissioners—state intervention in the language domain—would create a real crisis that would threaten national unity, rather than further it. This was the point of view of anglophones hostile to the idea of a federal language-planning policy. As long as bilingualism was limited to Quebec, they would be content.

In his analysis of the hearings that the Commission held in Moncton in 1964, historian Joël Belliveau recalls that, according to many anglophone intervenors, everything was fine in terms of linguistic and cultural cohabitation in their province. Some of them even claimed that no language tensions existed between anglophones and Acadians. The mayor of Moncton, Leonard Jones, proposed the abolition of French-language schools in his province so that young people could be educated in a single language and culture. In his mind that step would simplify the preservation of harmonious relations between the two communities. When the francophones present at this session showed little reaction, their silence annoyed the Commission co-chair, who was from Quebec. Laurendeau rationalized this lack of reaction by citing the weight of the Acadian past and the imbalance of demography and linguistics that seemed to have led to a political culture based on compromise.

The prospect that the federal state could enact a policy that would include providing bilingual administrative services, language training, and the use of French as the language of work, at least within the federal public service, raised great fears. Some groups firmly believed that bilingualism would undermine national unity. Organizations such as the Voice of Canada League, whose motto was "One National Loyalty, One National Language, One Canada," or the Canadian National Association, whose motto was "One Language for Canada," encouraged Canadians to speak out and bring their protest to political leaders to persuade them to reject the inquiry's diagnosis of the Canadian patient and the solutions proposed to reduce, or even cure, the symptoms of the ailment.[22]

Nevertheless, some people, while sharing the Laurendeau-Dunton Commission's verdict that a crisis was at hand, feared that the solution of institutional bilingualism would in turn create a new crisis resulting from the non-inclusion of other ethnic groups in the symbolic order. The immigrant communities dreaded an amendment of the Canadian Constitution that would take only Quebec demands into account.

In 1966 the Laurendeau-Dunton Commission received sixty-two briefs from a sector that the commissioners called the "third force," and was later known as "allophone groups." Some fifty-six of these briefs came from institutional networks. Some communities encouraged the Commission to propose policies to strengthen the bilingual nature of Canada—the Japanese-Canadian Citizens' Association, for example. However, this organization made sure to encourage the commissioners to explore the means of helping other ethnic groups maintain their own cultures. The representatives of ethnic groups nonetheless expressed a sense of uneasiness. They feared that the transformation of national symbols aimed at recognizing the two founding peoples would result in their own exclusion. The Canadian Polish Congress explicitly expressed its concerns, arguing that the notion of two founding peoples left no space open for the other ethnic communities.[23] Prior to the beginning of the hearing, the Canada Ethnic Press Federation even asked the Commission to replace the term "biculturalism" with "multiculturalism" in its designation.[24]

Among the groups, the various Ukrainian organizations were without question among those who best grasped the issues. They deemed that the Commission would attract the attention of political leaders and that its recommendations would not go unheeded. They used the public hearings and mobilized their network of connections and interests to make the commissioners, if not the political leaders, take into account the demands of their community, in particular its vision of Canada and of the place granted to ethnic groups. Ukrainian organizations submitted some thirty briefs in which they insisted on the unacceptability of biculturalism—because, they said, the origins of Canada were multicultural. The bilingualism solution should take into account the demographic weight of certain ethnic groups, in particular the Ukrainians. If the state were considering involvement in the field of language, it should recognize other languages in addition to French and English.[25]

The Ukrainian representatives were relying on the support of Senator Paul Yuzyk. He relayed complaints from members of his community who were fighting against the slightest political desire to restructure Canadian symbols within a framework of constitutional reform that would recognize Canada as a pact between two founding peoples. To do so would be to infringe on the rights of Canadians from other ethnic groups, which, according to the 1961 Census, made up 26 per cent of the Canadian population. Yuzyk did not want the contribution of these communities to be neglected; he believed that their contribution to the development of Canada was as important as that of the so-called founding peoples, even if their roots on Canadian soil went back only about a hundred years. The senator took pleasure in reminding people that Canada had never been bicultural. The presence of Aboriginals prior to the arrival of Europeans and the multi-ethnic composition of the Anglo-Saxon group undermined the myth of biculturalism. Later, during an examination of the bill on Official Languages in 1969, Yuzyk reminded federal members that they were denying the demands of communities who spoke a language other than French and English.[26]

While some ethno-cultural groups abstained from submitting briefs to the Laurendeau-Dunton Commission, this decision did not mean that they had chosen not to participate. Quite the contrary: they expressed themselves by sending letters and participating in seminars on the renewal of the Canadian Constitution and the place of ethnic groups in this constitutional re-engineering. In one session in 1963, leaders of the Canadian Jewish Congress expressed their reservations regarding the mandate of the Commission that was defining Canada as a partnership based on the notion of equality between two founding peoples. The Congress was concerned about a constitutional recognition of the notion of two founding peoples and feared that if legislators went down this path, they would be ignoring the contribution of other ethnic groups in the development of Canada. Other organizations, such as the Italian Immigrant Aid Society, were not at all offended by the Commission's mandate and the desire to encourage the state to act merely in the areas of bilingualism and biculturalism.[27]

The pulse of the nation. Caricature of the Laurendeau-Dunton Commission by John Collins, *The Gazette* (Montreal), ca 1965.

In addition to receiving briefs and letters and organizing public hearings, the Laurendeau-Dunton Commission sought the opinion of experts. The expert witnesses would have a heavy influence on building the knowledge necessary to the later efforts of decision-making and defining of policies. In the end the Laurendeau-Dunton Commission devoted "more time to research in social science," in the words of its research director, and paid "more attention" to that research "than any other commission, except for the Rowell-Sirois Commission," citing a total of 145 studies.[28] In a report appended to the first volume of the commissioners' report—on official languages—Michael Oliver specified that the main objective of the Commission's Research Office was clearly to provide relevant data for the making of recommendations, but it also had another goal: the creation of a large research group, which no Canadian university could pull together, to undertake proactive studies of interconnected problems. The Commission thus greatly stimulated the development of social sciences in the country and helped prepare the changing of the guard by hiring 137 graduate students as contract workers.[29]

How did the members of this research group function? As in other sectors of state activity, they first of all willingly adopted a problem-based approach. They divided the overall question by type of issue to be analysed and expertise required for each type. According to this classification scheme, the Research Office produced studies broken down into different areas such as official languages (six studies), the work world (thirty-three), the education sector (twenty-four), cultural groups other than the two founding peoples (sixteen), arts and literature (six), media (twelve), the national capital (one), federal bodies (five), volunteer associations (six), and various other studies (thirty-six). The problem-based approach also made it possible to centralize the work of the experts, in the way that medical or hard science teams worked in a lab. Led by political scientists Michael Oliver and Léon Dion, the Commission's research team followed the same model: each expert produced a report within his domain of expertise, and the reports then went to a central body—the Research Office—which proposed the fruit of the thinking to the commissioners.

In thematically constructing the subject of the study, the problem-based approach widened the outlook by allowing comparisons. For example, examining international situations, which offered certain resemblances with Canada, could provide insight for analyses and reflection. This comparative approach, which confirmed the commissioners' scientific approach as well as their openness to the rest of the world, was one of Laurendeau's initial motivations. He wanted to

study "abroad, and closely—countries such as Belgium and Switzerland—the way societies facing the same questions [as ours] resolved
them."[30] In the Commission's report, Belgium, Finland, Switzerland,
and South Africa became benchmarks in the sketching of solutions to
the Canadian language problems. Pointing out that "even an international language like French, under certain sociological conditions,
can wither away,"[31] the Laurendeau-Dunton Commission used several
research projects that contributed to a comprehensive scientific survey.

The Laurendeau-Dunton Commission's objective of applying scientific expertise derived from a second approach to political
decision-making: the distinctively Canadian managerial rationality.
Based on a monopoly exercised by the experts on risk assessment and
management, the managerial rationality approach granted an inferior
role to the uninitiated, limiting it to the development of acceptable risk
standards. Therefore, in the studies produced by the Research Office
the briefs and other statements originating from civil society were
granted rather scant attention, except when they supported the verdict
of the experts. Managerial rationality is also based on a tendency to deny
the existence of scientific controversies—rather than revealing them,
as would be the case in a conflicting perspectives approach. The scientific experts at the Laurendeau-Dunton Commission seemed to reach
an implicit consensus: the language situation was already sufficiently
controversial within society. Furthermore, they found it important not
to add fuel to the fire by noting divergences in interpretation among
experts. What's more, any such controversy would diminish their capacity to persuade political decision-makers to take appropriate action.

The combination of these two methodological approaches had
a concrete impact on the content and designs of the studies. Oliver
explained the process: the experts' work at the Commission was
to assist in developing useful models for analysing a Canadian society made up of two linguistic communities. Consequently, the main
assumption was no longer based on the premises of assimilation and
resistance to assimilation—an assumption frequently put forward by
intervenors from civil society—but rather on an enduring interaction
between groups that preserved their specific cultural characteristics. In
addition, the research director wanted to spread the good news among
the citizens. The studies were presented as a source of information for

those who were studying "Canadian Affairs" and, through them, for the entire "Canadian public." [32]

The studies, particularly when they documented the place that francophones occupied in the social hierarchy, were echoed in the public sphere. Many intervenors commented bluntly on conclusions about the economic inferiority of French Canadians in Quebec and how studies of the average income of a worker in 1961 in Quebec ranked French Canadians in twelfth place among the fourteen ethnic groups listed (see Table 2).

Table 2

Average income of male salaried workers by ethnic origin, Quebec 1961

Origin	Annual Revenue ($)	Index
All origins	3,469	100
British	4,940	142.4
Scandinavian	4,939	142.4
Dutch	4,891	140.9
Jewish	4,851	139.8
Russian	4,828	139.1
German	4,254	122.6
Polish	3,984	114.8
Asiatic	3,734	107.6
Ukrainian	3,733	107.6
Other European	3,547	102.4
Hungarian	3,537	101.9
French	3,185	91.8
Italian	2,938	84.6
Aboriginal	2,112	60.8

Source: Royal Commission on Bilingualism and Biculturalism, Report, Table 5, Labour Income, Book III, Ottawa, Queen's Printer, 1969, p.23.

While the creation of the Laurendeau-Dunton Commission was a means of channelling the voice of citizens, the federal state was also resorting to the surveillance of individuals and groups who were demanding unilingualism in Quebec. The Royal Canadian Mounted Police was gathering information on individuals and groups such as the Mouvement pour l'unilinguisme français au Québec, the Front du Québec français, created in 1969, and the Mouvement pour l'intégration scolaire, whose members were protesting against the lack of services in French and demanding the proclamation of French as the only official language in Quebec. In addition, RCMP officers would send reports to their superiors on the scale of demonstrations, such as the one held in March 1969 organized by Opération McGill français or those organized in Montreal and Quebec City against Bill 63, which was tabled in October 1969 by the Union Nationale government of Jean-Jacques Bertrand. The surveillance involved gathering newspaper articles and sending reports on press conferences and other public activities organized by groups and militants supporting the cause of French unilingualism. Officers who infiltrated these groups and scrutinized the public actions—or got information from municipal police—sought to detect the presence of external influences, quantify the strength of the independence movement with the groups, and attempt to determine their potential for violence during the demonstrations, as in the case of Opération McGill français.[33]

As it turned out, the language turmoil was hitting Quebec hard. In 1968, right in the middle of a political crisis, the Quebec government under Jean-Jacques Bertrand also created a commission, headed by linguist Jean-Denis Gendron.

Commission of Inquiry on the Situation of the French Language and the Language Rights of Francophones

Mandate, Order-in-Council (December 9, 1968)

With respect to an inquiry into the situation of the French language in Quebec and the measures needed to ensure the full development of the citizens of Quebec and their language rights;

Given the complexity of the language problem in Quebec and the urgency of finding solutions;

Given the responsibility that Quebec has regarding the language of the majority of its citizens;

Given the need for a language policy that takes into account the nature of Quebec in North America and its relations with the other Canadian provinces and the federal government;

Whereas it is critical to undertake an inquiry on the situation of the French language in Quebec;

Whereas, for similar motives, it is essential to find the most suitable means that will guarantee the exercise of the language rights of the majority while respecting the rights of the minority;

IT IS ORDERED, therefore, on the motion of the premier:

That a Commission be created ... to gather evidence and report on the situation of French as the language of use in Quebec, and to recommend measures to guarantee:

a) the language rights of the majority as well as the protection of the rights of the minority;

b) the full development and dissemination of the French language in all sectors of activity, at once in educational, cultural, social, and economic areas.[34]

> Source: Québec, Rapport de la Commission d'enquête sur la situation de la langue française et sur les droits linguistiques au Quebec, Livre 1, La langue de travail. La situation du français dans les activités de travail et de consommation des Québécois, Quebec (Prov.), Official Publisher, December 1972, pp.iv-v.

– – – – – – – – – – – – – – – – – –

On December 31, 1972, following four years of inquiry, the commissioner published a three-volume report dealing with language rights and the situation of French in work and the marketplace, and amongst ethnic groups. The Gendron Commission received 155 briefs from individuals and organizations. In their analysis of the input, historians Jean Hamelin and André Côté found that Quebec society was deeply divided on the question of any state action pertaining to language matters. The anglophone and business communities were hostile to government intervention and preferred the status quo. Business representatives justified their position by invoking the imperatives of the North American economy, in which the use of English dominated, and the dependence of Quebec on foreign economic markets. The organizations involved in the education system favoured the implementation of a language policy that would include, among other things, the regulation of access to English schools. According to political scientists Donat J. Taddeo and Raymond C. Taras, in their study of the Italian community and the language debate, the Commission des écoles catholiques de Montréal (CÉCM, Catholic School Board of Montreal) recommended that tests be established to measure the English-language knowledge of anyone who wanted to send their children to an English school. The Catholic School Board also proposed another criterion to regulate access to English schools: that children had to have at least one parent educated in English in Quebec before they could attend an English school. Finally, one brief signalled the emergence of a new voice in the discussion, that of the First Nations. In a submission written almost exclusively in Mohawk, the Kahn-Tineta community of the Caughnawaga (Kahnawake) reserve reminded the commissioners of the importance of respecting treaties.[35]

At the end of their study Hamelin and Côté raised the question of representation—asking how representative the organizations and individuals were who submitted the 155 briefs to the Commission. The historians did not try to determine which groups and individuals were actually representative of the organizations and communities for which they claimed to speak. Furthermore, Hamelin and Côté argued that these various organizations had tended to use the Commission to enhance their own power and influence. The citizens' voices did not stop with the submission of a brief. On the contrary, while they awaited the tabling of the Commission's report, organizations and individuals continued to pursue their cause, gauging their influence and preparing for battle, this time with the aim of winning the favour of political leaders.

For the Gendron Commission the list of briefs received from ethnic community organizations was surprisingly different compared to that of the Laurendeau-Dunton Commission. The Gendron Commission received only fourteen briefs from "allophone groups." That result was partly because many such groups in Quebec were either poorly organized or not organized at all. In addition, as they showed in their relations with provincial policy-makers, the leaders of the ethnic groups preferred using unofficial contacts. Indeed, in April and June 1970, the members of the Gendron Commission met with some thirty school principals and representatives of various ethnic groups to hear their grievances.[36] Finally, the ethnic groups were focused on the federal scene and the work of the Laurendeau-Dunton Commission. It was the Ukrainians especially who organized around the language issue in Canada, and given that the community was not very big in Quebec—it was rooted primarily in Western Canada—the Ukrainian institutional lobby was, not surprisingly, less active within the framework of the Gendron Commission.

Adopting the same model as the Laurendeau-Dunton Commission, the Gendron Commission based its work on scientific expertise supported by social sciences methodologies.[37] In 1970 and 1971 sociologist Serge Carlos of the Université de Montréal interviewed five thousand individuals on the language they used at work, and he found that about 64 per cent of the francophones and anglophones interviewed worked exclusively in their respective mother tongues. The situation was a bit more troubling in Montreal, the economic capital of Quebec. Only 46 per cent of francophones worked exclusively in French in the metropolis. Furthermore, 48 per cent of the francophones used both languages at work. As for the anglophones, whatever their profession and line of activity, and for those grouped under the term "other"—citizens whose mother tongue was neither French nor English—English remained the language of work. According to the study, 14 per cent of the allophones worked exclusively in French, while 40 per cent of them used both languages. The sociologist's analyses revealed, "It is more costly for a francophone than an anglophone worker to rise in the hierarchy at work. Bilingualism is imposed on the former, while unilingualism is accepted for the latter."[38] Confronted with this situation, the francophones interviewed supported state intervention.[39] Other studies documented francophone underrepresentation in management positions within companies established in Quebec.

The holders of this knowledge, the scientific experts, spread anxiety about the future of French-speaking people. Quebecers may have wanted to maintain their demographic weight within the Canadian federation and promote economic development in French, but a public consensus was emerging: the need to integrate immigrants into the francophone majority.[40] However, to guarantee their own economic success, the newcomers preferred to be trained in English. Consequently, they sent their children to English schools. Elsewhere in Canada the problem was the capacity to gain access to French education, from kindergarten to university—which explains the extent to which the schools were a critical issue in language-planning policy. Tensions between individual rights and the common good, between short-term economic development and long-term social progress, were vigorously expressed.

For its part, the Laurendeau-Dunton Commission tabled a series of recommendations between 1967 and 1971. It proposed the rollout of measures to promote French-language rights outside Quebec as a means of eliminating one of the causes of francophone discontent about the functioning of Confederation. The Commission recommended that a true bilingual policy be implemented within the federal jurisdiction. It suggested that Ontario, New Brunswick, and the National Capital Region become officially bilingual. It also proposed the adoption of measures to promote the use of French in businesses. One of the major elements of the proposed bilingualism policy was the creation of bilingual districts in areas in which French-speaking or English-speaking minority groups made up 10 per cent of the population, based on the geographic divisions used in Canadian censuses. This was a concession to the territorial principle—official status only within a defined territory—in the implementation of institutional bilingualism. Within these districts, "official language minority groups"—an expression the Commission used to distinguish these people from other ethnic groups and francophones in Quebec—would have access not only to federal, provincial, and municipal services, but also to public schooling, in their own language.

With regard to education, by promoting the two languages across the country the commissioners were rejecting the territorial principle, which was a constituent principle of the Belgian language-planning policy. Observing that the principle had not solved the conflicts between communities in Belgium, they added that "the legal restrictions on the right of Belgian parents to choose the language in which their children are to be taught" formed a constraint "that few Canadians would accept."[41] The commissioners knew that the francophones in Canada would not accept losing their right to send their children to schools in which French was the language of instruction. They recommended the recognition of the right of parents to educate their children in one or the other official language, wherever there was a sufficient number of francophones or anglophones. It was therefore necessary to solve the question of access to French schools in English-speaking provinces—and the need for such a settlement became particularly urgent in Ontario and New Brunswick.[42]

Urging the state to act

While the debates on the language issue in the public sphere led the federal and provincial states to examine the place of French in the administrative practices of their institutions, the scant progress made on the issue fuelled the disgruntlement of citizens who were demanding decisive actions.

In addition to the creation of the Laurendeau-Dunton Commission, the federal government under Pearson adopted various measures to appease francophone public opinion, which, as political scientist Daniel Bourgeois indicates, was becoming impatient with the procrastination of the federal machinery of government in providing services in French. In April 1966 the prime minister announced the launch of language-training programs for civil servants, the use of one or the other official language within the bureaucracy and in communications between civil servants and the population, and a hiring policy that would take into account proficiency in the official languages.

In Quebec debates on language were part of the extensive symbolic re-engineering of the Quiet Revolution. It was a period when the provincial state started to become more active not only in jurisdictions relating to the powers it had been granted in the Constitution, such as education and social services, but also in new sectors, such as culture and international relations. On the language-issue front, the Quebec state created the Office de la langue française in 1961, which it integrated into the Ministère des affaires culturelles. (In 2002 the bureau later became known as the Office québécois de la langue française.)

Did the creation of the Office herald the implementation of a language-planning policy based on the notion of unilingualism as advocated by many experts, individuals, and organizations? In Quebec the Liberal government of Jean Lesage rejected this solution. In 1963 the minister of Cultural Affairs, Georges-Émile Lapalme, declared in the Legislative Assembly that the Canadian Constitution provided the guidelines for state actions and that it would be unconstitutional to proclaim French as the only official language in Quebec. The position of the Lesage government and the Liberal Party was to make French the primary language in Quebec, a position that was reiterated at a special meeting of the Fédération des étudiants libéraux on October 23, 1965. During the meeting, the participants rejected a resolution presented by Liberal students from the Université de Montréal that urged the Quebec government to proclaim French as the only official language in the province.[43]

Following the 1966 provincial elections the Union Nationale government inherited the language issue. But the events in Saint-Léonard unsettled the government of Jean-Jacques Bertrand. The education minister, Jean-Guy Cardinal, acted rather hastily. Following the failure of Bill 85 the previous year, Cardinal succeeded in getting what was now called (as of December 1968) the National Assembly to enact the Loi pour promouvoir la langue française au Québec, known as Bill 63 (L.Q., 18 Élisabeth II 1969, c.9). This law granted parents free choice regarding the language of education for their children. The Quebec Liberal Party, then the official opposition, also accepted the principle of free choice. Section 4 of the law still entrusted the Office de la langue française with the responsibility of advising the government on measures that were most likely to encourage the use of French in the workplace and make French the primary language of public signage. The state agency retained the responsibility for promoting the proper use of French.

The anglophones and business people reacted favourably to the law, but not so the francophones. Deeply opposed to Bill 63, members Yves Michaud, Jérôme Proulx, and Antonio Flamand broke from their respective parties to sit as independent members of the National Assembly. In this stand they echoed the disgruntlement of citizens, many of whom vigorously stated their discontent in briefs, petitions, and public demonstrations. In his study of the Quebec students' movement in the 1960s, Jean-Philippe Warren mentions the major mobilization of students against Bill 63. In October 1969, ten thousand

Demonstration against Bill 63, Montreal, October 1969. Photograph by
Michel Elliott.

students shouted their opposition during a meeting at the Université
de Montréal. A few days later, some fifty thousand people, students and
private citizens, gathered in front of the Quebec Parliament to denounce
the action taken by the Bertrand government. Some students organized
strikes in schools and CEGEPs to indicate their opposition to the bill. It
was nevertheless the Front du Québec français, created by the Société
Saint-Jean-Baptiste de Montréal, joining forces in particular with the
Confédération des syndicats nationaux, Association québécoise des
professeurs de français, and Syndicat des écrivains québécois, which
co-ordinated the opposition. Led by François-Albert Angers, editor of
L'Action nationale, the Front pursued several objectives: defeat Bill 63,
make French the official language in Quebec, and oblige the Quebec
state to implement a comprehensive language-planning policy.[44] Angers
organized press conferences and demonstrations, in particular in
Montreal and Quebec. The discontent created by Bill 63 helped lead
to the defeat of the Union Nationale in the 1970 provincial elections.

     In the anglophone provinces, concerns surrounding education
prompted francophone parents to demand school reforms. Since the

issues of constitutional amendments and francophone rights were dominating the discussions between provinces and the federal government, the institutional networks took advantage of the situation to propose their solution. The French-Canadian institutional networks began to consider the idea of a federal Department of Education with a two-headed structure—one administration exclusively in charge of the francophone minorities in Canada, the other watching over the anglophones in Quebec. As early as December 1963 participants in a meeting of the Association canadienne des éducateurs de langue française (ACÉLF), convened to prepare a brief for the Laurendeau-Dunton Commission, had discussed the idea. The proposition annoyed the Quebec delegates and the director of the Service du Canada français d'outre-frontières, an organization overseeing the relations between the Quebec state and French-language minority groups. The director doubted that the creation of a federal department was the appropriate solution to solve the thorny problem of access to French education for French-language minority groups. In the discussions that followed within the machinery of government in Quebec, people had trouble hiding the irritation caused by the proposal. Despite these objections, the ACÉLF brief suggested that the Laurendeau-Dunton Commission examine the possibility of creating a federal department.[45]

On January 24, 1966, a Liberal MP from New Brunswick, Jean-Eudes Dubé, forged ahead and proposed the creation of a federal Department of Education and Culture. The Ottawa daily *Le Droit* supported the project. The Conseil de la vie française en Amérique had quite the opposite point of view. It was categorically opposed to the idea, with its sensitivity to objections coming from Quebec made quite clear: "to entrust the fate of minorities to a federal Department of Education is entrusting it to the federal political power. The history of Confederation has taught us that the only Canadian government that sought to be fair to minorities was defeated and not a single party has wanted to risk its future on this issue."[46] The Conseil proposed to assign this matter to a commission, which would be free from the pressures exercised by politicians.[47]

The solution of creating a federal Department of Education gathered little support. Indeed, federal politicians had their hands full with the provinces' demands, in particular those of Quebec, which was moving along full speed in its Quiet Revolution. In the wake of major controversies over taxation and the international involvement of the Quebec state and municipalities, a federal intrusion in an area in which provinces had exclusive jurisdiction would unduly fan the flames. For its part, the Laurendeau-Dunton Commission also did not recommend the creation of such a department. It suggested instead that the federal government take upon itself the additional costs that the provinces would incur for education provided to official-language minority groups.[48]

Beyond the proposal for a federal department, parents renewed their efforts to increase the proportion of French used in schools. The political context seemed favourable because provinces were announcing policies aimed at making French a language of instruction in the education system.

In Ontario the network of French private high schools was in bad shape. It was suffering from major financial problems that were threatening its existence, and it was unable to educate youth to meet the demands of the job market. Not only did it need to improve the quality of education, but it also had to increase the access of young francophones to secondary education. The disturbing situation in the high-school system gained the sympathy of some provincial bureaucrats and politicians, and especially that of Premier John P. Robarts, who was aware of both the relations between Quebec and the rest of Canada, and the issue of the rights of francophones in his own province. Taking a different path than the federal and Quebec governments, which had created commissions of inquiry to channel the debates on language matters, the premier of Ontario created the Ontario Advisory Committee on Confederation (OACC).

Launched in January 1965 and dissolved in 1971, the OACC assembled a group of civil servants and academics from among the most renowned names in Canada, including historian Donald Creighton, political scientist Paul Fox, Trent University president Thomas Symons, and the research director of the Canadian Labour Council, Eugene Forsey. Two francophones, Roger Séguin, president of the Association canadienne-française d'éducation d'Ontario, and Father Lucien Matte, president of Laurentian University, participated as the spokesmen for the francophone community.

The OACC's mandate was to examine Ontario's role within Confederation. At its first meeting, on March 19, 1965, the Committee entrusted to one of its three subcommittees, the Cultural Affairs Subcommittee, the task of analysing the relationship between Quebec and Ontario, the issue of the rights of francophones in Ontario—in particular regarding secondary education—and the notion of establishing a provincial language-planning policy. Several members of the Committee believed that legislative action by the Ontario government to support Franco-Ontarians would set a good example of leadership that might have an effect nationally and be a spur to improving relations between francophones and anglophones in the country.[49] According to the Subcommittee members, any project aimed at recognizing the rights of Franco-Ontarians would be following the logic of the crisis as stated by the Laurendeau-Dunton Commission: a conflict between two majorities, the francophones in Quebec and the anglophones throughout Canada. The question of the place and rights of Franco-Ontarians was in a certain manner a specific case adding proof that political leaders were now being driven by a new spirit. The hope was that this new energy would convince francophones in Quebec that the country had changed, as demonstrated by a revolution in thinking sweeping through Ontario. Still, the spirit had a major limitation, which was the recognition of French as an official language. Some members of the Committee, such as Creighton and Forsey, categorically rejected official bilingualism as a solution in Ontario, and they were joined in this by Premier Robarts, who was particularly fearful of a popular backlash on the issue. He saw signs of antagonism in letters he received from Ontario citizens who expressed their deep hostility towards bilingualism. One MPP even reminded him that declaring French as an official language would harm social peace and spread discord within the provincial Progressive-Conservative Party.[50]

In 1966, and despite Creighton's opposition, the OACC recommended that French become one of two official languages. Probably taking into account the reservations of the University of Toronto historian, and especially those of the Ontario premier, the Committee proposed that the recognition of French as an official language in Ontario be introduced in stages. In that way, it was supposed, the measure would not radically transform the provincial symbolical order—it was feared that people would no longer be capable of identifying with that order, hence creating a feeling of alienation. Given the necessities of *realpolitik*, the objective of making French an official language would represent the end result of a process whose timetable would be determined by the legislator.[51]

Pragmatism also characterized discussions on the Laurendeau-Dunton Commission's recommendation for bilingual districts. The OACC believed that Quebec would object to the creation of a bilingual district in the federal capital that would include an area on the Quebec side of the Ottawa River; Quebec's objections would prevent the matter from evolving rapidly. Aware that the Ontario government also had to come to a decision on this matter, the members of the OACC favoured a step-by-step approach in dealing with it. The province would create bilingual districts through administrative measures, which was a much more discreet manner of proceeding than passing new legislation. The members of the OACC feared that enacting a law would allow the opponents of bilingualism to regroup and derail the state action.[52]

The Ontario government moved to adopt OACC's proposals and strategies. Anxious not to slip off track, the political leaders made sure that the changes implemented did not undermine the provincial symbolic order and representation of the collective "We." The legislative changes were therefore not going to alter the province's constitution. In August 1967 Premier Robarts revealed his intention to solve the sensitive question of French-language high schools: to be granted access to state financing, they would have to be non-denominational. His education minister, William Davis, created a special committee, chaired by Roland Bériault, to examine the possibility of creating a network of French public high schools. Tabled in 1968, the Bériault Report supported this solution and recommended the creation of French-language advisory committees that would be responsible for working with public school boards. Based on the recommendations in the report, Davis sponsored the enactment of bills 140 and 141 by the Legislative Assembly (L.O.,17 Elizabeth II, 1968, c.121 and 122). This legislation made possible, among other things, the establishment of public French-language secondary schools or classes "where the numbers warrant." The statements by the Robarts government concerning the use of French in the Ontario Legislative Assembly and the

provision of services in French by some Ontario departments demonstrated the will to proceed step-by-step with the implementation of
institutional bilingualism.[53]

This state activism forced Franco-Ontarians to examine the
links between religion and education as the cornerstones of their collective cultural identity. Already, in December 1966, the Association
des écoles secondaires françaises privées had approved the project
of French-language public high schools. A decisive convention of
the Association canadienne-française d'éducation d'Ontario, which
addressed the issues of francophone identity and nationalism, was held
in February 1967. Many participants and onlookers expected the meeting to be characterized by divisiveness and tensions between partisans
of secular French public high schools and those who believed that language and faith were inseparable and the key element in the collective
identity of francophones in Ontario; but the feared confrontation did
not materialize. Indeed, the ACFÉO leaders received the support of the
francophone bishops for the French public high-schools project. They
advised the reluctant delegates that the anglophone bishops would
refuse to support any other approach. The English-speaking clergy
was requesting that the provincial government finance separate high
schools, to be attended by Catholics. Concerned with the interests of
the Franco-Ontarian community, the francophone bishops supported
the Association's project because it solved the question of secondary
education. Confronted by these conditions, the delegates rallied around
the ACFÉO leaders. The bishop of Ottawa, Mgr. Joseph-Aurèle Plourde,
then healed the wounds of those who had defended the link between
language and faith. In a presentation to members of the Richelieu Club
in Ottawa, he reminded them that being non-denominational was only
a façade because, after all, the teachers and students would be Catholics
and the Ministry of Education was allowing the teaching of religion.[54]

In New Brunswick a reform movement was transforming the
province. The elections of the Liberals in 1960 and the swearing-in of
the first Acadian premier, Louis J. Robichaud, led to a series of major
changes. Following the tabling of a report from the Royal Commission
on Finance and Municipal Taxation, called the Byrne Commission,
the Liberal government created the Equal Opportunity Program in
1965. From then on, the state, rather than municipalities, took on the

financing of health-care institutions, social services, and education. In 1962, in the field of education, the Royal Commission on Higher Education, chaired by John J. Deutsch, proposed the creation of a French-language university. In the next year, the Robichaud government followed up with the creation of the Université de Moncton, which included six colleges situated in Moncton, Shippagan, Edmundston, and Bathurst (the school in Bathurst closed its doors in 1975). A major school reform led to the creation of French-language high schools and the reduction of the number of school districts. As of 1968, the first French-language high schools were opened.

As it turned out, legal conflicts increased the number of high schools set up by school districts. Several districts had mixed populations, which meant that they managed both schools attended by anglophones and those attended by Acadians. Some Acadians demanded the splitting of these mixed school districts, the recognition of the linguistic duality within these administrative entities and within the provincial Department of Education, and the creation of homogeneous sectors. The demands led to considerable debate in the Acadian community—in particular in Moncton in 1967 when community members challenged the framework of the "consociational" democracy. While anglophones complained that splitting mixed school districts would be a kind of separatism, members of the Acadian elites saw the move as an attempt to put an end not just to cohabitation between the two main linguistic communities in the province but also to the use of compromise as a means of solving conflicts between the communities. All the demands expressed by certain Acadians were coming at a very bad time. It seemed they might derail the government's reforms. In 1969, to avoid these conflicts and to pull the rug from under the feet of activists who wanted homogeneous structures, the Robichaud administration proposed a compromise solution to establish two superintendent positions in the mixed school districts: one for French-language schools and one for English-language schools. Both superintendents would report to the same director.

Despite the debate on the organization of mixed school districts, the school reform was well received among Acadians. The changes would, it was thought, improve the quality of French education given that the level of illiteracy was 11.1 per cent among Acadians, compared

to 6.1 per cent for anglophones. By taking on the expenditures relating to education, the state's intention was to increase the resources of
the Acadian school boards. The expenditures in County Kent, which
was predominantly Acadian, were only $132 per student, while in a
predominantly anglophone county they reached $331 per student.[55]

The reforms raised new expectations. They were criticized
by some for not remedying quickly enough the inequalities between
Acadian and anglophone communities. The example of fisheries, a key
economic activity in the Acadian peninsula, was often evoked. Fishing
was a seasonal activity, and the unemployment rate in the region was
higher than the provincial average—which was 11 per cent. As soon
as they took ownership of the fishing industry, the Acadian activists
promoted a community and co-operative shift to break Acadia out of
its economic underdevelopment.

– – – – –

The efforts deployed to channel the voices of citizens through commissions of inquiry, in tandem with monitoring of the situation by
the RCMP, prevented violence from breaking out over the tensions.
But in no way did these factors eliminate, from the list of priorities of
state leaders, the need to manage the language issue. On the contrary:
expectations remained high, and the pressures were numerous—
which was particularly evident in the provinces of New Brunswick and
Ontario.

In Quebec the attempt to solve the language dispute by enacting
Bill 63 made the issue even more complex. The intervenors became
more numerous and active, and the strong expression of the public's
voice empowered the citizens who were becoming increasingly involved
in an energetic activism, demanding rapid state intervention. Furthermore, studies by demographers spread doubt regarding the vitality of
the French language. They indicated a decrease in the birth rate among
francophones and saw a language shift taking place. Such a situation
was beneficial mostly to the anglophone community given that allophones whose first language was neither French nor English preferred
taking the route of mastering English to improve their integration in the
workforce and further their socio-economic mobility. The prevailing
research fuelled the determination of those who believed that French

unilingualism was the only solution to the French language problem. They argued that unilingualism would foster state actions favouring a fairer distribution of resources among citizens, in particular among those who were suffering the repercussions of socio-economic domination. As a result the language issue became part of a push to develop and pursue the common good.

Faced with pressures from its citizens, the federal government was forced to act on the language issue. Its action took into account the grievances and demands of francophones in Quebec and of the French-speaking minority groups elsewhere, of allophone groups—in particular the Ukrainian leaders—and of anglophones. Pockets of English-speaking people grumbled at the advent of institutional bilingualism. These divergent interests and conflicts surrounding the language issue influenced the measures that the federal state was preparing to take in the field of language. The homogenization of the population within the territory was at stake, and it would be a homogenization that could no longer rest on the foundation of a single ethnic group.

CHAPTER 5

ACTION

Language laws, 1969-82

Nous savons
que nous ne sommes pas seuls.
- Michèle Lalonde, *Speak White*

Nous ne voulons plus ressembler
à ceux qui nous acceptent
à condition que nous effacions
toute trace d'histoire personnelle.
- Gérald Leblanc, *Éloge du chiac*

From 1969 to 1982, confronted by the mobilization of citizens and laden with the recommendations of the recent commissions of inquiry, state leaders began implementing language-planning policies. The initiatives grew out of more comprehensive policies that promoted national unity. In addition to being grounded in the emergence of new symbolic orders aiming to secure the allegiance of citizens, the objective of national unity entailed the homogenization of the political community within the state territory, as a nation-state. In so doing, the state political leaders favoured the use of law—with its charters, legislation, and regulations—to safeguard social peace and contain controversies such as the language issue. In theory, more homogeneous political communities—secured through state machinery and the widespread use of official legal resources and procedures—would allow for tighter control and the gradual reduction of social conflicts.

The federal and provincial states formulated policies that attested, in both their sense of choice and their implementation, not just to a political will, but also to the capacity of pressure groups and citizens to influence the legislator. Once they had decided to intervene in matters of language, the states had to pass legislation on the scope of the recognized rights; they also had to establish a balance between collective and individual rights. In the enforcement of the laws, they had to choose between the principles of personality and territoriality. Finally, they had to implement a policy based on obligations that could essentially be either active or passive, making sure that no minority group—especially francophones—would be deprived of any right.

Ottawa's solution: institutional bilingualism

With the enactment of Canada's Official Languages Act in 1969 (S.C., 18 Elizabeth II 1968-69, c.54), the federal government established its language-planning policy based on the principle of personality. Contrary to the Laurendeau-Dunton Commission, which encouraged the federal state to take into account the territorial distribution of francophone and anglophone groups, Prime Minister Pierre Elliott Trudeau made language an individual right, dissociated from culture. As a result, the various federal authorities would have to provide services to citizens in both official languages, no matter where those citizens lived. A commissioner of Official Languages was appointed to watch over the implementation of the law and empowered to investigate complaints from people who found themselves not being served in one of the official languages by a federal agency. Under the leadership of the dynamic Gérard Pelletier until 1972, the Secretary of State Department provided subsidies to organizations such as chambers of commerce and professional and cultural associations that wanted to use one or the other of the official languages in their activities, and in particular it proposed simultaneous interpretation services for general meetings. Finally, the federal state—seeking to shape Canadian citizens who would be more in keeping with a bilingual Canada from sea to sea—became deeply involved in promoting individual bilingualism by targeting youth.

- - - - - - - - - - - - - - - -

Canada's Official Languages Act
(S.C., 18 Elizabeth II 1968-69, c. 54)

Section 2: The English and French languages are the official languages of Canada for all purposes of the Parliament and Government of Canada, and possess and enjoy equality of status and equal rights and privileges as to their use in all the institutions of the Parliament and Government of Canada.

Section 13 (1): A bilingual district established under this Act shall be an area delineated by reference to the boundaries of any or all of the following, namely, a census district established pursuant to the *Statistics Act*, a local government or school district, or a federal or provincial electoral district or region.

(2) An area described in subsection (1) may be established as a bilingual district or be included in whole or in part within a bilingual district if

(a) both of the official languages are spoken as a mother tongue by persons residing in the area; and

(b) the number of persons who are in the linguistic minority in the area in respect of an official language spoken as a mother tongue is at least ten per cent of the total number of persons residing in the area.

(3) Notwithstanding subsection (2), where the number of persons in the linguistic minority in an area described in subsection (1) is less than the percentage required under subsection (2), the area may be established as a bilingual district if before the coming into force of this Act the services of departments and agencies of the Government of Canada were customarily made available to residents of the area in both official languages.

(4) No alteration of the limits of any bilingual district established under this Act shall be made unless such district would, if the proposed alteration of its limits were made, continue to comply with the requirements of this section respecting the establishment of bilingual districts under this Act.

(5) No proclamation establishing or altering the limits of any bilingual district shall be issued under this Act before such time as the Governor in Council has received from a Bilingual Districts Advisory Board appointed as described in section 14 a report setting out its findings and conclusions

including its recommendations if any relating thereto and at least ninety days have elapsed from the day a copy of the report was laid before Parliament pursuant to section 17.

(6) A proclamation establishing or altering the limits of any bilingual district shall take effect in relation to any such district on such day, not later than twelve months after the issue of the proclamation, as may be fixed therein in relation to that district.

Section 19 (1): There shall be a Commissioner of Official Languages for Canada, hereinafter in this Act called the Commissioner.

(2) The Commissioner shall be appointed by Commission under the Great Seal after approval of the appointment by resolution of the Senate and House of Commons.

(3) Subject to this section, the Commissioner holds office during good behaviour for a term of seven years, but may be removed by the Governor in Council at any time on address of the Senate and House of Commons.

(4) The Commissioner, upon the expiration of his first or any subsequent term of office, is eligible to be re-appointed for a further term not exceeding seven years.

(5) The term of office of the Commissioner ceases upon his attaining sixty-five years of age, but he shall continue in office thereafter until his successor is appointed notwithstanding the expiration of such term.

Source: University of Ottawa, Site for Language Management in Canada, http://www.slmc.uottawa.ca/?q=leg_official_language_act_1969.

‑ ‑

This law was part of a major transformation of Canada's symbolic order. In a response to the diagnosis of the members of the Laurendeau-Dunton Commission, the Trudeau government proclaimed the equality of the French and English languages as a way of guaranteeing national unity. Indeed, during the parliamentary debates on the Official Languages Act, the Liberals used the argument of national unity to silence opponents, declaring that the Official Languages Act would reinforce the links between Canadians. They faced little opposition given that the three other parties—Progressive Conservative Party, New Democratic Party (NDP), and Ralliement Créditiste du Canada—supported the bill in principle. However, some MPs echoed groups and individuals who were hostile to a change that would so deeply alter the Canadian symbolic order. Some Progressive Conservative MPs feared that public service jobs would no longer be accessible to unilingual anglophones. Others claimed that the bill was a solution to a problem that was situated primarily in Central Canada. Some wondered if other languages, such as Ukrainian, Polish, or German, should not also become official languages. The Créditiste MP René Matte relayed criticisms expressed in the Quebec francophone milieu regarding bilingualism. He was of the view that the Official Languages Act would not change anything about the reality of bilingualism, which he regarded as the cause of the Canadian crisis. Furthermore, English would always be dominant in the relations between both languages.[1]

Although the major anglophone newspapers and some intellectuals in English Canada applauded the enactment of the Official Languages Act, many citizens remained sceptical, and, as historian José Igartua notes, special interest groups became more active. A survey by the Canadian Institute of Public Opinion revealed that the project of institutional bilingualism and creation of bilingual districts enjoyed great support among francophones, but among the anglophones polled, 49.5 per cent were opposed, with the greatest opposition in the Prairies while Ontario and British Columbia were a little less intensely concerned, with opposition reaching 50 per cent. Only in the Maritimes did the majority of respondents support the project. The pool of opponents simplified the work of organizations hostile to official bilingualism, such as the Single Canada League and the Dominion of Canada Party, which expressed their opposition through letters to federal members of Parliament and letters to the editors of various dailies. They denounced the law on the grounds that it would undermine national unity, increase the expenditures of the federal public service, and be discriminatory. They believed that it would unduly favour the career advancement of francophones and prevent unilingual anglophones from working in the public service. This last point suggested that the new law was contrary to the Canadian Bill of Rights, which had been enacted by the federal government of John Diefenbaker in 1960.

In 1974 a regulation amended the federal Consumer Packaging and Labelling Act. From then on, French and English had to appear on all packaged and labelled products. This new French-language

LAC, PA-047484

Joseph T. Thorson (1889-1978), former federal minister and judge, opposed to bilingualism. Photo by Arthur Roy.

presence—seen, for instance, on boxes of Corn Flakes cereal—triggered the imagination of numerous cartoonists in their comments on the official bilingualism policy. Despite the exemptions set out in the regulation, especially for local products and trial tests, the opponents of bilingualism were fulminating. They declaimed that the federal government would impose the use of French everywhere, even in their breakfast bowls.

One of the fiercest opponents of institutional bilingualism was Joseph Thorarinn Thorson, a former Liberal member of Parliament and cabinet minister and former judge of the Exchequer Court of Canada who became the president of the Canadian Citizenship Council in the 1960s. Viscerally opposed to the recognition of linguistic duality, he crossed the country in 1969 to mobilize citizens in the hope of blocking the enactment of the federal law. He encouraged them to write to their members of Parliament on the issue. In 1970 he created and directed the Single Canada League, a Canada-wide organization rallying opponents to the federal law. His determination to derail the legislation led the former judge to take his cause before the courts.

Thorson believed that, without amending the Constitution Act of 1867, the federal state did not have the power to legislate on language matters to extend the reach of its Section 133. In no way was the former judge discouraged by the enactment of the Official Languages Act. On the contrary, he believed, the law should raise concerns on the part of each and every Canadian because the cost of institutional bilingualism would be absorbed by everyone's taxes. Consequently, the law would be prejudicial to all Canadians, including himself.

In 1970 the Supreme Court of Ontario dismissed his case. Some two years later the Ontario Court of Appeal did the same. Both courts stated that the Official Languages Act did not cause Thorson any prejudice. Despite these defeats, he became more determined than ever to lodge an appeal. On January 22, 1974, the Supreme Court of Canada heard the case and recognized Thorson as applicant. He could therefore demand that the courts rule on the constitutionality of the Official Languages Act.

Less than a month later Thorson tested his legal argumentation in front of the judges of the Supreme Court of Canada, this time acting as a lawyer in the case of the mayor of Moncton. Leonard Jones was contesting a ruling of the New Brunswick courts authorizing a trial to be held in French for a student accused of having attacked him when he was leaving Moncton City Hall in 1972. The mayor was requesting that the courts rule on the constitutionality of the official languages laws of the federal and provincial governments. Lawyer Thorson declared before the judges of the Supreme Court that the federal government was not authorized to legislate on language matters. In the case of New Brunswick, the Official Languages Act was deemed to be *ultra vires* (or beyond one's legal power or authority) because Section 133 of the Constitution did not apply to that province. On April 2, 1974, the Supreme Court of Canada dismissed the cause and ruled that the federal and New Brunswick governments did have the power to legislate on language matters. Following this defeat, Thorson abandoned his legal battle. He encouraged his supporters and all the opponents of the law to punish the Trudeau government during the next federal elections.[2] In the end the situation was not without irony because the actions of

Jones, Thorson, and other opponents of institutional bilingualism contributed to the recognition of the powers of states and, consequently,
the rights of language minorities in the country.

During his battle, Thorson relied on the sympathy of historian
Donald Creighton, with whom he had been corresponding since 1968.
Creighton published two scathing articles on the language issue and the
rights of francophones. In his "Myth of Biculturalism" he denounced
the notion of a Canada defined as a partnership between two founding
peoples, arguing that no historical proof existed to support this interpretation of Confederation. The University of Toronto historian went
on the attack again in June 1977, with an article published in *Maclean's*
magazine in which he reacted to the election of the Parti Québécois
and the debate on the Charter of the French Language. In "No More
Concessions," Creighton declared that the Quebec law contravened
Section 133 of the Constitution Act of 1867. In addition, he pressed
the federal politicians to stop making concessions to Quebec. What's
more, the federal state should abandon official bilingualism, among
other things, because Quebecers were on the verge of abandoning
Confederation.[3]

Although the anglophone intelligentsia reacted coolly to Creighton's point of view, among groups hostile to bilingualism the response
was quite the opposite. The Toronto historian had a symbolic stature,
and these groups drew on his articles to refine their arguments in their
battle against official bilingualism, despite the defeat that the Supreme
Court had inflicted on Thorson in 1974. Indeed, the opponents espoused
a conspiracy theory to explain the decision taken by the federal state to
legislate on language matters. According to this theory, Prime Minister
Trudeau was executing a Machiavellian plan aimed at transforming Canada into a country dominated by francophones. The Official Languages
Act was seen as one of the steps in the strategy concocted by Trudeau
and his clique to turn Canada into a unilingual French country and, in
so doing, to destroy English Canada. Jock V. Andrew, a retired soldier,
and his bestseller *Bilingual Today. French Tomorrow: Trudeau's Master Plan
and How It Can Be Stopped*, published in 1977, perhaps best encapsu-
lates this conspiracy theory.[4] The 1976 election of the Parti Québécois
inspired the opponents of bilingualism to regroup within a new Alliance
for the Preservation of English in Canada (APEC).

Among francophones, reactions varied. In Quebec the supporters of French unilingualism compared the Official Languages Act to a legal tool aimed at protecting English at time when the province was in total linguistic turmoil. Elsewhere, the leaders of the minority groups' institutional network welcomed the federal law, even if it was not entrenched in the Canadian Constitution. However, they greatly feared that a political party hostile to bilingualism would gain the majority of seats in the next federal election, form the government, and abolish the law or simply render it inoperative. They also pointed out that the law did not recognize the notion of two founding peoples and that it privileged individual rights to the detriment of collective rights.[5]

The Official Languages Act was but a step in the alteration of the Canadian symbolic order. On October 8, 1971, the Trudeau government introduced a multiculturalism policy and made official the goal of respect for cultural pluralism in the country. The federal state had taken into consideration the criticisms of the Official Languages Act, in particular those expressed by members of ethnic groups. Representatives of the Ukrainian community had forcefully pointed out that they had been trivialized and reduced to the rank of second-class citizens. The feeling stemmed from the reaction to the public discourse that presented Ukrainian as a foreign language that was not entitled to special protection by the federal state.[6] For their part, the leaders of the institutional network of francophone minority groups were recalcitrant. As historian Stéphane Savard recounts, the leaders of what became known, as of 1968, as the Association canadienne-française de l'Ontario (ACFO) were unhappy because the policy likened language to a simple communication tool dissociated from culture. They believed that if the federal state discarded biculturalism, it would never enact a law on the two official cultures.[7] The Quebec state shared the ACFO leaders' reading of the situation. In 1971, faithful to the "principle of equality between the two founding peoples," Liberal premier Robert Bourassa stated that multiculturalism was "difficult to reconcile with Quebec's reality, with its dominant presence of French language and culture and, in addition, an important minority of English language and culture, and numerous minorities of other languages and cultures." As the advocate of a cultural sovereignty policy, Bourassa assigned to the Quebec state "the role of prime custodian in its territory of the permanency of French language and culture within the North-American context," with "all the means at its disposal" and always without "the slightest discrimination towards other cultures."[8]

Although the idea of multiculturalism raised hopes as well as reservations when it came to its implementation, the federal state provided scant financial resources. In fact, the promotion of multiculturalism often amounted to subsidies for allophone organizations, the organization of seminars, and publication of works, and support for the presence of allophones at the Canada Day celebrations on Parliament Hill and elsewhere in the country. Nevertheless, Ottawa did make moves to provide new financial support for the Aboriginal peoples of Canada. Jean Chrétien, then federal minister of Aboriginal Affairs and Northern Development, announced the establishment of a cultural and education centres program that would support measures being put in place to teach Inuit, First Nations, and Métis languages. The federal state was reacting to some of the pressures from the National Indian Brotherhood, which set out its first policy on "Indian Control of Indian Education" in 1972 after recognizing the rampant assimilation and acculturation taking place among Aboriginal peoples.

As regards the official bilingualism policy, the Department of the Secretary of State created a Social Action Branch in charge of supporting official languages minority groups. The Branch granted provincial francophone and anglophone minority group associations subsidies aimed at strengthening the organizations by covering part of their operating expenditures. The funds also financed the creation of socio-cultural action programs and the opening of cultural centres for francophone and anglophone minority groups.

The federal state came up against some barriers in the implementation of its official language policy. The creation of bilingual districts was based on the co-operation of the provinces, which procrastinated on the matter. In Quebec, although Education Minister François Cloutier suggested in February 1971 that the province be proclaimed a bilingual district, Premier Bourassa did not see the usefulness of this step given the proposals put forward by the Trudeau government at a constitutional conference held in Victoria, B.C., in June.[9] For its part, Ontario decided it would not make French an official language in the province; creating bilingual districts would run counter to its own language-planning policy. If it were to support bilingual districts, the province would have to restructure its symbolic order, a choice categorically rejected by Premier John P. Robarts and, as of 1971, his successor, William Davis. While taking part in discussions with their federal counterparts, Ontario public servants indicated that on this file the province intended to leave the stage wide open to Ottawa. They also expected that the popular backlash, at least in Ontario, would be such that the federal government would back down. Ontario intended to pursue its step-by-step policy based on the implementation of administrative measures that did not involve either the tabling of a law in the Legislative Assembly or an amendment to the provincial constitution; according to provincial political leaders, such actions would provoke hostility among the population.[10]

In the West the opposition of citizens, in particular of allophone groups, provided ammunition to the provinces. Already displeased by how the federal state's Official Languages Act and multiculturalism policy had split language and culture, the representatives of the Ukrainian community certainly did not appreciate the prospect of bilingual districts. Ukrainians tended to believe that the solution did not correspond to the socio-linguistic reality of the Western provinces, where francophones represented less than 5 per cent of the population, a smaller proportion than in Central Canada and the Maritimes. Indeed, bilingual districts could end up closing the door to the potential constitutional recognition of the languages of other ethnic communities whose people, like the French Canadians, had played a role in the social and economic development of Canada since their arrival.[11] Alberta, through the voice of its premiers Harry E. Strom and, after him, Peter Lougheed, swiftly rejected the bilingual districts policy.

A study by Daniel Bourgeois reveals that, alongside the opposition of the provinces, the indifference of the Fédération des francophones hors Québec (FFHQ), and the objections of various groups, the federal public servants associated with the implementation of the bilingual districts project had finally seen the impossibility of the directive. They had multiple objections. Mapping the boundaries of the districts would be a complex and delicate task. Furthermore, the implementation would crystallize the opposition to bilingualism—an opposition that rejected any transformation of Canadian symbols. Finally, some public servants declared that bilingual districts already existed in the federal state's administrative practice, even though they were not officially recognized as such. Consequently, Ottawa abandoned its bilingual districts policy in 1976.

The federal state then decided that it would increase its allocation of financial resources to the promotion of official languages, the provision of services in both languages, and, especially, minority-languages education. However, this last element of the Official Languages Act came under the constitutional jurisdiction of the provinces. As historian Matthew Hayday demonstrates, the federal state searched for ways of nurturing minority-language education and encouraging members of French-speaking minority groups to attend schools in which French was taught. These steps had to be taken without provoking opposition from Quebec, which was preoccupied with protecting its own powers in the field of education.

In its area of jurisdiction, the Department of the Secretary of State managed the Bilingualism in Education Program, which became the Official Languages in Education Program in 1979. To begin with, it contributed funds to the provinces, hoping that the amounts allocated would end up in schools attended by members of official-language minority groups. In this regard, many social actors were soon disenchanted. Federal public servants sympathetic to the cause of minority-language education, francophone parents, and anglophones favourable to bilingualism—who launched an association called Canadian Parents for French in 1977—all became aware of the limits of federal action. Indeed, Canadian Parents for French became quite vocal about it. As a beneficiary of support from the Department of the Secretary of State, and with contacts throughout the country, this organization pressured the provinces to allocate the amounts received from the federal state to French and English education. In addition, it reminded the provinces that the federal grants must be used to establish French immersion programs, which were very popular among members of the anglophone middle classes. The provincial states dragged their feet, invoking, as did Ontario, the school boards' decision-making power with regard to the allocation of resources to French education. The matter of education in French minority communities proved the limits of the federal state's action within the framework of the Official Languages Act. Different tools had to be assembled to solve the matter.

For the federal state, one of these tools was the enshrinement of individual rights in the Constitution. In a 1969 document, *The Constitution and the People of Canada: An Approach to the Objectives of Confederation, the Rights of People and the Institutions of Government*, the Trudeau government announced that it would include individual rights for minority-language education in the Constitution. It attempted to do so during the constitutional negotiations, which fell through in 1971 following the failure of the Victoria Conference. The federal leaders returned with their Charter of Rights proposal in 1977 and, a year later, with another document, *A Time for Action: Highlights of the Federal Government's Proposals for Renewal of the Canadian Federation*. The project included provisions relating to the education of francophone and anglophone minority groups, where numbers warranted.[12]

During discussions on the enshrinement of a Charter of Rights and Freedoms, the Fédération des francophones hors Québec actively tried to force the hand of the provinces regarding education. The creation in 1975 of the FFHQ, which did not include any francophone organization from Quebec, was a symbolic and historic gesture marking an acknowledgement of the breakup of French Canada. In its push for significant gains the FFHQ intended to take advantage of the particular political circumstances—and especially the sense of urgency surrounding the constitutional file following the November 1976 election of the Parti Québécois, led by René Lévesque.

In a spectacular move in 1977, the FFHQ published *Les héritiers de Lord Durham*. The report reminded people that the election of the Parti Québécois meant that "Quebec has decided to actively forge its own destiny. As such, its attitude is exemplary and the francophones outside of Quebec respect it and are inspired by it."[13] The profile of the Canadian Francophonie outlined in the document endorsed the representations spread by nationalist groups in Quebec, which suggested that the Francophonie was anaemic and even doomed to vanish in some cases. Consequently, the FFHQ emphasized the high assimilation rates among francophone groups in some provinces. To curb those rates, francophones outside of Quebec could not rely on the support of their provinces because, except in New Brunswick, they refused to declare French as an official language. In an echo of the situation in Quebec, they perceived the low fertility rate among francophone women as undermining generational renewal and long-term demographic growth. In addition, they believed that the vitality of the francophone communities was being sapped by exogamous marriages—that is, unions with non-francophones—and, with the exception of those in New Brunswick, the meagre capacity to integrate immigrants. The opportunity to communicate in French was still greatly inadequate, and, finally, the low rate of education resulting from overcautious state policies regarding the use of French as a language of instruction placed French-speaking minority groups in a precarious socio-economic situation.

At the end of this bleak assessment, the FFHQ presented an initial list of demands, which became more specific with the publication in 1979 of a document entitled *Pour ne plus être . . . sans pays*. In its quest to put an end to the problem of "genocide" and "dispossession" that characterized the experience of francophone minority groups, the FFHQ became bold. The organization demanded the creation of a republican regime, the enshrinement of the Charter of Rights and Freedoms in the Constitution, and a constitutional status for the language rights of official-language minorities, cultural duality, and a special status for Aboriginals. On the issue of education, every child was to have access to primary and secondary education in one or the other of the official languages. In addition, the Fédération demanded the right for parents to send French-speaking children to the so-called homogeneous schools. In this case, the FFHQ was rejecting the option of bilingual schools, which some provinces had selected as a means of providing French-language education. It hoped to finally gain for francophones the right to manage their schools and the recognition of French as an official language in Ontario and Manitoba.

Faced with the FFHQ's new protest discourse and the increase in its militant political activism, the federal government was forced to act. In addition, the political circumstances preceding the referendum on sovereignty association in 1980 was prompting it to respond rapidly. Federal politicians also increased the financial support provided to provincial francophone minority groups; and the federal state created new programs, including one to support court challenges in order to provide financial help to individuals and groups wanting to have recourse to the courts to gain recognition of their rights.

In this tense political climate, a spark seemed likely to provoke a conflagration. In 1976 a major controversy pitted the federal state against the Canadian Air Traffic Control Association (CATCA), which was protesting the use of French in communications between certain air controllers and pilots in Quebec. At the end of June, a portion of the CATCA members went a strike on the issue in a number of Canadian cities. It was their way of demonstrating their strong opposition to the federal Transport Department's desire to increase the official use of French in its Quebec operations and, according to CATCA, elsewhere in the country. The Department had been authorizing the use of both official languages in five small airports in Quebec since 1974. The federal minister of Transport, Otto Lang, promised to extend this practice to all of Quebec, including the Mirabel international airport. CATCA and its president, Jim Livingston, rushed to raise citizens' awareness, but especially to alert the federal state concerning the dangers facing air control if French were to be used in communications between pilots and controllers. As for the pilots, who were members of the Canadian Air Line Pilots Association (CALPA), many of them, supported by their president, Kenneth Maley, refused to fly their planes. Citing, as an example, an incident that took place at the Quebec airport in 1974, they stated that the security of flights was not guaranteed. The pilots' action led Air Canada and CP Air to cancel several scheduled flights from June 20 to June 28 in 1976.

Although English was the international language in aviation communications,[14] the Quebec air controllers voiced their dissent. They denounced the actions of their Association and the fears being fuelled about air-traffic security in Canada. They pointed out that bilingualism in aviation communications was a standard practice in several airports.[15] Finally, for at least a year CALPA had been leading a deliberate campaign aimed at media and members of Parliament, spreading information on the risks of planes colliding. According to journalist William Johnson, this campaign of public opinion manipulation was aimed at dismantling the policy allowing bilingual aviation communications in Quebec.[16]

Despite denunciations by Prime Minister Trudeau and his condemnation of the fear campaign conducted in the media, the pilots' strike forced Ottawa to make major concessions. The Trudeau government resigned itself to the creation of a commission of inquiry to study bilingualism in communications between pilots and air controllers. Although the commission's report concluded that air traffic was in no way threatened by the use of bilingualism in Quebec, the transport minister agreed to submit the issue to the House of Commons. Led by Roger Demers, the Association des gens de l'air du Québec denounced what it saw as a concession made to anglophone pilots and air controllers. Moreover, the Liberal government's solution to the pilots' strike drove Jean Marchand to resign his position as federal minister of the Environment.

Quebec's common good: from freedom of choice to unilingualism

From 1969 to 1982 in Quebec, the Liberal and then especially the Parti Québécois governments developed other types of language-planning policies. Their choices were based on the Quebec political leaders' interpretation of the specific circumstances at the time: a tense climate, exacerbated by the power relationship between a francophone majority protesting increasingly against the socio-economic order and the unfavourable status of its language, an anglophone minority concerned with its preservation, and immigrant groups wanting to integrate in the best possible way. Consequently, the Quebec political leaders, based on their abiding belief in the common good, recognized French first as an official language, and then as the common public language, and in doing so established the contours of a culture of convergence that would be capable of integrating all of Quebec's citizens. This direction triggered conflicts with the federal state, which was itself working on a Canada-wide interpretation of the issue and was determined to fight against the perception that a French-speaking community was viable only in Quebec.

In the 1970s, in a kind of competition with the federal state—sometimes falling behind, sometimes in response to Ottawa's actions—the Quebec state undertook its own transformation of the symbolic order on its terrain. It both recognized the distinct character of its society and sought to find a balance between the exercise of individual rights and the search for the common good. This transformation was necessary; international migratory movements were significantly altering the social fabric of the province; the disparities between classes, ethno-linguistic groups, and regions were increasing; and social tensions were becoming more and more palpable. In constructing this new social order, successive governments in Quebec took up positions according to their objectives regarding the preservation of ties with Canada—which meant cultural sovereignty for Bourassa's Liberal government and sovereignty association under Lévesque's Parti Québécois. The new symbolic order in Quebec, like its Canadian equivalent, fell within the dual politics of national unity—a nation, in this case enclosed within the Quebec territory—and the pursuit of social peace. Among the manifestations of this political direction in 1975 were the enactment of the Charter of Human Rights and Freedoms and the implementation of language-planning policies.

Tabled on December 31, 1972, the report of the Gendron Commission acknowledged the integration of Quebec within the North American economy—an economic reality that explained the patterns of linguistic behaviour among the Quebec population, the use of English in the workplace, and, especially, the economic logic behind the language choices made by members of the allophone communities. The scant control that francophones had over economic activities intensified the pressure to use English in businesses. Given these findings, the Commission recommended that the Quebec state establish "French as the common language of Quebecers," which meant that it would be "the instrument of communication in contacts between French and non-French Quebecers."[17] French was also to be used in the workplace. Demographers, for their part, had encouraged the Commission to focus on language shifts as an area of state intervention, in the context of a reduction in the fertility rate of francophone women. However, this reduction was part of a trend in the Western world and signalled a general change in society's view of procreation. The report nonetheless remained silent on the issue of the language of instruction. The Commission deemed that Bill 63 had solved that question; therefore, it would be better to wait and measure the impact of the law before reopening the file.[18]

Following these recommendations, the language-planning policies swung back and forth between two methods of guaranteeing the promotion of French: persuasion and coercion. They also intended to change tendencies that demographers and other scientific experts had observed in the language of work in Montreal and the language choices of immigrants.

Even though it had just been re-elected in October 1973, the Bourassa government was subject to intense pressures. As a result, François Cloutier, the minister in charge of the language portfolio, proceeded with his solution. Enacted in July 1974, the Official Language Act (S.Q. 1974, c. 6), known as Bill 22, declared French to be the official language in Quebec. The government relied on persuasion to encourage employers to support French in their workplaces. The law also provided for the creation of the Régie de la langue française, an office that would have the authority to intervene and conduct investigations. Finally, with regard to the language of instruction, Quebec introduced a limited range of choices. Section 43 of the law imposed assessment tests on the knowledge of English, and the results of those tests were to determine who could have access to instruction in that language.

Bill 22 made many people quite unhappy. The francophones were divided: some accused the law of being timid, while the Alliance des professeurs de Montréal, the Comité central des parents of the CÉCM, and the Commission des écoles catholiques de Montréal itself bluntly denounced it. In vain did they put pressure on the government to render French schooling mandatory for all except the anglophone minority. For its part, as historian Miguel Simão Andrade points out, the CÉCM called on the Bourassa government to promote an increase in enrolment in French-language schools in Montreal. With allophones massively choosing to send their children to English schools, the CÉCM urged the government to intervene to change this pattern. For its part, the Mouvement Québec français demanded that the state declare French to be the only official language in Quebec.

The measures regulating access to English schools shocked the Quebec Federation of Home and School Associations and other spokespersons from the anglophone community. For the first time they were confronted with a challenge to the power relations that they

Seminar on the French language organized by the Mouvement Québec français, 1974. Left to right: Normand Cherry of the Union nationale, François Cloutier, Minister of Education, the moderator André Payette, and Yves Michaud of the Parti Québécois. Photo by Michel Elliott.

had previously found so accommodating. John Ciaccia and George Springate, two Liberal members of the National Assembly, voted against Bill 22; they were excluded from the caucus. Some anglophone activists applied to the courts, seeking to have the law invalidated. In his ruling in April 1976, Judge Jules Deschênes recognized the constitutionality of the legislation. Other members of the anglophone community—in actions that received extensive media coverage—used the enactment of Bill 22 as a pretext to leave Quebec and settle elsewhere in Canada. More than sixty thousand anglophones signed a petition asking the federal government to disallow the provincial law; Ottawa refused to do so. Still, although the Trudeau government refused to give in to the demands of the anglophone activists, it nevertheless put other measures into motion. When the voicing of public sentiment gave rise to concern because of an assumed potential for violence, the RCMP took pains to collect information on individuals and groups advocating French unilingualism. Within

Demonstration against Bill 22 in Quebec, 1974.

its surveillance operation labelled Operation G, the RCMP asked its agents in Quebec to identify individuals, groups, unions and student organizations, and members of political parties—especially the Parti Québécois—that might resort to violence to influence the actions of the Bourassa government.[19]

Among the allophone communities, the Italian community was by far making the most headlines, as historian Paul-André Linteau and sociologists Claude Painchaud and Richard Poulin indicate. Established by Pietro Rizzoto in 1972, the Fédération des associations italiennes du Québec (FAIQ) favoured the implementation of a new language policy. According to political scientists Donat J. Taddeo and Raymond C. Taras, the FAIQ proposed that all the children of new immigrants attend French schools. Following three years of mandatory French schooling, parents could choose between a French-language and English-language school. However, the FAIQ made sure to specify that members of ethnic communities already settled in Quebec—the majority of Italians, for instance—would be exempted from this obligation. In addition, children attending French schools could also learn the other official language.

Despite the FAIQ's support for Bill 22, the Bourassa government turned a deaf ear to the demands of the organization in relation to the language of instruction. Some members of the FAIQ left the Fédération and in 1974 established the Consiglio Educativo Italo-Canadese, which brought together members of the Catholic clergy, business community, and education sector. Chaired by Angelo Montini, the organization fought against Bill 22 and the tests determining accessibility to English-language schools. The Consiglio made headlines when it opened clandestine classes in schools that were part of Catholic school boards. By January 1975 it was providing courses every Saturday morning for parents who had children of five or six years old, teaching them how to prepare their children to pass the admission exams.

The discontent intensified during the back-to-school period in September 1975, which was the beginning of the implementation of Bill 22 regarding access to English schools. Allophone parents, especially those who wanted to send their children to English schools but were unable to do so because the youth had failed the language-knowledge test, had to make a choice: conform or not to Bill 22. In refusing to register their children in French schools, they would be committing an act of civil disobedience. Moreover, they noticed that some school boards were much more tolerant than were others in applying the law. Supported by the Italian clergy and the Consiglio, some Italian parents put pressure on school boards and government to amend the law.

A number of Italian parents in Saint-Léonard, in particular those who lived in the territory of the Jérôme-Le Royer School Board, sent their children to English Protestant schools. Their action prompted members of the Italian clergy to write to the archbishop of Montreal, Mgr. Paul Grégoire, in September 1976, to denounce the situation. In the letter, trying to gain the sympathy of the archbishop, the priests expressed the sadness they felt in watching Italian Catholic parents send their children to English Protestant schools and thus sacrifice the religious beliefs of the children. In so doing, the priests were echoing the arguments used by numerous French Canadians during the school crises at the beginning of the twentieth century in anglophone provinces. With the Catholic Church becoming a stakeholder in the language debate, the archbishop had difficulty concealing his annoyance regarding the letter. He asked the signatories to explain the objectives of Bill 22 to their flocks. Furthermore, he was doubtful that the young Italians would lose their Catholic faith because they attended Protestant schools.

In 1976 other members of the anglophone Catholic clergy intervened in the debate by pressuring the education minister, Jean Bienvenue, to suspend the sections of the law pertaining to access to English schools. The minister refused to do so. He was not inclined to agree with these opponents because he believed that the members of the Italian community should manifest their will to integrate by choosing French-language schools.

Frustrated by what it perceived as being a form of inaction, the Consiglio took a critical stance towards the Quebec Liberal Party during the 1976 provincial elections. It informed the Liberals that they could no longer rely on the unconditional support of the Italian community. This position did not prevent the organization from supporting Liberal candidates in some ridings.

The Parti Québécois victory signalled a shift in tone with regard to the management of the language file. Instead of reacting to specific cases, the lawmakers now intended to clarify the language issue by adopting an overall approach, focused on the common good, in order to reassure francophones on the future of their language. An indication of this rather republican tendency was that Premier Lévesque, despite his reservations, gave the responsibility for implementing this general policy to Camille Laurin, minister of state for Cultural Development, rather than to the minister of Education. Tenacious and determined, Laurin surrounded himself with a team of experts in social and human sciences: sociologists Guy Rocher—who became deputy minister—and Fernand Dumont, linguist Jean-Claude Corbeil, the union leader— and then chief of staff—Henri Laberge, and others who took on the development of a white paper on French-language policy for Quebec. The minister's intention was clear. It consisted of accomplishing "a decisive action for the liberation and promotion of Quebec workers" because "for all our ordinary people," he said, "using the national language is their way of life." [20]

Following the tabling of the white paper in April 1977, the Quebec National Assembly enacted the Charter of the French Language (S.Q. 1977, c.7), also known as Bill 101, in August. Designed to be "in keeping with a new perception of the worth of national cultures

Camille Laurin (1922–99), Minister of State for Cultural Development from 1977 to 1980 and father of the Charter of the French Language. Photo by Eugen Kedl.

in all parts of the earth, and of the obligation of every people to contribute in its special way to the international community," the Charter established French as "the language of Government and the Law." It also made it "the normal and everyday language of work, instruction, communication, commerce and business."[21]

Charter of the French Language (1977)

Section 1: French is the official language of Québec. ...

Section 7: French is the language of the legislature and the courts in Québec. ...

Section 58: Public signs and posters and commercial advertising must be in French. They may also be both in French and in another language provided that French is markedly predominant. However, the Government may determine, by regulation, the places, cases, conditions or circumstances where public signs and posters and commercial advertising must be in French only, where French need not be predominant or where such signs, posters and advertising may be in another language only. ...

Section 72: Instruction in the kindergarten classes and in the elementary and secondary schools shall be in French, except where this chapter allows otherwise. ...

Section 73: Notwithstanding Section 72, the following children, at the request of one of their parents, may receive instruction in English:

a) a child whose father or mother received elementary instruction in English in Québec, provided that that instruction constitutes the major part of the elementary instruction he or she received in Québec;

b) a child whose father or mother was residing in Québec on 26 August 1977 and had received elementary instruction in English outside Québec, provided that that instruction constitutes the major part of the elementary instruction he or she received outside Québec.

c) a child who, in his last year in school in Québec before 26 August 1977, was receiving instruction in English in a public kindergarten class or in an elementary or secondary school;

d) the younger brothers and sisters of that child as defined in subsection c.

Source: Quebec, Office québécois de la langue française,
English Section, Charter of the French Language,
http://www.oqlf.gouv.qc.ca/english/charter/index.html.

The Charter of the French Language established fundamental language rights relating to the use of French by all citizens (Sect. 2–6) and recognized French as the language of legislation and courts (Sect. 7–13). With regard to education (Sect. 72–88), Bill 101 limited access to primary and secondary English schools to children whose father or mother had received instruction in English in Quebec—a provision referred to as the "Quebec clause." Given the massive assimilation of immigrants into anglophone groups and the consequences of this condition for the viability of the French language, the Charter aimed to put an end to children from immigrant allophone communities attending English primary and secondary schools. As linguist Jean-Claude Corbeil notes, 90.3 per cent of the children of allophones living in Montreal attended English schools in 1972–73. Among francophones in Montreal the proportion was only 2.9 per cent.

In addition to regulating the explosive issue of the language of instruction, the Quebec state implemented measures to ensure the francization of the workplace (Sect. 41–50), which, among other things, obliged businesses with more than fifty employees to hold a francization certificate. As well, to ensure that French would from then on be the language of commerce and business, French unilingualism became the standard for commercial advertising (Sect. 51–71).

The government designated the Office de la langue française to monitor the enforcement of the law. To support the minister in the development of language policy, the law anticipated the creation of the Conseil de la langue française. In using legislation to reach their objectives of national unity and social peace within Quebec's territory, the state leaders claimed to be acting "in a spirit of fairness and open-mindedness." This spirit applied not only to the ethnic minorities, but also to the First Nations, Métis, and Inuit because it recognized their right "to preserve and develop their original language and culture."[22] Finally, the Quebec political leaders reiterated their concern for the anglophone minority in Quebec. Lévesque declared that "the government must treat [the anglophone community] in a civilized manner" and not "act as an aggressor towards the minority."[23] In accepting "the hand held out by the member for D'Arcy McGee," the Liberal MNA Victor Goldbloom, when Bill 101 was enacted, Laurin reflected, "In fact, we respect and appreciate too much the anglophone community in Quebec not to show it the greatest friendship and open-mindedness possible."[24]

More than just a simple measure to protect the language, the Charter of the French Language presented an overall solution to the problem of the status of French in Quebec, and was the expression of a commitment to the common good of people throughout all the territory. It was accompanied in 1978 by a cultural development policy that was part of "a common, collective project of a modern and democratic society,"[25] and by an agreement between the federal and Quebec states on the selection of immigrants, known as the Cullen-Couture Agreement. Finally, the work of the Office de la langue française and Conseil de la langue française provided the political leaders with the knowledge needed for any future intervention. This knowledge was not confined to the Quebec territory; it was also drawn from various international experiences in the field of language planning. Therefore, one of the missions of the Office de la langue française in 1979 was to investigate language planning in Israel. Pierre-Étienne Laporte found that, though there was "a general consensus on the status of Hebrew as national language" in Israel, "this was not the case in Quebec" for the French language because "the political and technical aspects of the language issue remain entangled." In Israel, the public servant noted, "The existence of a single sovereign state authority provides a uniformity of results in the work of standardizing terminology, which is not always possible here because of the overlap between jurisdictions." [26]

At the time of the enactment of the Charter of the French Language, reactions in francophone milieus, in particular among unions, nationalist organizations, and citizens, were generally favourable to the new law; some groups, such as the Mouvement Québec français, asked that access to English schools be even more restricted. Others, such as the spokespersons for the Conseil du patronat du Québec [Quebec employers' council] and the chambers of commerce, who were preoccupied with the economic health of Quebec, especially with Montreal's capacity to remain an important economic metropolis, were more cautious. They argued in favour of choice for parents in matters of education. Anger was growing within the anglophone community. The dailies *The Gazette* and *Montreal Star* opened their pages to the opponents to the Charter—to people who disputed the calls for openness and worried about the challenges faced by the English language. These opponents emphasized that some companies were moving their headquarters out of the province, as in the cases of the insurance company Sun Life and chocolate producer Cadbury. They insisted on the harmful consequences of the Charter on economic activities in Quebec, especially in Montreal. As political scientist Josée Legault indicates, the language laws gave rise to a new framework of identity, within which English Quebecers would henceforth be perceived as a minority.

Although Bill 101 gave rise to strong reactions in the business community, some companies decided to adapt to the new environment. The management of the Ontario-based Canadian Tire chain, for example, agreed to increase the use of French in the company's internal communications and purchase more advertising space in the francophone media. Commercial interests also dictated Canadian Tire's desire to convert to French: its competitor Rona was benefiting from a favourable perception among francophone consumers. Given that the company wanted to increase its share of the market and shed its English-Canadian image, its managers got down to the business of francizing its operations in Quebec. They even considered changing their corporate name to "La Société Canadian Tire L^{tée}," an idea they finally abandoned because Bill 101 did not oblige them to do so.[27]

According to political scientists Lucie Noël and Garth Stevenson, several anglophone associations then decided to speak up. Established by Alex K. Paterson and Storrs McCall, the Positive Action Committee/Comité d'action positive denounced the implementation of restrictions on access to English schools and the abolition of English as a language of use in the National Assembly and courts. Noting the departure of many anglophones to other provinces, the organization launched a campaign in The Gazette and Montreal Star to encourage people to remain in Quebec. Another organization, Participation Quebec, opted for a dialogue with francophones. It did so while continuing its battle against the irritants in Bill 101, such as the restrictions on attendance in English schools, commercial advertising, and business names. With support from the federal Department of the Secretary of State, which sought to create in Quebec a counterpart to the Fédération des francophones hors Québec, the Council of Quebec Minorities/Conseil des minorités du Québec came into being in 1978. Most of these organizations restrained themselves from intervening in the 1980 referendum debate, except for the Positive Action Committee, which advocated the preservation of Canadian unity. Finally, another organization was created in 1978, the Freedom of Choice Movement/Mouvement de la liberté, which became famous for its extreme positions. As an advocate of the abolition of Bill 101, this group opposed any law aimed at promoting the French language, including the enshrinement of language rights in the Canadian Constitution. Led by a member of the National Assembly, William Frederick Shaw, the Freedom of Choice Movement established itself as a political party that presented a dozen or so candidates in the 1981 provincial elections. All of them ended up biting the dust.

Among members of ethnic minority groups the situation was slightly different. According to political scientists Donat J. Taddeo and Raymond C. Taras, it was the Quebec wing of the new National Congress of Italian Canadians—created in 1975 in Toronto to unite

© Musée McCord, M989.363.96

The anglophone community in Quebec strongly opposed Bill 101. Cartoon by Aislin, *The Gazette* (Montreal), 1988.

all the Italian communities in Canada—that expressed the views of Italian Quebecers. In the debates surrounding the Charter of the French Language, the Italian community's organization had supported the decision to oblige the children of immigrants to attend French schools. Yet it also argued for an exemption that would allow ethnic communities already rooted in Quebec to keep their freedom of choice. The Lévesque government rejected the suggestion. As of September 1977, Italian parents faced new rules governing access to English schools. Now the parents had an alternative: accept the new law and its provisions, or go against the law and find an English school principal who would be amenable to welcoming their children. The Quebec wing of the Congress fought to normalize the children's illegal situation by demanding amnesty for them, which the Quebec state refused to do.

The Charter of the French Language, aimed at strengthening the link with citizenship, especially among immigrants, was, then, not exempt from controversy. Although opposition continued to be expressed through the voice of citizens, it moved more and more into the realm of the courts, which reduced the number of protagonists from the public sphere and increased the power of legal experts. Following a challenge to a section of Bill 101 brought forward by a Montreal lawyer, the Supreme Court of Canada, in *Attorney General of Quebec v. Blaikie et al.* ([1979] 2 S.C.R. 1016), rendered void the provisions relating to the use of the French language only in the legislature and courts, pursuant to Section 133 of the Constitution Act of 1867. This first victory encouraged the various anglophone groups to unite, and in 1982 they created an organization to advocate for their community, with financial support provided by the state. From then on this pressure group, Alliance Quebec, favoured legal challenges.

The election of the Parti Québécois also marked the beginning of a new chapter in the relations between the Quebec state and French-speaking minority groups. The Parti Québécois outlined the advantages of a sovereign Quebec and tried to reassure anyone who feared the potential consequences of the accession of Quebec to political sovereignty. In April 1977 the minister of Intergovernmental Affairs, Claude Morin, communicated the thrust of the Quebec policy to francophone groups. He promised them that the Quebec state intended to do away with the practice of double standards relating to the rights of minority groups in official-language policies in Canada. If Quebecers chose political sovereignty in a referendum, the Quebec state would use its political weight to advance the cause of francophones outside of Quebec. What was essential at that moment was for Quebec to acknowledge that it had a "moral" responsibility towards francophone minorities.

This moral responsibility was transformed into actions. The Quebec state recognized the FFHQ as the official representative of French-speaking minority groups. It increased the assistance it provided to these groups through the creation of technical and financial support programs. In 1974 and 1975 that government support amounted to

$588,000; after the election of the Parti Québécois it tripled. In 1978 and 1979 it reached $3 million. Moreover, the Quebec government's efforts were paltry compared to the amounts granted by the federal Department of the Secretary of State. The Social Action Branch of the department had a budget of $3,625,000 in 1976; it increased considerably, to more than $70 million, by the beginning of the 1980s.[28]

The Quebec state put forward its own solution to the problem of access to education in French within the provinces that were predominately English-speaking. In 1977 Premier Lévesque presented his provincial counterparts with a plan for a new agreement on education. The Quebec state proposed negotiations with the interested provinces to establish a reciprocal agreement: anglophones living in Quebec who came from other provinces would have the same rights as established English Quebecers; and francophones living in anglophone provinces would have the same rights as those guaranteed to anglophones in Quebec. This proposal brought together multiple objectives: to avoid, or prevent, federal intervention within a provincial jurisdiction; to prompt the other provinces to take action on the issue of language rights, in particular the rights of "their" francophone minorities; and to reassure francophones and demonstrate, by this action, the sense of moral responsibility that the Quebec state had for their well-being.

The federal government immediately enjoined premiers to categorically reject the offer presented by the Parti Québécois government, which they did. Still, in February 1978 the provincial leaders promised to take action to improve access to education in French, where numbers warranted. Nevertheless, each province was free to act as it pleased in applying this principle.[29]

For their part, the leaders of francophone minority groups feared that the negotiations would lead to the multiplication of language regimes that would differ from one province to another. Moreover, it was feared that reciprocal agreements would change the identity discourse of minority communities by altering the terms of the prevailing national duality. If provincial governments negotiated with Quebec, the federal state would be shut out of the process. As for the francophone and Acadian minorities who linked their identity to a national project, they saw themselves being relegated to the rank of provincial language minorities.

The multiple provincial language policies

In the other provinces the commitment to language planning was different because it stemmed from the recognition of a Canadian symbolic order promoted by the federal state. Given that the objectives of other provinces were different from those of Quebec, their various language-planning policies revealed the more or less timid political will of leaders concerned about a potential anti-francophone backlash. Even while the provinces necessarily took into account the activism of individuals and groups advocating the provision of French services, their actions were restricted by the strength of the opposition to bilingualism. Although the English-Canadian provinces had been accepting the financial aid granted by the federal state for French education and French immersion since 1969, francophone communities, parents in favour of French immersion, and the national Parents for French organization found these funds to be insufficient. In some cases the resources did not even reach the targeted beneficiaries. Finally, as in the English community in Quebec, the elites of the francophone minorities relied on institutionalized pressure groups, which received federal financial assistance and used official legal resources to promote their cause. Posing as the representatives of their communities, these flourishing groups had a tendency to dominate public debate.

Ontario implemented a language-planning policy to accommodate the rights of francophones—but did not substantially alter the province's symbolic order to match Canadian conditions as a whole. The province targeted five issues: education, legal services, public service, operations of the Legislative Assembly, and municipalities.[30]

Following the enactment of bills 140 and 141 in May 1968, the battle for access to French education in Ontario was transferred to school boards, which now had the authority to open French-language high schools when a minimum of twenty students were in need or when ten francophone taxpayers made the request. In several cases the school boards, often elected by anglophone parents, refused to establish French-language schools even when the required number of francophones called for the action. In other cases boards chose to establish French classes within English high schools. This was not a satisfactory solution because it meant that English remained the primary language of use within schools attended by francophones.

Francophone parents and school trustees discovered the limits of their influence on school boards, as illustrated by conflicts that emerged in Sturgeon Falls, Kapuskasing, Cornwall, and Windsor-Essex. In Windsor-Essex the education minister obliged the school board to establish a French-language high school only after a conflict that had lasted for eight years. In 1979, in Penetanguishene, a new crisis broke out. Following the Simcoe school board's refusal to create a French-language school, some francophones accomplished the sensational feat of opening the Huronie high school. The school opening benefited from formidable support, in particular that of Jean-Robert Gauthier, federal member of Parliament, Pierre Elliott Trudeau (at the time the leader of the official opposition in Ottawa), the Office of the Commissioner of Official Languages, official representatives of the Ontario and federal NDP, and the provincial Liberal Party. In 1980, at the end of a gruelling battle, the francophones gained the right to establish a French-language high school, which opened its doors two years later.

As historian Michael D. Behiels recounts, these battles led Franco-Ontarians to recognize the basic lack of determination on the part of the Ministry of Education, which often refused to intervene for fear of disrupting the school boards' decision-making process. School management became the new major issue for the francophone parents. In 1975 the Ottawa-Carleton French-language Advisory Committee requested the establishment of French-language school boards for the Catholic and public schools in the region. The hope was that the establishment of French-language boards could serve as a model in other locations in Ontario. The Progressive Conservative government under Bill Davis entrusted the question to Henry Mayo, who in his report on the redistribution of the Ottawa-Carleton region proposed the creation of a French-language Catholic school board. Premier Davis did not favour this recommendation, and the Ministry of Education rejected it, preferring the creation of francophone sections within existing Catholic and public school boards in the region. The Franco-Ontarians could not, then, manage their schools directly because their influence was limited by the power of the school boards making the decisions.

The constitutional amendments of 1982, in particular the inclusion of Section 23 on instruction for French- and English-speaking minority groups in the Canadian Charter of Rights and Freedoms, and the intervention of courts, would lead to a favourable outcome for the Franco-Ontarians' demands.

In 1976 a pilot project in the field of legal services allowed the use of French in criminal cases brought before the provincial court in Sudbury. A year later the attorney general included the regions of the National Capital and Eastern Ontario in the pilot project. Still, it was not until 1984 that the Courts of Justice Act would recognize the use of French in courts.

With regard to the three other issues for intervention—the Legislative Assembly, the public service, and municipalities—the Legislative Assembly adopted a motion in 1968 that gave the elected members the right to speak in English or French during parliamentary business. That same year some public servants and members of the Legislature took the first courses in French-language training. A year later Ontario reached a cultural agreement with Quebec focusing in particular on language, education, and provincial services as areas for intervention. Ontario wanted to provide services in both languages in locales in which francophones made up a significant number of the population. In addition, the province established a translation bureau to assist the ministries. As for the French services that municipalities could provide, the issue involved the powers of another order of government. Even though municipalities were the "creatures" of the provinces, the Conservative governments of Robarts and Davis proceeded cautiously. The Robarts government amended the Municipal Act so that municipalities could provide services in both languages.[31]

A study conducted by Brigitte Bureau indicates that in the 1970s the provincial step-by-step approach to providing services in French caused anger among some Franco-Ontarians. With militants like Jacqueline Pelletier, they created the movement C'est l'temps (It's time) to denounce the use of unilingual traffic tickets and forms that needed to be filled to get a driver's licence or renew a licence plate. In 1977 some Franco-Ontarians did not hesitate to refuse filling out unilingual forms to renew their licence plates, even if it meant going to jail.

According to some people, the government's step-by-step approach to the establishment of French services demonstrated a lack of political will. In 1977 delegates at the annual meeting of the Association canadienne-française de l'Ontario demanded the recognition of French as an official language, which the Davis government rejected. The ACFO intensified its pressure by sending letters, signing petitions, and tabling a brief. In 1978 Albert Roy, a member of the Liberal opposition at Queen's Park, tabled a private member's bill on the implementation of French services, which died on the order paper—a result that, as Matthew Hayday says, greatly troubled the ACFO. The Alliance for the Preservation of English in Canada also became agitated and launched a letter campaign to oppose the provision of French services in the province. During the talks leading up to the patriation of the Canadian Constitution in 1982, Trudeau failed in his attempt to persuade Davis to move towards a proclamation of French as an official language in Ontario, in contrast to New Brunswick, where Premier Richard Hatfield willingly accepted the constitutional recognition of bilingualism in his province. Fearing a popular backlash and, especially, firmly believing in the soundness of its approach to language issues, the Davis government favoured a policy that focused on administrative measures.

In 1968 in New Brunswick, on the heels of the Acadian students' strike in Moncton and the tabling of the Laurendeau-Dunton Commission's report, the government of Louis J. Robichaud introduced its own language-planning policy, which was enacted a year later by the Legislative Assembly. At the Federal-Provincial Conference on the Constitution held in 1968, the premier informed his federal and provincial colleagues that he would respect the recommendations of the Laurendeau-Dunton Commission and that his province would become bilingual. In recalling the events surrounding the preparation of the New Brunswick Official Languages Act (S.N.B., 1969, c. 14), public servant Robert Pichette mentioned that Father Clément Cormier, the first president of the Université de Moncton and a member of the Laurendeau-Dunton Commission, offered suggestions on the first draft of the bill. Father Cormier encouraged the Robichaud government to establish bilingual districts in the province and to oblige municipalities to provide bilingual services. The premier rejected these suggestions because he believed that the pressure on municipalities to provide services in both languages should come directly from the citizens. On the issue of bilingual districts, Robichaud did not want to link the provision of provincial bilingual services to the fluctuating borders of the districts, which necessarily reflected internal migration movements.

Inspired by the Canadian Official Languages Act, the New Brunswick Act proclaimed the equality of French and English and promoted the implementation of provincial services in both languages. It empowered municipalities to adopt, by resolution, the use of one or the other official language in municipal council meetings. It remained silent on the implementation of this measure in several major sectors of activity, in particular professional bodies, unions, the private sector, and health.

This provincial law triggered various reactions. Many Acadians noted the limits in the new regulations. There were delays imposed before the implementation of some parts of the law. Moreover, the law did not make any provision for a monitoring agency, contrary to the practice of the federal government, which had an Office of the Commissioner of Official Languages. Finally, the legislator remained silent on the issue of management of schools.

Some members of the anglophone community were fiercely opposed to the law. Groups such as the Canadian Loyalist Association, created in 1968, and the Orange Lodge of New Brunswick gave voice to their recriminations. These ideologically conservative groups were opposed to state activism, especially when it led to what they considered a radical transformation of the provincial ethos. Indeed, the Canadian Loyalist Association declared that the bilingualism policy was but a step towards the political dispossession of anglophones because it would support the takeover of the country by francophones. The Moncton section of the Orange Lodge of New Brunswick proposed the enactment of a law that would make English the only official language in the country. In his study of the opposition to the reforms launched by the Robichaud government, political scientist Chedly Belkhodja states that the two anglophone groups were in the crosshairs of the Royal Canadian Mounted Police.

Those two groups were not the only targets of police surveillance. The RCMP also opened a file on the Dominion of Canada English Speaking Association, with which Mayor Leonard Jones was associated. Although the police force deemed that this organization was not inclined to use physical violence, the officers were aware that its activism represented a form of symbolic violence. As the RCMP noted, the hostility to institutional bilingualism stimulated the resentment of Acadians.[32] Given the activism of Acadians and students at the Université de Moncton, the federal police feared outbursts of violence among these groups.

In 1972 the battle for bilingualism led its supporters to put pressure on municipalities, which then became the battlefield. Yet the Moncton case probably cooled the enthusiasm of the bilingual activists elsewhere in New Brunswick. Although francophones represented 32 per cent of the city's population, Mayor Jones refused to provide French services, going as far as seeing the project of twinning with the City of Lafayette in Louisiana as a conspiracy to promote bilingualism.[33] For its part, the Comité pour le bilinguisme à Moncton, made up of students and professors from the Université de Moncton and citizens concerned about the lack of bilingual municipal services, increased its public interventions to force the hand of the mayor. He did not shy away from declaring on every platform that bilingualism would lead to political discrimination and divide the community rather than unite it. This battle had a very large symbolic reach: any victory against a recognized opponent of bilingualism could well have a ripple effect elsewhere in the province. However, the Comité failed despite its efforts, in particular its lobbying for the implementation of bilingual services. Indeed, Jones leveraged his popularity among the opponents of bilingualism to gain re-election as mayor in 1973 and then leap into federal politics in 1974 as an independent member for the Moncton riding. In addition to the resolute opposition from Mayor Jones, the Comité pour le bilinguisme à Moncton faced divisions among Moncton citizens and other Acadians.[34]

The issue of school management was mobilizing the Acadian community. Members of the community rejected bilingual school boards because those bodies did not meet their own concerns. The Société des Acadiens et des Acadiennes du Nouveau-Brunswick (SAANB) and the Association des enseignants francophones du Nouveau-Brunswick (AEFNB) demanded the implementation of distinct school boards for anglophones and francophones. As Hayday indicates, the opponents of bilingualism organized a postcard campaign in 1978. They demanded that English be declared the official language of the province and that the government stop using taxpayers' money to finance French education and French immersion programs. Confronted with these conflicting demands, the Hatfield government acted cautiously. Following the 1974 provincial elections, it divided the Department of Education into two sections, anglophone and francophone, each with power over programs and the evaluation of primary and secondary schools. It then created a task force that in 1980 recommended the elimination of bilingual school districts and the creation of homogeneous linguistic school boards.

At the end of the 1970s and beginning of the 1980s, activism in Acadia thrived, all the more so because the grievances were numerous. The promises made during the Robichaud era were long in coming, and the Acadians in the northeast of the province were still living in a situation of precariousness and economic underdevelopment. In 1972, as historian Léon Thériault states, "In their progression towards a more just society, the Acadian people of New Brunswick" had to realize that "Acadianizing the political machine, where and when it concerned them, had become as important as gaining French schools, French hospitals, etc." [35] Founded in 1972, the Parti acadien advocated more just social policies for disadvantaged citizens—policies that would be implemented through the creation of a new province. The successive presidents of the party, Euclide Chiasson and especially Donatien Gaudet as of 1979, were particularly active on this front.

Faced with the growth of this political party, which was translating into reality the growing dissatisfaction of Acadians, the Hatfield government could not remain silent. In 1981 the Legislative Assembly passed An Act Recognizing the Equality of the Two Official Linguistic Communities in New Brunswick, called Bill 88 (S.N.B. 1981, c.O-1.1). Based on the principle of separate development, the Act recognized the right of each community to have distinct cultural, educational, and social institutions. Jean-Maurice Simard, the sponsor of the bill and president of the Treasury Board, pointed out that one of the targeted objectives was to reduce the pace of language assimilation among Acadians. At first the SAANB, through its president Aurèle Thériault, expressed reservations about the bill, which it said was too vague.

For its part, the Fédération des étudiants de l'Université de Moncton rejected the bill completely, because the organization wanted the province of New Brunswick to recognize Acadians as a people, rather than, as provided by the bill, as a community. The Liberal opposition and its leader Joseph Daigle, as well as several members from the anglophone community, also denounced the provincial bill, some of them because they feared that its enactment would strengthen the position of the Parti acadien and eventually lead to the breakup of the province. Later the SAANB changed its mind in reaction to a campaign led by Jean-Maurice Simard.[36] The Hatfield government pursued its strategy of appeasement by mandating its director general for official languages, Bernard Poirier, and the dean of the Faculty of Law at the Université de Moncton, Michel Bastarache, to undertake a comprehensive assessment of the language situation and review the Official Languages Act of 1969. Tabled in 1982, the impressive Bastarache-Poirier report presented ninety-six proposals relating to services provided to citizens in both languages. The most controversial involved the duality of services guaranteed to both linguistic communities. Because of the potential costs and the opposition of anglophone activists, Hatfield wavered before proposing the establishment of yet another task force on the issue.

In the other provinces legislators intervened in matters of language and education either because they were prompted by parents, members of the francophone minority groups network, and Canadian Parents for French, or because of the work that the Laurendeau-Dunton Commission did in raising awareness. Their will to take action can also be explained by a shift in political orientation, as happened, for example, in Alberta after the departure of Premier Ernest Manning, who was hostile towards bilingualism. In 1967 even *The Edmonton Journal* criticized Manning's position, estimating that his opposition to the recognition of the rights of francophones in Alberta harmed the efforts deployed to solve the Canadian crisis. The change was also felt in Manitoba in 1969 when the NDP formed a majority government led by Edward Schreyer, who received support from Laurent Desjardins, the Liberal member from Saint-Boniface.

In 1967 the provinces of Manitoba and Saskatchewan, followed by Alberta in 1968, increased the number of hours dedicated to French instruction. Then, in the 1970s, the Prairie provinces allowed instruction to be provided entirely in French in schools attended by francophones. This was the case in Manitoba as of 1970.[37] However, the efforts deployed by the provinces to increase French instruction met with many difficulties. In the case of Alberta, as Hayday's analysis reveals, the province did benefit from federal grants to promote the use of French as a language of instruction in school. But faced with the problem of recruiting qualified teachers with a good command of French, the Department of Education refused to allocate additional funds to attract teachers from outside of Alberta. Finally, parents were divided regarding the demand for the creation of homogeneous French-language schools that would favour children's acquisition of the language. Some believed that socio-economic realities reminded people daily of the need to instead master English. The Association canadienne-française de l'Alberta (ACFA) would nevertheless end up supporting the demand for homogeneous schools at the beginning of the 1980s.

The province of British Columbia was sympathetic to the project of the Fédération canadienne-française de la Colombie-Britannique and encouraged the establishment of a non-denominational school network for francophones. During the 1960s the francophones in British Columbia had been faced with the opposition of the provincial premier, William A.C. Bennett. In 1977, the Social Credit government of Bill Bennett—son of the previous premier—enacted Bill 33 (R.S.B.C. 1996, c.216), which provided financing for private schools, whether denominational or not. From the start, the private French schools were able to take advantage of this financial support.[38]

In 1975 in Manitoba, businessman Georges Forest challenged the validity of parking tickets written in English only. He used as argument Section 23 of the Manitoba Act (1870, 33 Victoria, c.3) to reject the validity of the Act to Provide that the English Language Shall Be the Official Language of the Province of Manitoba (1890 [Man.], 53 Victoria, c.14). On December 13, 1979, the same day that it rendered its judgment on the *Blaikie* matter, the Supreme Court of Canada recognized in its judgment on the matter of *Attorney General of Manitoba v. Forest* ([1979] 2 S.C.R. 1032) the unconstitutionality of the 1890 law. Sterling Lyon's Conservative government dragged its heels, as political scientist Raymond Hébert indicates. The Manitoba political leaders believed that provinces had exclusive jurisdiction over the definition of language rights, rights that were not guaranteed in the 1867 Constitution, according to Premier Lyon. The inaction stemmed in part from its opposition to the proposal made by the Trudeau government to enshrine language rights in the Canadian Constitution. Reluctantly, the Manitoba political leaders had to accept the recognition of French and English as official languages in the province. Consequently, they established a secretariat in 1981 to be in charge of providing French services to the population. The Société franco-manitobaine applauded the actions, but privately deplored the weakness of the provincial language-planning policy. On the other hand, the issue of the invalidity of the provincial laws enacted since 1890 was still not solved, and the NDP government of Howard Pawley would have to undertake this task after its election in 1981.

– – – – –

With the enactment of the Official Languages Act in 1969, the federal state, through the Trudeau government, took the first step in restructuring the Canadian symbolic order. The mobilization of citizens endured, and it fed all the more the crisis diagnosed by the Laurendeau-Dunton Commission, a crisis perceived as threatening the unity of the country and the public interest. Loyal to the logic of liberalism—an art of separation, according to philosopher Michael Walzer—Trudeau believed that the common good would be established by ensuring the good of individuals. Therefore, individual rights had to prevail over collective rights. By ensuring individual rights, such as the right to services in one's mother tongue, the state could resolve social conflicts that existed throughout Canada. The federal language-planning policy followed this logic in a more or less coherent way for the period.

In seeking to prove that French was viable outside of Quebec, the federal state attempted to resolve the problem of access to French education. It did, however, measure the limits of its action. In addition to abandoning bilingual districts, the access to education in the official languages was a matter that caused frustration. The French-speaking minority groups realized that the provinces were dragging their feet and that those who took action did so, as in Ontario, by entrusting the management of the issue to school boards, which were controlled by the anglophone majority.

Through its actions relating to language, the federal state hindered the choices available to the Quebec state for its language policy. Since the issue presented itself differently in Quebec—the problem being the recognition of the rights of the francophone majority, as originally subjected to an unfavourable power relationship—the successive governments of Robert Bourassa and especially of René Lévesque adopted a more republican approach to the management of the language situation. Because the Quebec political leaders favoured a notion of the common good that focused on collective rights to better guarantee individual development, they gambled that policies with a more global outlook would in the long run resolve the social conflicts caused by language divisions.

These language-planning policies transformed the identity references of the various communities. Even though their intention was to provide equal treatment with regard to language rights, the policies stabilized the power relationships in given territories between a majority and a minority that henceforth recognized themselves as such. In a Canada that was basically anglophone and presented itself officially as bilingual and multicultural, francophone minorities had gained the legal means to defend their rights and their vitality, and now had the capacity to sustain their collective existence. In Quebec the francophones could consider themselves as the majority in relation to a new minority, the Anglo-Quebecers. Refusing to accept a minority status, the Anglo-Quebecers challenged bills 22 and 101. With its focus on individual rights, Canadian liberalism became a trump card in their battle, because they believed that the language laws restrained their freedom of choice. While the management of schools was the new issue of francophone minority groups, for English Quebecers the issue of individual freedoms was predominant.

Whether the issue was institutional or administrative bilingualism or unilingualism, the new language policies triggered the mobilization of numerous opponents. In some cases the criticisms expressed did not prevent the state from moving forward. In other cases the opponents of bilingualism did not yield, despite unfavourable rulings from the courts. They remained vigilant and weakened the determination of governments in various provinces, at least where there was a will to act. Sometimes, as in Ontario, the opponents' actions fortified the political leaders in their choice of language policy. In May 1980, following the population's refusal to grant the Quebec government a mandate to negotiate sovereignty-association, the power relationship was altered. The resumption of constitutional negotiations would once again transform the language situation.

CHAPTER 6

LAW AND LANGUAGE SINCE 1982

- -

Parlez-nous de votre Charte
de la beauté vermeille de vos automnes
du funeste octobre
et aussi du Noblet . . .
nous sommes cent peuples venus de loin
pour vous dire que vous n'êtes pas seuls.
  - Marco Micone, *Speak What*

Il feuillette le billet aller-retour de sa langue.
Le billet prend feu et se recroqueville dans le cendrier de sa bouche. . . .
The invisible man had a country.
Now he can't even remember its name.
  - Patrice Desbiens, *L'Homme invisible/The Invisible Man*

Eka aimiani,
nuiten aimuna.
  - Joséphine Bacon, *Moelle/Uinn*
    (*Bâtons à message/Tshissinuashitakana*)

The patriation of the Constitution in 1982 and the constitutional enshrinement of the Charter of Rights and Freedoms produced major changes in language policies and their implementation. They also altered the political cultures of Canada and Quebec.

At the federal level and in English-Canadian provinces, the emphasis on law and court decisions strengthened the model of a nation long promoted by Pierre Elliott Trudeau. Individuals and groups from francophone minority communities now often turned to the law in demanding the full recognition of the rights that went along with the ideal of a bilingual nation. In Quebec itself citizens and associations employed the law and the courts to challenge the Quebec model of a nation and its promotion of French as the common public language. In doing so they were taking actions founded on an individualist notion of language rights.

After 1982 new conditions were in place. Language remained an instrument of nation-building, but the terms for shaping the nation were transformed under the impetus of a new strategy: the recourse to Canadian courts and to international organizations, in particular the United Nations. With the enshrinement of the Charter of Rights and Freedoms in the Constitution Act of 1982, and the development of the international justice system based on the promotion of individual rights, new experts entered the field: lawyers and lawmakers. These new actors contributed to an increase in the activism of courts; they took on the responsibility of interpreting the legal provisions and even became promoters of political causes.

With this recourse to the formality of law, the informal expressions of public mobilization, such as demonstrations and other means of protest, became less effective and to some degree lost legitimacy in the eye of state authorities. Consequently, attempts to mobilize against violations of Bill 101 in Quebec or the closure of Hôpital Montfort in Ontario had less impact on authorities. Instead, court rulings guided their decisions on these matters.

Law as the new language environment

At the heart of the advent of the new language environment was a specific event: the patriation of the Canadian Constitution on April 16, 1982. It was an issue that, since the 1960s, had been addressed at numerous meetings. Beginning with the election of Jean Lesage's Liberals in 1960, various Quebec governments demanded a new distribution of powers between the federal state and the provinces—a reform that could be carried out either through decentralization, with each province receiving new powers, or by the granting of a special status to Quebec. If the political leaders were to select the second option to accommodate Quebec's demands, they would also be allowing the constitutional recognition of another concept of the Canadian experience: that of the two founding peoples. Each would occupy a specific territory: Quebec would henceforth become the nation-state of francophones; and Canada, the nation-state of anglophones. At the beginning of the 1960s, the theories surrounding two founding peoples and the recognition of their equality gained sympathy among the main federal political parties, as well as among some intellectuals and opinion-makers in daily newspapers.

In 1965, when Trudeau took the plunge into federal politics by joining the Liberal Party, he arrived with precise ideas on constitutional matters. According to this former law professor, Canada did not need either to change the powers of the federal and provincial states or to recognize a special status for Quebec. On the contrary, the Constitution needed a charter to protect the fundamental rights and freedoms of Canadians and, by the same token, to prevent states from limiting those rights. Finally, Trudeau believed that the Constitution should include what he perceived to be key features of the country—elements such as linguistic duality, the ethnic mosaic, and the protection of the school rights of language minorities.

In time Trudeau's constitutional agenda gained support among the intelligentsia and the main anglophone daily newspapers. Following the enactment of the Official Languages Act and the multicultural policy, the theory of two founding peoples lost ground and was supplanted by principles that were seen as being more neutral: the equality of the two linguistic communities, and the co-existence of various equal cultures within the same entity. In accepting this idea—the equality of languages and cultures rather than the equality of nations—the anglophone intelligentsia and daily newspapers began criticizing Quebec's demands. Any constitutional concession granted to Quebec, they argued, would undermine the new Canadian vision of society. They believed that linguistic equality and cultural diversity constituted the key components of the social contract that linked Canadians to their state; these conditions were the foundation of the new Canadian civic nationalism. In the 1970s it remained to be seen how this civic contract could be enshrined in the Canadian Constitution.

The opportunity to take action arose after the 1980 Quebec Referendum, which upset the predominant power relationship between a Quebec tempted by political sovereignty and a Canada preoccupied with the preservation of its integrity. During the constitutional talks that followed, René Lévesque's Parti Québécois government opposed the federal project, in particular the enshrinement of a Charter of Rights and Freedoms. Such a charter would limit Quebec's powers relating to language, among other rights. In the hope of defeating the federal project the Quebec premier entered into an alliance with seven of his provincial counterparts. The "Gang of Eight" collapsed when the Trudeau government agreed to amend some elements of the constitutional project, in particular by including a "notwithstanding" clause in the Charter of Rights and Freedoms. The constitutional negotiations ended in November 1981 with the signing of an agreement on the patriation of the Constitution Act, the enshrinement of a Charter of Rights and Freedoms in the Constitution, and the inclusion of an amending formula. Quebec did not sign the agreement.

During the constitutional talks, the Fédération des francophones hors Québec opposed the proposals put forward by the Trudeau government on matters relating to education in the languages of both minority groups. The organization's leaders advocated the recognition of the equality of the two founding peoples as the interpretive principle of the Constitution, a suggestion that the prime minister categorically rejected because it was contrary to his concepts of federalism and the appropriate relations between francophones and anglophones. Despite this rebuttal, the FFHQ pursued its battle by targeting fifteen or so members of Parliament and federal ministers, including Marc Lalonde, Roméo Leblanc, Jeanne Sauvé, Serge Joyal, and Jean-Robert Gauthier. It not only issued its demands to them but also, especially, in the days preceding the conclusion of the talks in 1981, reacted to the various scenarios that were circulating on the amendment of the Constitution. Because of the positions taken by the Fédération, tensions between the organization and some members of Parliament and senators emerged. The FFHQ feared that access to education in French would be limited by the application of the criterion summarized in the formula "where numbers warrant." Furthermore, the FFHQ was demanding homogeneous schools and school boards, greater access to French instruction from primary to post-secondary education, and the governance of schools by francophones themselves.[1]

Canadian Charter of Rights and Freedoms (1982)

Section 16. (1) English and French are the official languages of Canada and have equality of status and equal rights and privileges as to their use in all institutions of the Parliament and government of Canada. ...

Section 17. (1) Everyone has the right to use English or French in any debates and other proceedings of Parliament. ...

Section 20. (1) Any member of the public in Canada has the right to communicate with, and to receive available services from, any head or central office of an institution of the Parliament or government of Canada in English or French, and has the same right with respect to any other office of any such institution where

(a) there is a significant demand for communications with and services from that office in such language;

(b) due to the nature of the office, it is reasonable that communications ... be available in both English and French. ...

Language of instruction

Section 23. (1) Citizens of Canada

(a) whose first language learned and still understood is that of the English or French linguistic minority population of the province in which they reside, or

(b) who have received their primary school instruction in Canada in English or French and reside in a province where the language in which they received that instruction is the language of the English or French linguistic minority population of the province,

have the right to have their children receive primary and secondary school instruction in that language in that province.

Continuity of language instruction

(2) Citizens of Canada of whom any child has received or is receiving primary or secondary school instruction in English or French in Canada, have

the right to have all their children receive primary and secondary school instruction in the same language.

Application where numbers warrant

(3) The right of citizens of Canada under subsections (1) and (2) to have their children receive primary and secondary school instruction in the language of the English or French linguistic minority population of a province

(a) applies wherever in the province the number of children of citizens who have such a right is sufficient to warrant the provision to them out of public funds of minority language instruction; and

(b) includes, where the number of those children so warrants, the right to have them receive that instruction in minority language educational facilities provided out of public funds.

Source: Canadian Charter of Rights and Freedoms,
http://laws.justice.gc.ca/eng/charter/
page-2.html#anchorbo-ga:l_l-gb:s_16.

— — — — — — — — — — — — — — — — —

With the enactment of the Constitution Act of 1982, language rights were from then on enshrined in the Constitution. Section 23 of the Charter of Rights and Freedoms recognized the right of Canadian citizens to educate their children in French or English in primary and secondary schools. The recognition applied to all Canadian citizens, in every province, wherever "the number of children of citizens who have such a right is sufficient to warrant the provision to them out of public funds of minority language instruction." This section obliterated the reciprocal agreements on education rights that the Parti Québécois government had proposed. It hindered in particular Bill 101 and its section dedicated to the question of access to English-language instruction.

The objective of Section 23 was to constitutionalize the rights of parents to educate their children in one or the other of the country's official languages. The section included the expression "educational facilities." During the discussions of the Special Joint Committee of the Senate and the House of Commons on the Constitution of Canada, Liberal MP Jean-Robert Gauthier had played a decisive role in the drafting of the text of Section 23, as his biographer Rolande Faucher recounts. Gauthier successfully proposed to his colleagues that the term "educational installations" be replaced by "minority-language educational facilities," in the hope that this formulation would encourage a generous interpretation by judges.

Following the constitutional enshrinement of the Charter of Rights and Freedoms, the federal state continued to implant its new symbolic order. In 1988 it amended the Official Languages Act. The new law granted federal public servants the right to use one or the other official language if they were working in the National Capital Region, elsewhere in Ontario, in New Brunswick, or in Quebec. It also granted the Commissioner of Official Languages the capacity to analyse all regulations being considered by the federal state. It also allowed courts to hear a complaint "within six months after the complaint is made" to the commissioner. The law imposed on the federal state the mandate of supporting the development of French and English minority communities. Finally, it obliged federal agencies in Canada and abroad to provide their services in both official languages, when the demand for and nature of the state services were warranted.[2]

Another legislative measure strengthened the role of federal language planning. In 2005 Bill S-3, sponsored by Jean-Robert Gauthier, now a senator, and supported by the Office of the Commissioner of Official Languages, amended a specific part of the Official Languages Act. It obliged the federal government "to enhance the vitality" and "support the development" of the English and French linguistic minority communities in Canada. Consequently, from then on federal authorities were obliged to take positive measures to implement this commitment. Furthermore, "the obligations stated in this part of the [law] can be the subject of court remedies."[3]

After 1982, then, maintenance of the new Canadian symbolic order depended upon a range of tools. In addition to the Charter of Rights and Freedoms and the language laws, the ideology of multiculturalism provided an especially valued focus. Already entrenched in the Charter, the policy became federal law in 1988. With the Act for the Preservation and Enhancement of Multiculturalism in Canada (1988, 37 Elizabeth II, c. 31), the Progressive Conservative government of Brian Mulroney sought to extend the mandate of the approach, without, however, changing its fundamental objectives. Although this measure did not have an essentially linguistic reach, it did have an impact on the language issue because it was meant to "preserve and enhance the use of languages other than English and French, while strengthening the status and use of the official languages of Canada" (Sect. 3-i), thanks, among other things, to those languages being taught. In addition, the federal authorities were obliged henceforth to "make use, as appropriate, of the language skills and cultural understanding of individuals of all origins" (Sect. 3.2-e). Therefore, although the extent of the measure was not universal, individuals were entitled to receive services in their mother tongue when dealing with the federal state, depending on the availability of public servants who spoke their particular language.

That necessity became more frequent as of the 1990s. Indeed, beginning in 1990, Canada started welcoming between 200,000 and 262,000 immigrants a year. According to the 2006 Census data, 70.2 per cent of foreign-born individuals spoke a language other than English or French. Among these newcomers, one out of five (18.6 per cent) spoke one of the various Chinese idioms, such as Cantonese or Mandarin; the other languages spoken were Italian, Punjabi, Spanish, German, Tagalog (or Filipino), and Arabic. Only a small proportion of the foreign-born population (3.1 per cent) reported French as their only mother tongue.[4] Although a large majority of immigrants (93.6 per cent) declared that they could converse in French or English, the increasing imbalance called for a strengthening of language-planning policies. Nevertheless, despite the high values placed on multiculturalism, the policy failed to meet its objectives from the 1990s on. As anthropologist Denyse Helly argues, given the constraints of fiscal austerity the mandate to strengthen Canadian unity was never efficiently fulfilled; moreover, the federal authorities essentially converted the policy into simple rhetoric.

Finally, yet another legal and constitutional mechanism came to play a role in language matters. In 1981, at the time of the negotiations surrounding the patriation of the Constitution, the Trudeau government had turned to the courts for assistance in imposing its symbolic order—a strategy supported by Bora Laskin, the chief justice of the Supreme Court of Canada. Following the very close results of the 1995 referendum on sovereignty-partnership, Prime Minister Chrétien and his minister of Intergovernmental Affairs, Stéphane Dion, once again resorted to this strategy to prevent the future accession of Quebec to political sovereignty; but the results were less clear-cut. The Supreme Court of Canada stated in its *Reference re Secession of Quebec* ([1998] 2 S.C.R. 217) that Quebec did not constitute a people and, therefore, did not enjoy the right to secede from the country. Still, democratic rights had to prevail, and consequently the Canadian state would be obliged to negotiate if a future referendum indicated a clear majority for the yes vote. In a ruling in which the influence of judges Antonio Lamer and especially Michel Bastarache was obvious, the highest court in the land established four principles underlying the entire Canadian Constitution: federalism, democracy, constitutionalism and the rule of law, and respect for minorities.

Reference re Secession of Quebec (1998)
[1998] 2 S.C.R. 217.

(2) Question 1

The Constitution is more than a written text. It embraces the entire global system of rules and principles which govern the exercise of constitutional authority.... It is necessary to make a more profound investigation of the underlying principles animating the whole of the Constitution, including the principles of federalism, democracy, constitutionalism and the rule of law, and respect for minorities. Those principles must inform our overall appreciation of the constitutional rights and obligations that would come into play in the event that a clear majority of Quebecers votes on a clear question in favour of secession....

81   The concern of our courts and governments to protect minorities has been prominent in recent years, particularly following the enactment of the *Charter*. Undoubtedly, one of the key considerations motivating the enactment of the *Charter*, and the process of constitutional judicial review that it entails, is the protection of minorities. However, it should not be forgotten that the protection of minority rights had a long history before the enactment of the *Charter*. Indeed, the protection of minority rights was clearly an essential consideration in the design of our constitutional structure even at the time of Confederation. ... Although Canada's record of upholding the rights of minorities is not a spotless one, that goal is one towards which Canadians have been striving since Confederation, and the process has not been without successes. The principle of protecting

minority rights continues to exercise influence in the operation and interpretation of our Constitution.

Source: http://scc.lexum.org/en/1998/1998scr2-217/1998scr2-217.html.

With regard specifically to minority languages, the last principle
of this finding strongly constrained the states and courts in any new
measure relating to the management of language. In addition, as philosopher Michel Seymour observes, the principle had a distinct basis
in a sense of community. The shift tempered the concept of individual
rights that had prevailed among activists since the Charter of Rights
and Freedoms was constitutionalized in 1982.

The Supreme Court's intervention had direct effects not only
on the constitutional file, but also on the language file. As a counter-
attack to the Referendum Clarity Bill, enacted in 1999 by the Chrétien
government, the Quebec government under Lucien Bouchard enacted
Bill 99 relating to the exercise of the fundamental rights and prerogatives of the people of Quebec and the Quebec state. The legislation
reaffirmed the powers, legitimacy, and sovereignty of the National
Assembly with regard to any potential infringement on the exercise
of its rights, including those relating to language. Bill 99 defined the
Quebec people as a majority of francophones, and it reaffirmed Section 1 of the Charter of the French Language and the legitimacy of
any unilingualism policy, while recognizing the contribution of First
Nations, Quebecers of all origins, and the anglophone community. The
bill triggered the opposition of the anglophone activists, who went back
to the courts in 2001 in an attempt to have it invalidated.

**An Act respecting the exercise of the fundamental
rights and prerogatives of the Québec people and
the Québec State, called Bill 99 (2000)
(S.Q.R. chapter E-20.2)**

Preamble
WHEREAS the Québec people, in the majority French-speaking, possesses
specific characteristics and a deep-rooted historical continuity in a territory
over which it exercises its rights through a modern national state, having

a government, a national assembly and impartial and independent courts of justice ...

WHEREAS the Abenaki, Algonquin, Attikamek, Cree, Huron, Innu, Malecite, Micmac, Mohawk, Naskapi and Inuit Nations exist within Québec, and whereas the principles associated with that recognition were set out in the resolution adopted by the National Assembly on 20 March 1985, in particular their right to autonomy within Québec;

WHEREAS there exists a Québec English-speaking community that enjoys long-established rights;

WHEREAS Québec recognizes the contribution made by Quebecers of all origins to its development ...

THE PARLIAMENT OF QUÉBEC ENACTS AS FOLLOWS: ...

8. The French language is the official language of Québec.

The duties and obligations relating to or arising from the status of the French language are established by the Charter of the French language.

The Québec State must promote the quality and influence of the French language. It shall pursue those objectives in a spirit of fairness and open-mindedness, respectful of the long-established rights of Québec's English-speaking community.

> Source: Quebec, National Assembly,
> http://www2.publicationsduquebec.gouv.qc.ca/
> dynamicSearch/telecharge.php?type=5&file=2000C46A.PDF.

— —

The decision in the *Reference re Secession of Quebec* became a powerful argument referred to in subsequent legal cases on language, including those on the opening of minority language schools in 2000 and on the Hôpital Montfort in 2001. It was also referred to by the Fédération des communautés francophones et acadienne du Canada in October 2006, when that organization challenged the Canadian state following a decision by the Conservative government of Stephen Harper to abolish the Court Challenges Program. Faced with the general outcry of the francophone associations, and based on a report drafted by Bernard Lord, former Conservative premier of New Brunswick, the Harper government in part withdrew its decision in 2008.

The language issue created divisions again during debates on a private member's bill, C-232, tabled in March 2010 by the Acadian

New Democrat member of Parliament Yvon Godin. The bill stipu-
lated that any new Supreme Court of Canada judges would thereafter
have to know both official languages. When the Senate examined
the bill, the opponents of bilingualism once again drew on familiar
arguments. The Canadian Constitution Foundation claimed that the
requirement was discriminatory because it would prevent unilingual
people from sitting on the highest court in the land. *The Globe and
Mail*, although deeming the objective to be noble, concluded that it
was sufficient to have interpreters doing the work of translation in
courts. For these opponents, knowledge of the laws and experience
in the field of law should be the only criteria used in the selection
of judges.

Mapping the interpretations of the Charter

Although in previous years the Quebec state had demonstrated
its resolve in matters of language—as when it had enacted the Charter
of the French Language—transformations in political culture at the
turn of the 1980s caused it to lose some of its edge. The result of the
May 1980 referendum had diminished its capacity to negotiate in the
framework of power relations with the federal state. In 1982 the new
Canadian symbolic order, to which Quebec did not adhere, nevertheless had an impact on the political management of diversity and the
determination of the common good, especially with regard to language
issues. Finally, transformations in Quebec society—the flourishing of
cultural pluralism, the increased tendency towards individualism, and
a hegemonic economic conception of social relations—were having an
effect on the decisions taken by Quebec authorities, as well as on the
political action of citizens. With the 1979 *Blaikie* ruling, it had become
obvious that the strategy of using the courts to resolve issues of language
use would be extensively employed in the last decades of the twentieth
century and the beginning of the twenty-first. As the judiciary replaced
the political, this strategy not only reduced even further the capacity
for intervention of elected politicians, but also limited the space for
action by citizens.

Enacted despite the opposition of the Quebec state, the Constitution Act of 1982 and the enshrinement of the Charter of Rights and

Freedoms provided powerful ammunition for pressure groups during the 1980s, and those bodies used the principle of individual rights to promote their political causes. A 1984 Supreme Court of Canada decision in the case of *Attorney General of Quebec v. Quebec Association of Protestant School Boards et al.* ([1984] 2 S.C.R. 66) upheld the rulings of the lower courts. It declared that the "Quebec clause," which limited access to English primary and secondary schools to children of parents who had received their primary education in English in Quebec, had no force of law.[5] Another later decision by the Supreme Court, in 2005, further determined the scope of the "Canada clause," pertaining to parents whose children have been instructed in English-language schools in Canada, as opposed to only in Quebec. With the ruling in the case of *Solski (Tutor of) v. Quebec (Attorney General)* ([2005] 1 S.C.R. 201), children of parents from other provinces were granted broader access to English schools if they had previously undergone a significant part of their schooling in the English language. Although the ruling recognized the constitutionality of the Charter of the French Language and that children of francophone families had the right to attend schools in their own language, numerous commentators, such as Josée Boileau in *Le Devoir*, worried about the "judicial mishmash" and "application difficulties" that arose when trying to "map flexibility."[6]

Political agendas and court rulings stemming from the activism of individuals and groups helped to keep the language issue alive in the public debate—as in the case of a ruling on attendance at "bridging schools" (*écoles-passerelles*), non-subsidized private schools that provided education in English. In its ruling on *Nguyen v. Quebec (Education, Recreation and Sports)* (2009 SCC 47), rendered in October 2009, the Supreme Court deemed that the absolute prohibition on choosing an educational path in an English bridging school was far too severe. Consequently, the ruling struck down Bill 104, which set a threshold on admissions to English schools. In addition to creating a breach in Bill 101, the *Nguyen* decision was an indication of another major shift, one in which rights were perceived as commodities. As sociologist Yves Martin points out—and a statement by the Conseil supérieur de la langue française affirmed in March 2010—a child now had the right to a language of instruction if his or her parents obtained that privilege by paying the tuition fees at a bridging school.[7]

Given the rule of law, it was the Quebec state's duty to monitor the enforcement of laws within its territory, without any exceptions. Following the election of the provincial Liberals in 1985, the Robert Bourassa government proposed amendments to Bill 101. At first the changes were all about so-called illegal students—a term used to describe students who attended an English school when they were not eligible to do so because their parents had not received their education in English in Canada. A task force set up by Minister of Education Claude Ryan found a total of 1,013 illegals, with 544 of them being of Italian origin. The Quebec wing of the National Congress of Italian Canadians requested that these students be granted amnesty. The Liberal government, endorsing this proposition, tabled a bill on the Eligibility of Certain Children for Instruction in English (S.Q. 1986, c.46). The daily newspapers were divided on the issue. While Lysiane Gagnon at *La Presse* denounced the principle of amnesty, Jean-Claude Leclerc at *Le Devoir* supported it, stating that such a measure by the Bourassa government would be a "reasonable solution."[8] Despite opposition from the Parti Québécois, the Société Saint-Jean-Baptiste, the Alliance des professeurs de Montréal, and the Centrale de l'enseignement du Québec, the National Assembly adopted the Bill in June 1986.

In 1986 two more Bills tabled in the National Assembly by the minister of Cultural Affairs, Lise Bacon, served to keep the language debate alive. Bill 140 provided for a restructuring of the duties assigned to the agencies in charge of enforcing Bill 101. In addition to transforming the Conseil de la langue française, the bill made provisions for the abolition of the Commission de protection de la langue française. The Office de la langue française was to be granted the powers of the Commission to investigate. Finally, the government reserved the right to issue directions on the language issue directly to the Office. The second piece of legislation, Bill 142, recognized the right of English-speaking individuals to health and social services in English.

The opposition to these bills was intense, particularly because of the great fear that the operations of the Office would be politicized. Citizens united in the Mouvement Québec français, combined with unions and nationalist groups, led the battle. The Parti Québécois distributed signs displaying the slogan, *"Ne touchez pas à la loi 101"* (Don't touch Bill 101). The situation grew more acrimonious when

Zellers stores decided they would no longer comply with the Bill 101 restrictions on commercial advertising. Faced with the disruption of social peace, the Conseil du patronat du Québec (Quebec Employers Council) and the Chambre de commerce de Montréal urged the Bourassa government to clarify its intentions regarding Bill 101. As a result of the strong mobilization, as Michel Plourde relates in his study, the Liberal government let Bill 140 die on the order paper of the National Assembly.

Passions were rekindled in December 1988 following a Supreme Court ruling in the case of *Ford v. Quebec (Attorney General)* ([1988] 2 S.C.R. 712), which overturned the sections of Bill 101 dealing with public signs. Although it recognized the objective of Bill 101, which was to protect and defend the French language in Quebec, the Supreme Court upheld the rulings of lower courts, stating that the obligation to use French only on signs infringed on the fundamental right of freedom of expression and the right to equality. Given the scope it gave to fundamental rights, based on a broad interpretation of the Canadian and Quebec charters of rights and freedoms, the verdict was astonishing. As sociologist Robert Vandycke indicates, concerning a neighbouring case in the United States, the U.S. Supreme Court had included commercial publicity in its definition of freedom of expression in 1942; but deemed that the status of that practice was weaker than that of freedom of opinion in issues of public interest. Notwithstanding the U.S. precedent, the Supreme Court of Canada ruling did not establish an official hierarchy among rights and freedoms, but it did lead to concern about the possibility of an informal hierarchy based on the minority position of francophones within Canada as a whole. Even while accepting the rule of the predominance of the French language, the judges had invalidated French unilingualism in public and commercial signage.[9]

For the militant nationalists in Quebec, these rulings—and especially the 1988 decision on *Ford*—generated a major mobilization, particularly manifested on the streets. The activists were convinced that they needed, especially, to be vigilant; their strategies were motivated by the conviction that the common good was fragile, especially in relation to language. For them, the principle of precaution had to take precedence to ensure the preservation and full development of the common good that had been so dearly gained in and then defended

Francization remains partial in gastronomy. Restaurant signs in Montreal in 1985.

by the Charter of the French Language. The nationalist groups, which included the Mouvement Québec français led by Guy Bouthillier, and the labour unions—the Union des artistes and Union des écrivains québécois—urged the Bourassa government to pass legislation to preserve the French face of commerce, especially in Montreal. That city became a battlefield for the supporters of Bill 101; it was the province's economic centre and the main destination of immigrants who had chosen Quebec as their new home. Given that the metropolis was presented as an outpost under siege, any retreat within it would result in disastrous consequences for all of the people of Quebec. Although the context was different, debate about the anglicization of Montreal evoked the survival discourse of 1960s activists who used that same analogy of outposts under siege. Not so long ago, those outposts made up of French-minority groups anywhere in Canada had fallen in the battle against assimilation; their loss had disastrous effects on all of French Canada, including Quebec. After the ruling on the *Ford* case in 1998 the argument took on a new dimension, with the metropolis now being perceived as the outpost of French Quebec.

The ruling on the *Ford* case was not unanimously condemned. Some anglophone commentators applauded the Supreme Court ruling on signage, as did Alliance Quebec. Through the voice of its president, Royal Orr, the pressure group welcomed the judgment and called on Quebec to amend Bill 101 accordingly. Other intervenors challenged the argument that the French language in Quebec was in a precarious position—an argument used to encourage the government not to comply with the Supreme Court ruling. They also criticized the claim that the French face of commerce had to be preserved in order to prompt the integration of immigrants into the francophone majority. Some, including philosopher Charles Taylor, noted that education, the labour market, and socialization also provided ways of integrating immigrants into the majority, and that these means were much more efficient than maintaining French as the only language used in commercial signage.

To ensure social peace, but to the detriment of attempts to reach agreement on constitutional amendments through what became known as the Meech Lake Accord, the Bourassa government stepped quickly to keep its feet in both camps. With Bill 178, sanctioned on December 21, 1988, the government relied on the authority of the notwithstanding clause set out in Section 33 of the Canadian Charter of Rights and Freedoms, to the effect that its provisions could "operate notwithstanding the provisions" made in the Constitution Act of 1982, and would "apply despite sections 3 and 10 of the (Quebec) Charter of Human Rights and Freedoms." Bill 178 maintained mandatory public signage in French only on the outside of businesses but allowed the use of another language inside, as long as French had a predominant position.

Although the activists in nationalist groups and other supporters of Bill 101 approved this recourse to the notwithstanding clause, they were preoccupied with the alterations brought to the Charter of French language. Therefore, on March 12 1989, some sixty thousand people demonstrated in Montreal, spreading from Lafontaine Park to the Champ-de-Mars, demanding the full and complete preservation of Bill 101. This massive demonstration was followed by others, including one that attracted several thousand people to Parliament Hill in Quebec City. The reliance on the notwithstanding clause also provoked general disapproval in English Canada, where numerous opponents to the Meech Lake Accord used the pretext of Bill 178 to justify their position. It also created a crisis within the Quebec Liberal Party. Demanding total compliance with individual rights, three anglophone cabinet ministers, including Clifford Lincoln, resigned before the end of the 1988 parliamentary session. Under Robert Libman's leadership, the new Equality Party came into being. Although it achieved relative success with the election of four candidates in the 1989 provincial election, it was in no position to seriously harm the Liberal Party because its electoral base was massively concentrated in anglophone and allophone ridings in Montreal. Its four members were defeated in the 1994 election; this included Richard Holden, who had, in the meantime, joined the Parti Québécois as a member for the riding of Westmount.

In using the notwithstanding clause the Bourassa government was aware of a further catch: the Constitution Act made it mandatory to re-examine the clause at the end of a five-year period. The Quebec government would have to pass further legislation. Furthermore, Quebec authorities had to take into account the opinion of the UN Committee on Human Rights, which recognized in May 1993, as the Supreme Court of Canada had previously done, that signage was

Aislin cartoon in *The Gazette* (Montreal), February 1989.

a fundamental right. As Vandycke points out, from then on no political strategy could disregard this new dimension. Consequently, the Bourassa government tabled Bill 86, which adjusted the provisions of the Charter of the French Language to require the clear predominance of French in commercial advertising, while granting space to other languages. According to linguist Jean-Claude Corbeil, the law abolished the Commission de surveillance—set up to ensure compliance with the law and to inquire into failures to comply (as brought to its attention by a third party or discovered by commission inspectors), which would be reinstated in 1997. Bill 86 came up against strong resistance from the francophone activists, including Pierre Bourgault, who argued, as his biographer Jean-François Nadeau notes, that it shattered the francophone majority's efforts to assert itself. But the fervour

Photothèque FTQ

Demonstration against Bill 178 in Montreal, March 1989. Photo by Serge Jongué.

around the issue was gone. Even though the Parti Québécois opposed the bill in the National Assembly, *realpolitik* prevailed. The potential for Quebec's accession to sovereignty, very solid in the post-Meech context, required that international opinions be taken into account and sights lowered.

In steering interpretations of the charters of rights and freedoms, the two rulings of 1984 and 1988 exposed the limits of the judicial strategies used by anglophone pressure groups. In 2001 a challenge to Bill 86 in the Quebec Court of Appeal regarding the predominance of French in advertising drew a blank. Then, as legal scholar Eugénie Brouillet points out, the Supreme Court refused to hear the appeal. Furthermore, in the opinion of the UN Committee on Human Rights, "Quebec's English community [did] not qualify for protection as a minority language group" because they were part of the Canadian English-speaking majority. Indicating that Bill 178 concerned all the citizens of Quebec, anglophones as well as francophones, the UN Committee concluded that the opponents of the Quebec measures on commercial signs "were not subjected to any discrimination based on their language." [10] From then on, the mobilization dried up. Except in rearguard skirmishes led by a few militant ideologues—such as the *angryphones* Howard Galganov, William Johnson, and Brent Tyler—the Charter of the French Language no longer prompted any systematic objections based on principle. Consequently, Stéphane Dion, the federal minister in charge of the Office of the Commissioner of Official Languages in 1998, readily acknowledged the legitimacy of the language protection measures in Bill 101, from the point of view of multilingual democracies.[11] As for *The Gazette*, though always quick to head to the ramparts in the 1980s, it had admitted after the 2005 *Solski* ruling that "by easing" fears of loss of identity, "Bill 101 created a language balance under which Quebec has prospered tolerably well."[12]

After the tight results of the October 1995 referendum on sovereignty-partnership, it was time for appeasement, at least according to a wish expressed by Quebec premier Lucien Bouchard in a speech delivered to the anglophone community at the Centaur Theatre. "In the language debate," he said, in referring to the common good, "the two great language groups in Quebec have now exited the era of upheavals to enter into a period of mutual interests."[13] Speaking to the Conseil national du Parti Québécois in September 1996, Bouchard pursued the same idea: "We are among democrats. It is our responsibility—in fact our duty—to protect the fundamental rights of our citizens." Therefore, it seemed to him necessary to "design a fair and stable language-planning policy that will ensure the permanency of French in Montreal and Quebec, and therefore ensure a better integration of newcomers," while watching over the "vitality of the anglophone community."[14]

With the objective of social peace having seemingly been reached on the language front, the Quebec state proceeded in three stages. First, in June 1997, it initiated the Act to Amend the Charter of the French Language, known as Bill 40, which remained faithful to the provisions of Bill 86. Second, in 1998, the Bouchard government introduced an amendment to Section 93 of the 1867 Constitution Act, making it possible to set in place linguistic school boards better adapted to the social reality of contemporary Quebec. Finally, in 2000 and 2001 the Commission des États généraux sur la situation et l'avenir de la langue française au Québec, known as the Larose Commission, began looking into the possibility of a comprehensive restructuring of the Charter of the French Language. To do so, it held consultations in every region of Quebec and collected 349 briefs not only from organizations representing community elites, but also from common citizens. Its final report, issued in 2001, offered two major recommendations for the development of the Quebec symbolic order. After noting the rupture in the language policy in the province because of "the historical Canadian approach that divides Quebec's identity according to an ethnic dividing line between French and English Canadians," the report said that it should be possible to promote "a civic approach that would build the identity of the people of Quebec on openness and inclusion thanks to a common language, French, and a common culture shaped by the contributions of all its components." The second recommendation advocated the establishment of Quebec citizenship.[15]

The Larose Commission's propositions were coolly received by Premier Bernard Landry's PQ government, which had other priorities, and went unheeded after the election of Jean Charest's Liberals in April 2003. From then on, for fear of waking a sleeping giant, Quebec authorities became very prudent regarding the language issue. The Charest government was plagued with controversy, in particular the issue of de-amalgamation of municipalities that had been merged by the previous PQ administration. The issue unfolded in a maze of language and community tensions in Montreal, and the bungling actions, after 2005, of what was now called the Office québécois de la langue française. Based on the conviction that "it was necessary to learn English for the individual and collective growth of Quebecers,"[16] to use the terms of National Assembly member Yvon Marcoux in 2003, the minister of Education, Recreation, and Sports, Jean-Marc Fournier, announced in June 2005 that instruction in English as a second language in the first year of primary school would be mandatory in the coming year. In taking this step the Charest government was fulfilling a campaign promise and proving the extent to which it valued bilingualism, despite the serious reservations of the Conseil supérieur de l'éducation, which questioned the pedagogical justification of the measure.

In 2007, without touching on the language issue directly, but referring back to the management of diversity, an intense controversy unsettled the political landscape in Quebec: the question of reasonable accommodations. The visible presence in the public sphere of ethnic communities practising a religion other than Christianity represented a challenge to the Quebec civic model based on secular principles, gender equality, and the primacy of French. The obsession with security after September 11, 2001, and the apprehensions caused by the real or presumed effects of Canadian multiculturalism combined to unleash a media storm. Faced with growing citizen discontent, Premier Charest created a commission of inquiry co-chaired by historian Gérard Bouchard and Charles Taylor. In May 2008, after touring Quebec, listening to 3,243 intervenors, and receiving 901 briefs—some addressing language concerns—the Bouchard-Taylor Commission tabled its report without providing any concrete recommendations on the question of language. The report's understanding of the issue was based on the civic concept of a nation. In response to the criticisms voiced on the fate of French in the public sphere, the commissioners stated, "The English that we must learn and speak today is not the English that Lord Durham sought to impose," but "the English that affords access to all knowledge and exchanges with all peoples of the world." Pleading for the practice of trilingualism, as seen in other "small nations," Bouchard and Taylor stated, "This question warrants the closest attention, otherwise a generation of young French-speakers risks being unfairly penalized." [17]

The issue of language also entered into Quebec's international relations, particularly because for a state that was not fully sovereign, language was a key means of gaining recognition. Since 1965 various Quebec governments had pegged their international policy on the doctrine set forth by Paul Gérin-Lajoie, which assumed the international extension of the province's internal powers in matters of health, education, and culture. It was a doctrine evidently challenged by federal authorities preoccupied with preserving the Canadian state's exclusive right to international representation of its peoples. The Quebec authorities' strategy relied on support received from some international agencies that had objectives related to the promotion of the French language. This was especially the case of the Francophone Summits, which, as historian Frédéric Bastien states, Quebec had been participating in since 1987 thanks to tacit support from France. In the Quebec Declaration of March 24, 1999, which put an emphasis on language, the minister for International Relations, Louise Beaudoin, brought the Gérin-Lajoie doctrine once again to the forefront. Within the context of the enactment of the federal Referendum Clarity Bill, the tone was clearly confrontational. The Quebec Declaration reasserted that "whereas Québec is the only territory in the Americas whose official and common language is French and whereas the National Assembly and the Government of Québec are the only francophone democratic institutions in the Americas," and also, "whereas the Québec people have a vital interest in the promotion and affirmation of cultural identity," Quebec was intent on participating in "all international forums dealing with education, language, culture and identity." [18] Later, as political scientist Nelson Michaud points out, Charest's Liberal government reduced the tension by recognizing that international relations were the exclusive domain of the federal state. In 2006 the minister of International Relations (who is also responsible for the Francophonie), Monique Gagnon-Tremblay, introduced a less challenging policy, simply establishing that the priority of the government was to "support the worldwide promotion and recognition of the French language." [19]

Meanwhile, the debate around the quality of language continued. Pierre Bourgault, who filmed a commercial celebrating the French language in 1988, was a regular speaker at forums on the improvement of the quality of French during the 1990s. At the end of the decade songwriter and interpreter Georges Dor revived the quarrel over the matter of French as spoken by Quebecers by publishing three essays: "Anna braillé ène shot" [She cried a lot], "Essai sur le langage parlé des Québécois [Essay on Quebecers' spoken language] and *Ta mé tu là?*" [Is your mother there?], and "Un autre essai sur le langage parlé des Québécois" [Another essay on Quebecers' spoken language].[20] Dor's words were curt; he denounced the very poor quality of the spoken language, especially among youth—despite the major financial investments that the state had been allocating to the school system since the 1960s—and in the media and on television. Rekindled by Dor, the controversy flamed even higher in the following decade. During the debate on the launch of a "pedagogical renewal" that started in the mid-2000s, opponents of government reform emphasized the laxity in the methods used to teach French, which focused on exercising the skills of the student rather than on the acquisition of knowledge of the subject. The controversy on the quality of language use continued to explode periodically in other contexts, such as the French used on television and radio by songwriters-interpreters and stand-up comedians, and on the Internet.

The vitality of minority communities and Aboriginal peoples

The relation between language and politics became particularly sensitive when it involved communities whose preservation, if not existence, remained precarious. People use spoken and written language as the means of communication not only to ensure social connectedness, but also to pass down collective historical and identity experiences from the past through the present and into the future. Language assimilation caused the dissolution of community links and severely destructured certain groups of people, especially if they were a minority within a territory and their members had difficulty gaining access to resources to ensure the development of their full potential. Given these social, economic, and cultural conditions, ensuring the language vitality of minority communities became a key entry in political agendas. The francophone and Acadian communities outside Quebec were well aware of this situation, as were the First Nations, Métis, and Inuit in Quebec and throughout Canada. After 1982 these communities and peoples, each in their own way, attempted to find the best way of addressing and resolving the issue.

A major phenomenon emerged among the francophones outside of Quebec, transforming their political relations: an increase in court referrals concerning language. The enshrinement of the Canadian Charter of Rights and Freedoms in the Constitution Act of 1982 encouraged francophone activists to use the resources of the judiciary to gain recognition of their rights and assurance of their community's vitality. The strategy took hold at once in 1982 because lobbying or citizen mobilization had serious limitations for minority groups in a democratic regime. As a result, the concept of the language issue changed. Language no longer referred solely to a political *problem*. Having become an object of judicial *litigation*, the issue gave rise to demands for legal resources to ensure its regulation.

During the last years of the twentieth century and at the beginning of the twenty-first, various rulings delivered on language rights—in particular the one interpreting Section 23 of the Canadian Charter of Rights and Freedoms on school governance—obliged the anglophone-led provinces to legislate in favour of francophones. While intensifying the emergence of expertise in the field of language among lawyers and other jurists, as jurists Michael Mandel and Mary Jane Mossman point out, referrals to court transformed those venues into political forums, including even cases that were strictly judicial matters. The 1999 ruling on *R. v. Beaulac* ([1999] 1 S.C.R. 768), in which the Supreme Court granted all accused persons the right to a trial in their language of choice everywhere in Canada, was proof of the new dialectics between the judiciary and the political. Indeed, in determining that an accused in a criminal case had the right to a trial in French, the Supreme Court based its interpretation of language rights on the need for law to be consistent with the preservation and development of official language minority groups in Canada.

In Ontario the question of language underwent a kind of thaw. The Association canadienne-française de l'Ontario, Association des enseignantes et des enseignants franco-ontariens, and some parents asked courts to determine if Section 23 of the Charter recognized their right to manage their own schools. In 1984 the Ontario Court of Appeal ruled that the right to education included the right to manage French-language schools. Two years later, the Ontario legislature amended the Education Act and granted francophones the right to manage their schools. In most cases, the provincial government established French sections within public or separate school boards. The French school trustees became responsible for the opening of schools, the hiring of personnel, and teaching programs. For their part, anglophone trustees were involved in and voted on school bus transportation, budgets, and the use of premises.

As researcher Brigitte Bureau demonstrates, cohabitation within school boards was not always free of conflicts. The French sections' quest for autonomy within school boards became the new cause. The Franco-Ontarian activists demanded structures similar to those of the autonomous French-language school boards in Toronto and the Ottawa-Carleton Region—boards that were created in 1988 to put an end to the quarrels between francophone and anglophone trustees. While in power from 1990 to 1995, the New Democratic Party government of Bob Rae expressed an intention to solve the school governance issue; but it was the Progressive Conservative government of Mike Harris that created twelve French-language school boards in 1998, of which eight were Catholic and four public, all managed by francophones.

Earlier, during the 1985 provincial election, the Association canadienne-française de l'Ontario had asked the parties to declare their intentions regarding a legal framework for French services. Unlike the Progressive Conservative Party, the Liberal Party and the New Democratic Party appeared to be favourable to taking the initiative. After the election, the formation of a minority Liberal government led by David Peterson, and supported by Rae's NDP, created a special situation. According to Bureau's study, the ACFO pressured the Liberals to act on the language issue and participated in the drafting of a bill on French services. Under the initiative of the minister responsible for Francophone Affairs, Bernard Grandmaître, the Legislative Assembly enacted the French Language Services Act (R.S.O. 1986, c. F-32), better known as Bill 8, in November 1986. The legislation guaranteed the provision of provincial services in French in designated bilingual regions, which meant regions in which francophones represented at least 10 per cent of the population, urban centres with more than five thousand francophones, and the regions designated bilingual prior to the promulgation of the law. The state entrusted the Office of Francophone Affairs with implementation of the law.

The reactions were mixed. The ACFO welcomed the new law and hoped that the ultimate step—a declaration of French as an official language—would not be long in coming. The opponents of bilingualism put pressure on their municipal councils even though they were excluded from the law, asking them to declare the principle of unilingualism in their jurisdictions—a measure that, if taken, would presumably make it possible to avoid the potential provincial requirements regarding French services. These opponents found a voice in the Alliance for the Preservation of English in Canada (APEC), which did not hesitate to launch a campaign of demagoguery aimed at feeding the conspiracy theory according to which the federal state and now the province of Ontario were planning to impose French education on unilingual anglophones. According to the pressure group, Bill 8 would prescribe the francization of all of the government ministries, all of the municipalities, and all of the businesses that had contracts with the provincial government. In addition—the APEC went on in its exaggeration—the other provinces would be enacting their own laws on French services, as in Ontario. The Association managed to mobilize a great number of citizens. In Sault Ste. Marie twenty-five thousand of them signed a petition against the use of French in municipal services. Under the leadership of Mayor Joe Fratesi, the municipal council of Sault Ste. Marie adopted a resolution in 1990 that made English the only official language in the municipality, a move that triggered a major crisis Canada-wide during the death pangs of the Meech Lake Accord. Still, a study by Don Stevenson and Richard Gilbert reveals that even though more than sixty municipalities copied the action taken by the Sault Ste. Marie council, the same number of cities in Ontario denounced the movement in support of English unilingualism. The Ontario Superior Court of Justice struck down the unilingual measures in 1994, arguing that they went beyond the powers of municipalities. Despite the opponents' rush to the barricades, the Peterson government did not backpedal on the issue—although it did shelve the possibility of declaring French to be one of the official languages in the province.

The election of the Progressive Conservatives under Mike Harris in 1995 marked the accession to power of a team of politicians who embraced a neo-conservative conception of the role of the state. With its famous action plan, "Common Sense Revolution," the Harris government proceeded with deregulation, administrative re-engineering, and budget cuts. Within these policies, the Ontario Health Services Restructuring Commission recommended the closing of the Hôpital Montfort, a hospital designed to provide French services in the regions of Ottawa and Eastern Ontario.

The francophone milieu reacted with astonishment and anger at the unilateral questioning of one of the jewels of the Franco-Ontarian institutional network. Under the presidency of Gisèle Lalonde, a committee supporting the preservation of the hospital, the Comité S.O.S. Montfort, launched an energetic campaign of public mobilization to prevent it from being closed. Driven by the ethics of vigilance, as

Demonstration of S.O.S. Montfort at the Westin Hotel, Ottawa, March 16, 1997.
Photo by Étienne Morin.

historian Marie LeBel puts it, the activists became deeply involved in this cause and were present in every forum. In this controversy, with the memory of the battles surrounding Regulation 17 being frequently evoked, the Comité S.O.S. Montfort achieved only modest success. In June 1997, faced with pressure from citizens, the Harris government conceded the opening of the psychiatric wing of the establishment, a half-measure that did not satisfy the supporters of the preservation of the entire hospital. The legal challenge was more successful: in November 1999, the Divisional Court of the Ontario Superior Court of Justice, followed by the Appeal Court of Ontario in December 2001, responded positively to the demands of the Franco-Ontarian pressure groups. The ruling in *Gisèle Lalonde, et al. v. Ontario (Health Services Restructuring Commission)* ([2001], 56 O.R. (3d), 577) stated that the closing of the hospital was contrary to the constitutional principle of protection of minorities specified in the *Reference re Secession of Quebec*. In February 2002, the Ontario government had to reconsider its decision. Not only was the Hôpital Montfort to remain open, but the Liberal government of Dalton McGuinty, elected in 2003, and the federal state invested in an expansion project to integrate the services of the former Ottawa military hospital.

The battle for the Hôpital Montfort stimulated the struggle for the recognition of French as an official language and the enshrinement of the rights of francophones in the Constitution. Despite pressure from Franco-Ontarians, in particular the Opération constitution group, co-chaired by Gisèle Lalonde and University of Ottawa law professor Marc Cousineau, the Harris government and later the McGuinty government stood firm on their positions. Fearing the threats against social peace, they refused to declare French an official language. However, a gesture of compromise was made to the Franco-Ontarian activists: in 2007 the Ontario Legislative Assembly amended Bill 8 to create the position of French Language Services Commissioner. Named by the government and not the Legislative Assembly, the commissioner was granted a renewable two-year mandate. In addition to receiving complaints from the public, the commissioner could undertake his or her own enquiries on French services provided by the ministries.

In New Brunswick the provincial authorities remained receptive· to the mutations in the Canadian symbolic order in dealing with their language-planning policy. This relative compliance provided them with a fallback strategy and the possibility of resorting once again to the policy of mutual accommodation if a controversy were to erupt between the two main ethno-linguistic groups. With the support of Premier Richard Hatfield, the Constitution Act of 1982 enshrined the bilingual status of the province. In winter 1993 the Frank McKenna Liberal government introduced an amendment on the internal constitution of New Brunswick, allowing the recognition of French as an official language of the province, similar to English.

Because court interventions in political debates had become more frequent with the enshrinement of the Canadian Charter of Rights and Freedoms, adjustments needed to be made to language planning in New Brunswick. In February 2000, Mario Charlebois, the owner of an apartment building, challenged the validity of a municipal decision and a construction standards ordinance because both texts had been published and printed in English only. In December 2001 the Appeal Court of New Brunswick in its ruling on *Charlebois v. Mowat and the*

City of Moncton ([2001] NBCA 117) obliged nineteen municipalities to translate their bylaws and called on the province to review the provisions of its Official Languages Act. Consequently, the *Charlebois* ruling had rather surprising indirect effects, given the recent history of Acadia. A sign of the times and an indication of the socio-economic progress that the Acadians had achieved in the northeast region of New Brunswick occurred in Moncton in 2002. Under Mayor Brian Murphy, and after acting as host to the Francophone Summit in 1999, Moncton became the first officially bilingual city in Canada. This ironic turn of fortune would have probably greatly displeased Leonard Jones.

In the middle of the 2000s the issue of health services in French also emerged in New Brunswick. Faced with the increasing costs of health care, the Liberal government of Shawn Graham undertook a reform of the provincial health-care system. The project, tabled in the Legislative Assembly in March 2008, provided for the establishment of two regional health authorities: the first body would combine the former English authorities; the second would combine one francophone and three bilingual authorities. At the outset the second authority was to become bilingual de facto, resulting in the elimination of unilingual French in the provision of services. According to the Société de l'Acadie du Nouveau-Brunswick and its president, Jean-Marie Nadeau, this provincial decision, which recalled the Hôpital Montfort episode in Ottawa, would deeply alter the governance of the francophone authorities.[21] In June 2009 both parties began to hone their judicial arsenals as the Acadian activists undertook proceedings against the New Brunswick government to make it comply with the francophone authorities' governance rights. Once again lawyers got down to work, including the former Supreme Court judge Michel Bastarache. In April 2010 the Graham government gave ground on the issue and abandoned its plan to eliminate the francophone regional health authority.

Judicial activism became particularly intense in the Western Canadian provinces. Because of their limited populations and dispersion, the francophone communities could not ensure a sustained and efficient mobilization of the expression of citizens' will. Furthermore, a latent hostility existed against the recognition of the French-speaking minority and institutional bilingualism, which often crippled the influence of francophone communities on provincial authorities. However, thanks to the Court Challenges Program established by the federal state, members of the francophone elites regrouped as an institutionalized pressure group and resorted to the courts to promote their cause.

At the beginning of the 1980s, the episode of the constitutional amendments relating to the language rights of Franco-Manitobans demonstrated the limits on the voices of citizens. With the election of the Howard Pawley NDP government in 1981, changes in the language policy started to emerge in Manitoba. The 1979 *Forest* ruling had forced the province to translate all of its laws. The task proved to be immense, which worried the political authorities because of the lack of legal translators and financial resources, and the real risks of having the Supreme Court reimpose bilingualism on the province. Indeed, after 1980 another Franco-Manitoban, Roger Bilodeau, had challenged an English-only parking ticket and demanded that the courts invalidate the law involved because it was enacted in English only. Faced with the difficulties relating to translation and fearing a new judicial defeat at the hands of the Supreme Court, the Pawley government began to promote the enactment of a constitutional amendment that would guarantee the right of Franco-Manitobans to receive services in their language. In return, the province would be released from its obligation to translate all of its laws, keeping only those enacted since 1970. As political scientist Raymond Hébert relates, Pawley presented his government's language policy to members of the Société franco-manitobaine in March 1982. According to this policy, Franco-Manitobans could communicate with their provincial government in their own language, official forms would be published in French, and French services would be provided, in particular to youth and the elderly, in regions in which francophones were concentrated. The Société franco-manitobaine responded very positively, welcoming the policy statement.

In 1983, supported by the federal government and the Société franco-manitobaine, the Pawley government tabled its constitutional amendment to the French-language guarantees. Manitoban Attorney General Roland Penner told members that the measure would make it possible to allocate to the development of the francophone community the amounts that had been previously going to the translation of all the laws. He insisted that school boards and municipalities were exempt from the scope of the amendment. It would nevertheless be possible, for those municipalities with a large number of francophones, to provide French services with financial support from the federal state.

From the outset the constitutional amendment gave rise to a major language crisis that united the opponents of bilingualism. Their leaders included members of the Manitoba Progressive Conservative Party led by former premier Sterling Lyon, and then by his successor Gary Filmon after December 1983. Lyon denounced the measure by challenging the Pawley government's motivations, in particular the assertion that the invalidation of all the provincial laws would create judicial chaos. According to the former premier, because Manitoba was not a bilingual province the NDP government was providing a misleading reading of Section 23 of the Manitoba Act. Finally, this flamboyant politician believed that the constitutional amendment was the result of lobbying by activists—or, as he called them, zealots. In speaking in these terms, Lyon denied the representative nature of the Société franco-manitobaine and activists supporting the francophone cause by demonizing them and caricaturing them as a small minority eager to impose their vision, to the detriment of the needs of the majority.

For their part, the New Democrats had a major dissident voice within their ranks, that of Russell Doern. This member of the legislature became restless and encouraged citizens to oppose the constitutional amendment project. As a result, more than fifteen thousand individuals signed a petition denouncing the provincial action on bilingualism. The tireless opponent even encouraged municipalities to organize referendums on the issue. Outside the political parties, the body of opponents included representatives of municipalities in rural Manitoba who did not want to be forced to provide services in French, and, according to Hébert, even some Ku Klux Klan militants.

Dissent also occurred in the ranks of the Franco-Manitobans, but for other reasons. Georges Forest, who was at the origin of the 1979 Supreme Court ruling, denounced the Pawley government's project because he believed that it allowed the government to escape its judicial obligations relating to translation. Given the agreement reached by the NDP government and the Société franco-manitobaine, Forest, along with other Franco-Manitobans, did not shy away from criticizing the representativeness of the community organization. In addition, the opposition of the fiery advocate of bilingualism spread outside the

Franco-Manitoban community and led him to wage his uncompromising fight against the constitutional amendment with provincial and federal political leaders.

Faced with this general outcry, Pawley and Penner launched a public information campaign and public hearings allowing citizens to provide their views on the issue. The process turned into a disaster. Far from creating sympathy for the amendment project, the citizens' forums became the favoured platform that opponents used to denounce bilingualism as a policy and symbol of Manitoba. The financial argument was invoked at every turn. Why invest in French services when the amounts would serve a more just cause if they were allocated to job creation at a time when the province and the country as a whole were experiencing a major economic recession?

Despite some support for the amendment project provided by organizations such as Alliance Quebec, the federal political parties, and ethno-cultural groups, the language storm did not subside. Some municipalities were bent on organizing a referendum on the constitutional amendment, despite the reservations of groups defending minority rights and the members of some churches, such as the Catholic Archbishop of Saint-Boniface, Mgr. Antoine Hacault, who were worried about the repercussions of direct democracy on the determination of language rights. All of this was to no avail; the majority of Manitoban citizens categorically rejected the NDP bill. The atmosphere became poisonous with the expression of hostility and francophobia. Already shaken by a fire that had destroyed their premises in January 1983, the leaders of the Société franco-manitobaine were granted police protection in response to death threats they had received.

The Pawley government threw in the towel in 1984. It resigned itself to the intervention of the Supreme Court of Canada, which duly rendered a ruling in June 1985: all the Manitoba laws were declared unconstitutional. To maintain public order, it was declared that the laws would remain valid until the expiration of the date set for their translation. The Province of Manitoba used the funds intended for the translation of the laws and implemented a policy for the provision of French services that did not, as they would have under the 1983 amendment proposal, have the support of any constitutional guarantees. Some activists of the French-speaking minority were left feeling very bitter.

The Manitoba experience had a great impact. From then on francophone activists in the other Prairie provinces went to the courts to gain recognition of their language rights. In Saskatchewan, judicial activism forced the provincial government to act. A Franco-Saskatchewanian, Father André Mercure, also challenged a ticket presented to him in English. He demanded the right to make his plea in French and contended that Section 110 of the Northwest Territories Act, enacted in 1877, guaranteed judicial and legislative bilingualism in the territories involved. When it was called upon to provide a decision on the status of French in its ruling on *R. v. Mercure* ([1988] 1 S.C.R. 234), the Supreme Court confirmed that Section 110 remained valid despite the enactment of the 1905 law creating the provinces of Saskatchewan and Alberta. However, the judges gave the legislators of those provinces the right to choose to act: they could declare their respective provinces bilingual or unilingual. To comply with part of the ruling, the legislative assemblies of Saskatchewan and Alberta enacted laws revoking Section 110 and ratifying retroactively the legislation and regulation enacted previously in English only.[22]

Nevertheless, the position of the Province of Alberta was once again challenged at the beginning of the twenty-first century, this time in a case involving a Franco-Albertan trucker, Gilles Caron. The case ended up in the courts in 2006. Claiming that his constitutional rights had been violated because the Alberta Highway Traffic Act had not been published in French, Caron disputed a ticket and, in so doing, the 1988 Alberta law that entrenched unilingualism in the province. In 2008, at the end of the trial—in which experts, including political scientist Edmund Aunger, provided opinions on the historical evidence—the Provincial Court of Alberta delivered its judgment in its ruling on *R. v. Caron* ([2008], A.B.P.C. 232). The court declared that, even before the enactment of the 1887 law creating the Northwest Territories, a constitutional guarantee protecting the language rights of francophones was already in place. Indeed, at the time of the first Métis insurrection in 1869–70, the governor general of Rupert's Land, John Young, had proclaimed on December 6, 1869, the basic respect for all the civil rights of the Métis and other inhabitants of those lands. This guarantee had never been revoked, and Young's proclamation was still being considered a constitutional document; thus the need to respect language rights remained in the entire territory of Rupert's Land in 1869, which included the Canadian Prairie provinces, as well as the Northwest Territories and Nunavut. The 1988 Alberta law entrenching unilingualism was therefore considered invalid. Yet the debate did not end there. In August 2009, after the Alberta government decided to refer the case to the highest court in the land, the Supreme Court of Canada agreed to hear the case.

At the end of the 1980s Alberta was also the scene of a major victory regarding the governance of schools by francophones. In taking their case to court, the activists did not hesitate to use Section 23 of the Charter of Rights and Freedoms relating to the language of instruction and the language of courts. The challenge began when a group of francophone parents in Edmonton, including Jean-Claude Mahé and Angéline Martel, established the Association Georges-et-Julia-Bugnet. The members of the association believed that French-language children needed more than the immersion programs and bilingual instruction of the time. They demanded the creation and governance of homogeneous French-language schools. For its part, the Province of Alberta countered that the school system did adequately serve the needs of francophones. Given the refusal to meet their demands, the parents' group decided to go to the courts for a decision on the scope of the Charter's Section 23. Represented by Michel Bastarache, they received financial support from the Court Challenges Program established by the Department of the Secretary of State. The Association also benefited from the intense sympathy of the Canadian Parents for French group, which believed that the Province of Alberta was not willing to respect its constitutional obligations. This organization's support was by no means insignificant. Indeed, French immersion programs had been in full expansion since the mid-1970s. As journalist Graham Fraser notes, the enthusiasm of parents regarding French immersion combined with the resulting funding from the federal state led to a strong rise in school attendance: in 1986, 177,824 young English Canadians took courses in French, which represented a 369 per cent increase in the school population since 1978.

However, the citizens' action taken up by the francophone parents caused friction with the Association canadienne-française de l'Alberta, which was hesitant about involving itself in the school issue. The events in Manitoba were still freshly rooted in their memories, and ACFA feared the backlash of the anglophone public if francophones gained the right to manage their own schools. These hesitations also reflected the divisions among francophones in the province on the issue of French-language education. Was it really necessary to demand homogeneous French-language schools? Would it not be preferable to send young francophones to schools in which English was one of two languages of instruction?

Finally, though, the ACFA did decide to promote the options of homogeneous and immersion schools. Despite the Manitoba precedent, the ACFA firmly believed that negotiations with the Lougheed government would lead to compromises and there would be no need to resort to the courts. But, faced with the categorical refusal of the Progressive Conservative government to act in favour of the francophones, ACFA fell into line with the activists of the Association Georges-et-Julia-Bugnet.

In the ruling on the *Mahé v. Alberta* ([1990] 1 S.C.R. 342) case, the Association Georges-et-Julia-Bugnet won a major victory relating to the governance of schools. The Supreme Court of Canada confirmed the right of language-minority parents, in this case francophones, to manage their schools to ensure that their language and culture flourished. The judges determined that Section 23 played a remedial role because of the prejudices relating to education that francophone minority groups had been subjected to in the past. The right to manage schools included the right to recruit the teaching staff, to appoint the staff in charge of managing the educational institution, and to allocate the funds required for education. As of 1993, the Government of Alberta established French-language school boards and granted francophones the right to manage their schools. The other provinces did the same in subsequent years. This did not stop francophone parents from dragging the provincial states into court again, if they believed that they were being deprived of their right to education in the language of the minority. As a result, in its ruling in the *Arsenault-Cameron v. Prince Edward Island* ([2000] 1 S.C.R. 3) case in 2000, the Supreme Court recognized the right of French-language school boards to manage and control the location of francophone schools.

Although the recourse to the judiciary characterized the defence of francophone and Acadian communities' language rights during this

period, political action was not forgotten. Given the profound consequences of the relations between language and politics, community
leaders passionately participated in the major constitutional discussions
and in the national debate that unfolded between the time of the election of the Progressive Conservative government of Brian Mulroney
in 1984 to the Quebec Referendum on sovereignty-partnership in
October 1995. With the return to power of Bourassa's Liberal Party, a
new period of negotiations was launched. In 1986 the Quebec minister
for Intergovernmental Affairs, Gil Rémillard, presented five conditions
required for the Quebec state to adhere to the Constitution Act of 1982,
one of which was the recognition of the distinct character of Quebec.
In 1987 the prime minister and the provincial premiers agreed on the
conditions and approved the constitutional changes drawn together in
the Meech Lake Accord, which the Parliament of Canada and every
legislative assembly were to adopt.

During the episode of the Meech Lake Accord, from 1987 to 1990,
the leaders of the francophone minority groups, political leaders, and
Quebec nationalist activists adopted objectives and strategies that ended
up clashing with each other. As the main institutional representative of
the Canadian francophones, the FFHQ reacted negatively to the Meech
Lake Accord. According to its president, Yvon Fontaine, the Accord was
a reconciliation between two majorities, Quebec and Canada, in which
there were no gains for minorities of one or the other official language.
The francophone leaders had hoped Quebec would get clarification on
the famed Section 23 of the Canadian Charter of Rights and Freedoms
and, among other things, on the question of the governance of schools.
What was even more serious, according to them, was that the Accord
could prevent francophone minority communities from demanding
new rights. Still, despite the internal divisions relating to support of the
Accord—in particular the strong opposition of the ACFA—the FFHQ
decided that it could not categorically oppose it. Following pressures
exercised by federal and Quebec political leaders, and also by leaders and associations of the francophone minority communities, such
as the Association canadienne-française de l'Ontario and Société des
Acadiens et Acadiennes du Nouveau-Brunswick, the Fédération ended
up supporting the constitutional agreement. The constitutional train
was moving, and the leaders of the FFHQ estimated that they should

get on board and then later ask for changes in direction. Consequently, they suggested that the definition of distinct society be altered to include francophone minority communities. They also proposed that the federal state and provinces be mandated with the duty to protect and promote language duality. Finally, the SAANB demanded that a recognition of the equality of the two official languages communities be enshrined in the Constitution Act in order to guarantee the symbolic order as exemplified in New Brunswick since 1981.

The Meech Lake Accord also vested in Quebec the responsibility of protecting and promoting its distinct character. On this point, the Fédération des francophones hors Québec and Alliance Quebec deemed that the term "protect" was insufficient. According to the FFHQ, "protection," contrary to "promotion," was limiting because it confined the legislator to a passive role in the execution of its obligations towards the Francophonie. As for Alliance Quebec, it feared that the clause on a distinct society could threaten language rights. The position of these organizations displeased the Quebec political leaders. According to Michel Doucet, lawyer and president of the SAANB from 1987 to 1989, Premier Bourassa and Intergovernmental Affairs Minister Rémillard were showing little willingness to support the demands of the FFHQ and the New Brunswick Acadians. The Bourassa government believed that the term "promote" would provide ammunition to the English Quebecers in their battle against the Quebec symbolic order, which was based on the protection and promotion of the French language.

Faced with the opposition of intellectuals, Aboriginal spokespersons, some provinces, and the majority of Canadian citizens, the Meech Lake Accord died in June 1990. This defeat sparked the resumption of constitutional talks, which led to the Charlottetown Accord of 1992. This time the Bourassa government accepted that the Constitution recognize that "Canadians and their governments are committed to the vitality and development of official language minority communities throughout Canada."[23] However, the majority of Canadian citizens rejected the Charlottetown Accord in the national referendum held later that same year.

In a move that caused bitterness in Quebec, the Fédération des communautés francophones et acadienne du Canada asked Quebecers to vote no in the 1995 provincial referendum. This gesture indicated the extent to which the leaders of the francophone minority institutional network and the Quebec political leaders had diverged since 1982. Their differences often led to clashes that revealed conflicting views on federalism. In Quebec the Liberal government of Bourassa wanted to increase the powers of the provincial state, while the following Péquiste government of Jacques Parizeau wanted to re-engineer the political structures so that two sovereign states would be recognized. The francophone minority groups adhered to a symmetrical vision of federalism. The provinces had a poor track record on the promotion of the rights of francophone groups, except for New Brunswick and, to a lesser extent, Ontario. Consequently, the leaders of the institutional network refused to accept that provinces assume new responsibilities in promoting minority rights. According to Quebec federalists who shared Bourassa's views, asymmetrical federalism, which was more respectful of the notion of Canadian diversity, offered a path that could lead to a solution. There was a conflict between the vision of Canadian duality and the means required to protect and promote it. Francophone minorities were part of a debate in which they did not fully control the variables.

While francophones in minority communities made significant gains, especially in the governance of their schools, the indicators of the vitality of these groups became the subject of abundant scientific research. For many, the language vitality of a group was measured by its demographic weight. It was without question Charles Castonguay, mathematician at the University of Ottawa, who had the most prolific response to this subject; he analysed from every angle the language vitality of Quebecers and francophone minority groups. His studies highlighted the demographic reduction of the francophone minority and their inability to ensure the renewal of generations.

It seemed that the decline could be explained by the drop in women's fertility, which was calculated at 1.58 child per woman in these communities since the 1980s. According to Castonguay's analyses, the Canadian Francophonie was in a situation of underfertility, with a deficit between generations. Underfertility, far from being a phenomenon exclusive to francophone groups, was a characteristic of all Western societies, with the exception of the United States and France. While many states were attempting to neutralize the effects by increasing the number of immigrants allowed in, francophone minority groups could not resort to this solution because they did not have the power of a state behind them. Furthermore, few francophone immigrants settled in English-speaking provinces. According to Castonguay, these provinces had very little attraction for French-speaking people, which prevented the renewal of the francophone populations through the contribution of immigrants.

In addition to the question of underfertility, another problem arose: that of the language shifts towards English. In another study published in 2002, Castonguay observed that the anglicization of franco-phones in minority communities had increased more rapidly than the francization of allophone groups in Quebec. These shifts corresponded to the gaps between the Census data on the mother tongue and language of use at home. Given the increase in exogamous marriages among francophones, the language of use at home had become increasingly English. The number of francophones was declining because of the low rate of fertility among women and the surge in assimilation. Previously, the high fertility rates among francophones had been a compensation mechanism offsetting language shifts: now this advantage seemed to have disappeared. Because of these general demographic trends, the vitality of francophone communities was uncertain. At the end of several years of research and study, Castonguay concluded that the demographic future of francophone minority communities was bleak and disturbing. Inevitably, the population in francophone minority communities was diminishing.

Like the analyses published by Father Richard Arès in the 1950s and 1960s, Castonguay's studies triggered intense reactions. They perturbed or, on the contrary, reinforced the position of those who believed—as the Quebec nationalists did, among others—that the Canadian Francophonie would soon disappear. Faced with the mathematician's pessimistic conclusions, many criticisms arose, in particular concerning the use of demographic data as the sole criteria for measuring the vitality of a group. Castonguay's critics considered this kind of measuring instrument restrictive and relative. Several sociologists, through institutional spokespersons, promoted another indicator: institutional vitality. They insisted on the dynamism of the institutional network, inspired as they were by sociologist Raymond Breton and his "institutional completeness" model. They believed that to evaluate the vitality of a minority group it was necessary to seize the group's capacity to structure its political, economic, and socio-cultural space through a network of organizations that satisfied the various needs of the community members, from crib to tomb. They therefore saw a high level of institutional completeness as being capable of limiting the rate of assimilation, particularly because francophones had at their disposal several activities and organizations in which they could participate.

The model of institutional completeness was the one preferred by the leaders of francophone minority communities. Insisting on the institutional vitality of their community, these leaders pressured the states to provide them with the financial support they needed to maintain and expand their network. They believed that by multiplying the institutions and increasing the communities' autonomy in govern-ance it would be possible to limit the rate of assimilation. Paradoxically, the bilingualism that the federal and provincial states were promoting became increasingly perceived as a policy furthering assimilation. In fact, from then on, francophones in minority communities demanded French-language homogeneous authorities, as had been the case with regard to health services in New Brunswick and at the Hôpital Montfort.

Another subject of concern was undeniably the increase in prestige of personal bilingualism as an identity characteristic of franco-phones in minority communities. According to some opinion leaders, personal bilingualism as an identity reference concealed the advances of assimilation in francophone communities. Others suggested that bilingualism was instead an indication of the emergence of a new rela-tion with the English language. For many francophones, the symbolism of English was changing: from the language of labour to the language of capital, and in the process becoming the language of trade and commerce. In the context of the globalization of trade, English—or rather *business English*—was perceived as a communications tool that helped not only to increase understanding between nations but also, especially, to facilitate international commerce. Consequently, French was becoming an added value. This perception placed the problems of assimilation, the strategies for the preservation of the mother tongue, and, in particular, the relations between French and English in a different perspective; but it did not represent the entire socio-economic reality in the field. Indeed, as economists Nicolas Béland and Maurice Beaudin and sociologist Éric Forgues observe in relation to the years 1970 to 2000, the wage gap between unilingual anglophones and bilingual people on the one hand and unilingual francophones on the other persisted in New Brunswick and still benefited the first group. It is only in Quebec, where francophones formed the majority, that these wage inequalities disappeared as of 1995.

The vitality of the language was not a concern only in francophone communities. It was a major challenge for people speaking Aboriginal languages in Quebec and elsewhere in Canada. First Nations peoples, Inuit, and Métis had for a very long time been experiencing the slights of marginalization and social exclusion: endemic poverty, social and economic underdevelopment, cultural alienation and assimilation, problems relating to alcoholism, drug addiction, suicide, and interpersonal violence. Faced with this increasingly intolerable situation, Aboriginal peoples started raising their voices during the 1960s, and were doing so with even more vigour by the 1980s. In the wake of Aboriginal demands, the language issue joined the list of priorities. The timid measures of the 1970s were far from sufficient, and the language situation had become clearly alarming. As political scientist Mary Jane Norris suggests, only a small proportion of the Aboriginal population in Canada—24 per cent, made up mostly of elders—was capable of speaking or understanding a First Nations, Inuit, or Métis language in 2001. UNESCO revealed in 2002 that of the 104 Aboriginal languages in Quebec and the rest of Canada, 19 were dying and 28 were dangerously threatened. Worst still, Cree, Ojibwa, and Inuit-Inupiaq languages were the only ones that were sure to survive. At least seven Aboriginal languages disappeared during the 1990s, becoming dead languages like the Beothuk, Nicola, Tsetsaut, Huron, Neutral, and Petun languages before them.

To ensure the cultural survival and vitality of these peoples, first and foremost their languages had to be officially recognized. Inspired by a study on Aboriginal language policies published in 1988, the Assembly of First Nations (AFN) and its chief, Georges Erasmus, opposed Bill C-37 on the establishment of a Canadian Heritage Languages Institute, which had been proposed by federal minister David Crombie. According to the AFN, First Nations languages were exclusive to the founding nations and were protected by the rights arising from treaties and federal legislation. The unfolding process and failure of the Charlottetown Accord, which had aimed to include in the 1982 Constitution Act the preservation of Aboriginal languages and cultures, did not diminish mobilization around the language issue, which was so strongly linked to the cultural dimension. Therefore, between 1989 and 1992, the AFN published a series of studies on this issue. In 1992 the group established its own Languages and Literacy Secretariat with the mandate, among other things, to promote the development of First Nations languages, raise community awareness, and lobby for an increase in legal protection and financing from the various state programs.

The Secretariat's actions were relatively effective: the 1996 Report of the Royal Commission on Aboriginal Peoples recommended funding for the survival and vitality of First Nations, Inuit, and Métis languages. However, even though the federal heritage minister introduced some measures as of 1997, the situation remained disturbing: the 1996 Census data showed no improvement, and federal support remained subject to fiscal austerity policies. With its strategy statements on Aboriginal languages in 2000 and 2004, the AFN put constant pressure on the federal state and, in May 2009, Ottawa agreed to study a Senate bill on the promotion of Aboriginal languages and the recognition and respect of Aboriginal language rights. Given that the process was very slow, legal recourse was also used, in particular by the Métis. Rendered by the Supreme Court in 2003, the ruling in the *R. v. Powley* ([2003] 2 S.C.R. 207) case recognized that the Métis had a distinct collective culture and identity separate from those of their ancestors, and that their culture and identity were distinct because of the use of the Michif language.

In Quebec the Aboriginal language situation presented itself in a slightly different manner. Of course, the trend towards linguistic assimilation remained just as strong. However, since the James Bay and Northern Quebec Agreement in 1975 and the Charter of the French Language in 1977, Quebec had explicitly recognized Aboriginal language rights on its territory. This recognition was established through fifteen principles adopted by the Lévesque government in 1983 and renewed in the Motion on the Recognition of Aboriginal Rights adopted by the National Assembly in 1985. Two principles dealt specifically with the language issue. First, the Quebec state recognized the right of the eleven Aboriginal Nations on Quebec territory to protect their culture, language, and customs. Then, the state extended the recognition to the right of Aboriginal peoples to own and control institutions related to their cultural, educational, and language needs. In 1989, within the framework of the policy on the preservation and development of Aboriginal languages in Quebec, the Secrétariat québécois aux affaires autochtones also set objectives regarding the protection and preservation of the linguistic and cultural heritage of Aboriginal nations. With regard to the issues of justice, health services, and signage, Aboriginal languages could be used in certain situations. In the field of education, the Charter of the French Language allowed for the use of Aboriginal languages in schools and made provisions for the establishment of school boards managed by Aboriginal people.

However, Quebec's Aboriginal language policy was confined mostly to a statement of principles; usually few financial resources were allocated to their implementation. Although the 2002 Paix des Braves (Agreement Respecting a New Relationship Between the Cree Nation and the Government of Quebec), reached between the chief of the Cree community, Ted Moses, and the premier of Quebec, Bernard Landry, seemed to herald a change, the 2004 agreement in principle between Quebec and the Innu on Nitassinan and the protection and development of their language had still not led to the ratification of a treaty by June 2009. These delays demonstrate the gap between good intentions and actions at the beginning of the twenty-first century.

– – – – –

In January 2008 *Le Journal de Montréal* carried out an investigation of French services in commercial establishments in the Montreal area. Pretending to be a unilingual anglophone, journalist Noée Murchison managed to get fifteen job offers that would put her in direct contact with clients. Among the fifteen employers, fourteen decided that, despite complaints from clients, the evident gaps in Murchison's knowledge of French were not important. Extensively commented on in the public sphere, the results of the investigation are still feeding the fears of anglicization that were expressed, among others, by René Roy, secretary-general of the Fédération des travailleurs du Québec, and songwriter Luc Plamondon. The results corroborated the conclusions of a study by the Office québécois de la langue française published in 2008, according to which a third of the stores and small businesses in Montreal employed personnel who did not have a functional knowledge of French.

Beyond illustrating the obvious weaknesses of the Quebec language-planning policy, Murchison's investigation revealed yet another connection between language and politics. In addition to the inequalities between capital and labour, the use of English symbolized the pervasive presence of market rules in determining the common good. The globalization of economic relations that had intensified since the 1980s resulted in an increase in value of an all-purpose language, *business English* or *Globish*, to the detriment of other idioms. The exclusive promotion of a single language for commerce and business tends to reinforce the actual order of things, with all of its socio-economic and political inequalities. Although some postmodernists are ecstatic about the marvels of the contemporary linguistic traffic, the phenomenon nevertheless provokes a generalized cultural impoverishment. In addition, it will sooner rather than later threaten the vitality of political communities, and in particular that of minority communities.

Murchison's investigation also revealed another general trend, which is the use of law to regulate social relations and solve political problems. Indeed, faced with the provision of unilingual services, clients whose rights have been impinged upon usually turn to the courts, be they administrative, as at the Office québécois de la langue française, or civil. The various strategies that citizens have long used to voice their concerns, such as boycotting or demonstrating, have lost part of their prestige because they are perceived as not being very effective. Since 1982 courts have become the preferred theatre for action on the language issue; problems relating to languages, in all their complexities, have been reduced to disputes filtered by law. Although the legal decisions sometimes favoured members of minority groups, they came nonetheless at the end of a long process requiring time and major human and financial resources. Furthermore, the initial relations of domination tended to subsist during, and often after, a resolution.

Finally, by becoming confined to courts, the language issue established a different relation with the sphere of politics. When language disputes became entrusted to law and its interpreters, citizens and their elected representatives became silent. Consequently, they lost part of their empowerment in the determination of the common good—with the *duties of living collectively* replacing the *will to live collectively*. A certain democratic deficit sank in, feeding cynicism and a lack of interest in the *public realm*. Will this new tendency persist? Who can tell?

CONCLUSION

*Mais pourquoi parler
De ce qui n'est là que pour douter des mots
Le silence d'un peuple tout entier
Est celui-là que regrettent les poèmes.*
  - Fernand Dumont, "La mémoire réconciliée" (*La Part de l'ombre*)

The interactions between language and politics provide a good indicator of the transformations that political cultures underwent from 1539 to the present. From the time that the first of his settlers arrived in the New World, the French king was intent on reinforcing his subjects' allegiance by ensuring not just the control but the standardization of their lives in every aspect. Language—with its deep ties to religion—was an issue that fell within this intense policy of homogenization. After the 1760 Conquest the drive both to maintain religious homogenization and to promote allegiance to a new sovereign, the British king, transcended the divisions that now came into being relating to language—even though those divisions remained very real.

A major change took place during the Age of Revolution. First came the political revolution: the 1789 overthrow of the system based on estates in France upset the benchmarks that had been in place since the Middle Ages. As Edmund Burke theorized, ethno-cultural attributes would define membership in a political community, and those attributes related to language;

consequently, the language of debates in the House of Assembly of Lower Canada in 1792 became a matter of concern for parliamentarians. The beginning of the nineteenth century was marked by a dual nationalization of languages. English was a key attribute of the British nation in the homeland and across the seas. Following the repression of the 1837–38 insurrections and the failure of the Patriotes' republican project, French became a target for those in power. Faced with the threat of assimilation after Lord Durham's report and the union of the two Canadas, the Canadians, now "French Canadians," had no other choice than to nationalize their language to ensure its survival in perilous circumstances. Language therefore became both the guardian of the faith and the guarantor of the nation after 1840.

With the advent of the Industrial Revolution, the turn of the nineteenth century witnessed a new form of socio-economic domination based on the division between capital and labour. In Great Britain's North American colonies, where a rising bourgeoisie took control of the political levers, the English language, the idiom of the Empire's business community, became the dominant voice in the acquisition of resources and development of commerce and industry. For numerous Acadians and French Canadians who needed to sell their labour power to survive, especially when they migrated towards cities or the United States, the French language became a barrier to success. Languages had become nationalized, acquiring cultural connotations and characteristics that mirrored the relations of socio-economic domination, though without ever being the exact replica of those relations. For many citizens in the nineteenth and twentieth centuries, capital was spoken in English, and labour in French.

In the Age of Revolution, the political desire to homogenize populations within a state's territory became more pressing than ever. Nevertheless, this need faced the new requirements of a liberal order aimed at ensuring economic development. With a great displacement of people causing migrations from one side of the Atlantic Ocean to the other, leaders of several provinces and of the Dominion of Canada sought to settle the migrants in new territories and assimilate them into the English-Canadian nation, which in turn led to two paradoxical phenomena: assimilation and accommodation. Arguing that they were adhering to British rights and freedoms, members of the

English-Canadian elites advocated the adoption of cultural and linguistic assimilation policies to preserve the predominance of English as Canada's language of use and key to its ethno-cultural identity. These policies triggered numerous religious and language conflicts in New Brunswick, Manitoba, Ontario, and elsewhere in Canada, in particular at the end of the nineteenth and the beginning of the twentieth centuries. The conflicts festered among the French-speaking national communities in these provinces. Acadians and French-Canadians had to resist the exercise of a homogenizing power that was seeking to diminish their distinctive characters. This experience led to the formation of a mutual accommodation plan: faced with open resistance that led to conflicts threatening civil peace, members of the community elites agreed on a *bonne entente* among themselves; this agreement on mutual understanding generated conciliation and compromise.

In the second half of the twentieth century, the political cultures in Canada and Quebec underwent new transformations. As a result of the international migratory flows and the development of new means of communications, cultural diversity flourished within the cities. Furthermore, in the wake of the democratization of education, the rise of individualism, and the growing hegemony of the market, the public sphere expanded and became fragmented. Faced with the vigour of the expression of citizens' will, the plan for mutual accommodation crumbled and the language issue once again became the focus of public debates. Inspired by the theses on decolonization aimed at lifting the yoke of economic domination, many citizens in Quebec and in francophone communities in other provinces saw the French language as a common good to be protected and promoted. From then on, the former community elites who had favoured informal relations were compelled to come to terms with multiple intervenors. As of the 1960s, these elites welcomed official state intervention in matters relating to civil society in order to preserve the social discipline that was being threatened by language tensions.

As the source of law and enforcer of rights, the state undertook to shape national unity—whether in Canada or Quebec—and social peace. Through language-planning policies, the state leaders—especially at the federal level and in Quebec—took on the mission of ensuring the provision of French services for citizens and of intervening in matters relating to the language of work and instruction, among others. Focusing on individual rights, as of 1969 the federal state banked on official bilingualism to satisfy these requirements, and, in so doing, it redefined the scope of political identity. In 1977, after some hesitation, the Quebec state implemented official unilingualism with the Charter of the French Language. As jurist scholar Eugénie Brouillet states, "The survival and flourishing of Quebec's cultural identity, especially through the protection of the French language, represents the shared aspirations and, therefore, a collective right of Quebecers."[1] As for the minority communities that had no hold on the machinery of state, the respect for language rights, especially with regard to education, and the preservation of the power relationship became focused in a recourse to courts and the vitality of institutional networks. Then too, as the dramatic situation of Aboriginal languages at the turn of the third millennium made clear, those directions do not always lead to success.

General trends in the language issue

Beyond the emphasis on differences of language, the political world as a whole represents as well a *community of discourse*, to use a well-known socio-linguistic term. Such a community is meant to share a network of communications between individuals who more or less agree on a language's uses, its value, and its social and political relevance. In Canada and Quebec, from 1539 to today, within the world of politics, as we have seen, the language issue was addressed according to three approaches: *how to live together*, the *duties of living together*, and the *will to live together*. Over a period of more than four centuries, these three approaches revealed the general trends in the relations between language and politics.

How to live together: the weight of citizens' actions

The *how to live together* approach represents the power struggle between the participants in the language issue—their strategies for exercising power and for resisting it. Since the advent of parliamentary democracy, one of the general trends in the relation between language and politics involves citizens' actions prior to the implementation of a state policy, during its development, and following its implementation.

Politics, it can never be sufficiently stressed, is an individual matter before it enters into the realms of ideas or abstract entities such as law and state. Over time characters emerge who strongly influence the notions surrounding the language issue within a political community; we need only recall Edmund Burke, Louis-Joseph Papineau, and Louis-Hippolyte La Fontaine prior to 1848; D'Alton McCarthy, Henri Bourassa, and Armand LaVergne at the end of the nineteenth century; Father Richard Arès and Brother Anonymous at the beginning of the Quiet Revolution; André Laurendeau at the time of the Royal Commission on Bilingualism and Biculturalism; Camille Laurin and the Charter of the French Language, and Pierre Elliott Trudeau with the Official Languages Act and the Canadian Charter of Rights and Freedoms; or Michel Bastarache, Pierre Bourgault, Georges Forest, and Gisèle Lalonde after 1982. When these individuals spoke out, none of them—with the exception of Laurin and Trudeau—had any decision-making power within a government. They were expressing themselves from outside the government system, sometimes in parliamentary forums, but mostly on other platforms in the public sphere. Their influence on the language issue was essentially rooted in how their ideas on the issue matched the state of mind of their fellow citizens. "In the battle to impose a legitimate vision," to take up the analysis of sociologist Pierre Bourdieu, these individuals "have a power proportional to their symbolic capital, which is to say to the recognition a group provides them." [2] In other words, they are spokespersons for citizens' actions.

Those actions are the primary precondition for any language policy. They are the deeds of social actors—citizens on their own or united in organizations and professional associations such as the ACFÉO, Société de l'Acadie du Nouveau-Brunswick, Alliance Quebec, Fédération des francophones hors Québec (which became the Fédération des communautés francophones et acadienne du Canada)—who immersed themselves in expressing their voices and adopting certain strategies to reach their objectives. Each of these social actors was capable of mobilizing, holding symbolic capital and possessing material resources—human and financial—that varied according to the needs. For example, some of the organizations could sustain the mobilization of their members for long periods of time in order to impose all their weight on decision-makers. Rapid and massive mobilization of citizens in Lower Canada against the union of the two Canadas in 1822 prevented London from moving in that direction. Language policies implemented by provincial states from 1880 to 1920 were also a measure of the actions of members of Anglo-Saxon communities who made up the majority in Canada. United in organizations such as the Equal Rights Association, this majority was shaken by the influx of immigrants. Its members advocated assimilation as a solution to managing cultural diversity, and they brought their full strength to bear on their provincial leaders. Nor should we forget the constant pressure exercised by the Quebec organizations that advocated for French unilingualism prior to the enactment of Bill 101, which led to demonstrations by tens of thousands of private citizens supporting their cause.

Other social actors could rely on the solidarity of their political communities, as long as their communication networks were maintained. That was the case in the huge mobilization in French Canada at the time of the enactment of Regulation 17, when Franco-Ontarian associations received support from their fellow citizens in Quebec. Other social actors, with a more limited access to material resources, relied on their own tenacity to change the order of things. Although some, such as parents Jean-Pierre Mahé and Angéline Martel, trucker Gilles Caron, and businessman Mario Charlebois, succeeded, others failed, sometimes at the end of their battles, as was the case for former judge Joseph T. Thorson.

The state leaders, especially those with ministerial duties, displayed meagre initiative with regard to the implementation of language policies, and for a very good reason. As political scientists would say, a top-down approach does not work with these policies: if they are simply the result of the executive's will, in consultation with civil servants, the policies will garner practically no legitimacy among the vast majority of citizens, who will turn them down point blank. The Constitution Act of 1982 is an eloquent example of such a case. Although Quebec did not ratify the act and still questions its legitimacy, the same does not apply throughout the rest of the country, where the vast majority of citizens have identified by and large with this symbol of belonging, and did so from the outset. Given that language policies build on legitimacy in order to reduce social divisions, these policies always emerge from the constant contest between the powers exercised by state leaders and the strategies of resistance—such as protests or mobilization—of citizens.

As a result, the language issue in its *how to live together* approach is a space of controversies. Within it, the implementation of language policies is characterized by tensions and social divisions leading to huge mobilizations of citizens—at various levels of intensity depending on the period—and to underground or open conflicts. This response is in the very nature of these policies because they aim to alter the symbolic order of a state and, in so doing, to define the criteria of belongingness to a political community.

In essence, these language policies alter the fundamental values of citizenship, which explains their high mobilizing potential. Other issues relating to fundamental values, such as abortion and the regulation of drugs and alcohol consumption, also trigger huge mobilizations because of their moral connotations; but they do not have the same objectives. In the case of political issues with moral connotations, mobilization is focused on the victory of moralizing concepts influenced by the religious beliefs of citizens. In the case of issues that touch on a sense of collective belonging, the mobilized citizens seek instead to promote the most extensive identification possible with the constitutive symbols of the political community, such as language.

The duties of living together: the permanency of law and norms

From 1539 on, two general trends within the language issue related specifically to the establishment of norms that regulate life in common, or the *duties of living together*. Here, as socio-linguist Bernard Spolsky notes, language policies are based on choices, but the choices are limited by a normative framework. The norms are official when they fall under a law and its application, especially when the law regulates the use and recognition of languages. They are less so when they involve the development of linguistic rules relating to the quality of the spoken and written language.

The first major trend in the *duties of living together* is that law plays a fundamental role in relations between language and politics.

Ever since the Ordinance of Villers-Cotterêts, dealing with, we strongly emphasize, the administration of justice, the sovereign—the king or the people through representatives within the state—was not content with providing good advice and mediation to solve language policies. The king used his royal power to reinstate public order and impose an official modus vivendi by legislating and regulating. It is remarkable how the state achieved a formalization of controversies and consensuses by using law as an instrument for regulating social divisions relating to language matters. Treaties, charters, laws, and regulations punctuate the relations between language and politics, from the Royal Proclamation of 1763 to the Canadian Charter of Rights and Freedoms in 1982, from the 1731 British Act on the Use of English Language in the Law Courts Made Obligatory to the Quebec Charter of the French Language in 1977 and the 1986 Ontario French Language Services Act.

Beyond legislative actions, the administration of justice attests to the primacy of law in language matters. The courts are major authorities, if not the main authority, in the historical progression of the question of language use. In other words, the legislative and executive authorities were often reduced to tagging along behind the judiciary, which was on the front line regulating controversies. That is why citizens granted such importance to judicial proceedings: they were the guarantors of language rights. In 1834 the 92 Resolutions were grievances held against the unilingualism of judges and, therefore, against their inability to administer justice adequately. In 1916 the verdict of the British Judicial Committee of the Privy Council on the legality of Regulation 17 confirmed that Franco-Ontarians had never been given the right to education in their language. In 1988 the Supreme Court of Canada's ruling on the *Ford* case repealed a major provision of the Charter of the French Language when it abolished the regulation requiring French-only public and commercial signs.

The intervention of courts in the processes surrounding the development and implementation of language policies preceded by far the enactment of the Canadian Charter of Rights and Freedoms. With the establishment of the state of law, the nineteenth century witnessed a number of citizens and interest groups resorting to the courts in hopes of having their point of view triumph in language matters. But the recourse to courts was not always a winning proposition: power relations within a political community prevailed in the end. In Manitoba the courts twice repealed the law abolishing French as an official language, once in 1892 and again in 1909, but the province ignored the judgments. Following the enactment of the Official Languages Act in 1969, Thorson pleaded unsuccessfully for the revocation of this legislative measure. On the other hand, the political leaders rapidly understood the potential use of the courts' verdicts as strategic instruments. During the school conflicts in Manitoba in 1890, the Conservative cabinet minister Joseph-Adolphe Chapleau sincerely hoped that the courts, exemplifying the impartiality of justice, would appease the conflicts and offer a solution to the crisis.

The entrenchment of the Canadian Charter of Rights and Freedoms in the Constitution Act of 1982 changed the role of the courts. From then on, judges had to take into account Section 23 of the Charter and assume a liberal approach in language matters because the legislator sought to make up for prejudices suffered by the francophone minority communities that had been deprived of access to education in their own language. By freely citing Section 23, activists from francophone communities achieved gains in the legal recognition of their rights. This reversal in power relations was likened by some to the "tyranny" of courts: faced with the activism of interest groups seeking to twist the arm of governments, the political leaders had seemingly become hostages of the judges' verdicts. This "tyranny" was hugely exaggerated, for two reasons relating to power relations and the allocation of resources. On the one hand, despite programs designed for minority francophone and anglophone groups seeking recourse to courts, the legal process was long, slow, and expensive. On the other hand, the political leaders always had the last word, either by invoking the notwithstanding clause—as Quebec did in 1988—or by enacting another law to correct the situation.

The *duties of living together* cannot be summed up only with regards to relations with a state, its laws, and its administration of justice. They also apply to the civil society, in which citizens establish norms of social distinctiveness pertaining to language—a distinctiveness that surfaces in the debates on the quality of language and its proper use. These debates represent another major trend from the sixteenth to the twenty-first centuries. Indeed, the issue of language quality has been a constant preoccupation, connecting always to values and the relations of political and socio-economic domination within a given community.

The political determination to achieve social homogenization within the territory of a state went hand in hand with "a theory of language equally centralizing and normalizing," as writer and essayist Lise Gauvin points out.[3] This determination dictated the norms pertaining to quality and the judgments based on those norms. Travellers visiting New France did not hesitate to praise the purity of the language spoken by the settlers, which was an eloquent indication of the success that came from promoting the king's language to the detriment of local dialects. After the Conquest a new relation of domination was imposed through another language: English. In addition, there was a break with France, where new norms of quality were being adopted, in particular at the time of the 1789 Revolution. In the first decades of the nineteenth century, John Lambert, Michel Bibaud, and Alexis de Tocqueville all recorded the growing gap between proper language and the Canadians' language—in which a flurry of anglicisms offered distinct signs of an identification with the dominators.

At the end of the nineteenth and beginning of the twentieth centuries, the discourse on language norms fragmented. The reality of Acadians and French Canadians was increasingly that of the factory in New England or otherwise of movement to a city, in a place where the language of machines, bosses, and social advancement was English. Furthermore, members of the bourgeoisie could once again travel to France. From then on, the discourse on the quality of language was transformed into a dual resistance. Narcisse-Henri-Édouard Faucher de Saint-Maurice and Jules-Paul Tardivel were praising dialects both to fight the infiltration of English and to establish a distinction with respect to Parisian norms. In the early twentieth century the tone became more critical; as supporters of liberal values, the members of the elites who were involved in groups such as the Société du parler français au Canada directed blame for language problems towards the individual. They set a norm pertaining to quality and attempted to establish some sort of social control, arguing in favour of individual responsibility and denouncing the pitiful state of the spoken and written French language. Still, their admonitions did not produce the expected results.

At the turn of the 1960s the debate on the quality of language received extensive media coverage with the publication of *Les Insolences du frère Untel*. It was a period of major mutations in the references to French-Canadian identity, with faith being dropped as a component of the nation. Furthermore, the debate surrounding *joual* brought forward the political issues relating to the democratization of education. From then on, language gained a significant added value and, as a result, the debates on quality provided the opportunity to question the role of the state in the management of language matters. At the end of the 1990s, criticisms were still focused on the poor quality of the French language, especially among the youth. The offensive led by Georges Dor was a harsh judgment on the efforts devoted to education over the past forty years, and a sad recognition of failure. The debate on the quality of language, which was not limited to Quebec and Acadia, touched a sensitive chord because language was a major identity reference, and the survival of the French-speaking minority remained precarious.

The will to live together: language between market and memory

A final general trend in the history of the relations between language and politics involves the *will to live together*. If the language issue has a permanent feature, it is definitely the tight and permanent link between language and the feeling of belonging to a historical community—its common identity references and its search for continuity between past and future. The sharing of a language between citizens creates a defined entity: because of its performative character, language allows the entity to manifest itself through a discourse, to be present within space and time, to last. To speak French, English, Italian, Ukrainian, Attikamek, Ojibwa, or Inukitut does not simply translate, through language, into a relation with the world. It also "makes society,"[4] especially by expressing social divisions and plans for the future. A language is above all the affirmation of a person's solidarity with other human beings. The French of Jean-Baptiste Poquelin, known as Molière, the English of William Shakespeare, the Innu of poet Rita Mestokosho: these are vital parts of humanity, in all their richness and diversity. In maintaining their languages, we are establishing more than a simple communicational contact; we are touching these humans across centuries—humans of multiple riches, humans who refuse to disappear.

Given the growing hegemony of market rules that govern social relations, the *will to live together*, which is at the heart of the language issue, risks withering away in many aspects, thereby creating serious consequences for the political world. In a time when citizens are being reduced to consumers, the response becomes a preference for a strictly utilitarian concept of language. In recent years the status of the English language has changed because the acceleration of economic exchanges between continents has made business English the lingua franca. Studies of young francophones, especially those living in minority situations, reveal that they do not perceive of English as a cultural threat, but rather as a simple instrument of communication. The promotion of a utilitarian language is unfolding to the detriment of other languages that have less access to resources and markets. Ancient realities freshly revived, assimilation within francophone minority communities, and the disappearance of many Aboriginal languages all have an impact on cultural diversity. These factors are also causing the loss of identity references and knowledge accumulated over many generations. The reality expressed by a language risks becoming more and more limited to economic interactions without reaching its full cultural and political richness. As Fernand Dumont says, "The silence of an entire people / is the one that poems lament." [5]

At the beginning of the third millennium, language remains thoroughly political—obviously political. Indeed, given the reorganization of the public sphere into discursive microcosms and the emergence of diverse identity references, new solidarities are taking shape, and they are triggering the voicing of the people's will within their political communities. Driven by mobilizations similar to the anti-globalist movements that are reviving causes such as nationalism and grassroots or local politics, this voicing of citizens' will is structured around issues such as cultural diversity and concepts of rights and freedoms that are less centred on the economy. These voices are using the multiple networks of high-speed electronic and digital communications to be heard. They are mobilizing new actors that are leading them into the heat of debates and struggles. At this time, when our research is ending and we are becoming silent, let us remember confidently: in the world around us it is both the memory and the vibrancy of citizens' voices that open the doors to the future.

Acknowledgements

The art of thanking is one of the most difficult, but also one of the most pleasant, there is. It is part of the conclusion of a work, when recognizing generosity covers with its veneer the product of the historian's toil. This explains the care we bring to expressing our gratitude because, as history combats forgetfulness, we certainly do not want to omit anybody. Please forgive us if, by misfortune, we may have.

A historical investigation is an adventure in seeking out the remnants of the past; it is a task in which discovery is constantly at hand. This discovery is collegial, rooted in the efforts of numerous people who are carrying out work in common. Therefore, our team of inquisitive, enthusiastic, and competent assistants is greatly appreciated. And so, too, we heartily thank the graduate students who took part in the gathering of information: David Dowe, Leanne Dustan, Mathieu Lapointe, Karen Macfarlane, Eric Payseur, and Jamie Trepanier at York University; and Olivier Côté, Gabriel Delisle, Émilie Guilbeault-Cayer, Mathieu Horth-Gagné, Alexandre Lévesque, Julien Massicotte, Patrick-Michel Noël, Isabelle Roy, and Stéphane Savard at Laval University. We are also grateful to York University's Faculty of Graduate Studies for the valued support it provided in this matter.

Discoveries take place in locations. Thanks to astute and thoughtful guides, the archive centres in New Brunswick, Ontario, and Quebec were sources flowing with precious material. We are very grateful to the personnel of the following organizations: the Centre d'études acadiennes in Moncton, including Kenneth Breau; the Provincial Archives of New Brunswick (Fredericton); the Division des archives et de la reconstitution des débats et la Bibliothèque de l'Assemblée nationale du Québec, and in particular Christian Blais, Marise Falardeau, Alain Gariépy, Geneviève Langlois, and Martin Pelletier; the Centre d'archives de Québec de la Bibliothèque et Archives nationales du Quebec, including Rénald Lessard and André Ruest; the Centre de recherche Lionel-Groulx and the National Archives of the Canadian Jewish Congress in Montreal; the McCord Museum, including Cerise Mahuzier; the photo library of the Fédération des travailleurs du Québec, and in particular Isabelle Gareau; Library and Archives Canada, including Alain Roy and Lynn Lafontaine; the Centre de recherche en civilisation canadienne-française (University of Ottawa), including its then-director, Yves Frenette, and its archivist, Nicole Bonsaint; and, finally, the Archives of Ontario in Toronto. We also wish to thank Senator Serge Joyal for his generous contribution to the iconography in this synthesis.

Discoveries also appear through the sharing of ideas and approaches. Throughout our work, friends and colleagues provided comments on parts of chapters, reacted to some assumptions, provided advice and suggestions, or generously offered us their knowledge and skills. We are deeply grateful to Sébastien Arcand, Jean-Pierre Beaud, Nicolas Béland, Justin Bisanswa, Daniel Bourgeois, Eugénie Brouillet, Robert Comeau, Nathalie Courcy, Michel De Waele, Jacques Faucher, Rolande Faucher, Pierre Foucher, Donald Fyson, Gilles Gallichan, Patrice Groulx, Matthew Hayday, Daniel Hickey, Richard Jones, Guy Laforest, Julien Massicotte, Roberto Perin, Alain Roy, Giuseppe-J. Turi, Stéphane Savard, Jocelyn Saint-Pierre, Nathalie Tousignant, and Jean-Philippe Warren. We are equally grateful to Christophe Horguelin at Éditions du Boréal, who accompanied us wisely and efficiently through the revision of the manuscript for the French edition.

This sharing also took place in a more a formal way during two scientific activities. In the fall of 2006 a graduate studies seminar was held at Laval University that provided a group of specialists in linguistics the opportunity to share their thoughts. The seminar received financial and logistics support from the Chaire pour le développement de la recherche sur la culture d'expression française en Amérique du Nord (CEFAN). We want to express our gratitude to its former incumbent, Jacques Mathieu, and his administrative assistant, Jeanne Valois. This analytical work on language policies continued at York University's

Glendon College, which hosted a symposium on March 29–30, 2007, to mark the fortieth anniversary of the tabling of the Laurendeau-Dunton Commission's first report. We are equally grateful to the principal of the College, Kenneth McRoberts, and his team, as well as to the Avie Bennett Historica-Dominion Institute Chair in Canadian History for the enthusiastic support it gave us.

For it to exist, a historical investigation needs resources. We thank the Social Sciences and Humanities Research Council of Canada for the generous support it awarded our project, "D'une réalité culturelle à un problème politique: les politiques linguistiques au Canada, 1960–1982 [From a cultural reality to a political problem: language policies in Canada, 1960–1982]," within the Official Languages Research and Dissemination Program.

To conclude, we are especially grateful to two people because of the key role they played in the completion of this work. Andrée Courtemanche was, as usual, one of these. Friend of one of the authors, partner and accomplice of the other, she advised us wisely from the beginning to the end of the project, while providing us with constant support and productive intellectual input. May she be granted here an indication of our most sincere and warm thanks.

All through this project, we benefited from the kind support of the Éditions du Boréal and our editor Paul-André Linteau. Thanks to his intellectual rigour, suggestions, and wise advice, and also his patience, he made it possible for us to complete this historical study that covers four hundred years of the history of the language issue in Canada and Quebec. Once again, and as always, we thank him most sincerely.

Finally, we thank Between the Lines and in particular Amanda Crocker for taking on the task of an English translation of our book; and Robert Clarke of BTL for his editorial work on this new version. Last, but not least, we sincerely want to thank Patricia Dumas for translating the original text into English.

Marcel Martel and Martin Pâquet

Abbreviations

ACFÉO   Association canadienne-française d'éducation d'Ontario [Ontario French-Canadian Association for Education]

ACFO   Association canadienne-française de l'Ontario [Ontario French-Canadian Association]

AO   Archives of Ontario

AVQ   Archives de la Ville de Québec

BANQ-Q   Bibliothèque et Archives nationales du Québec, centre de la capitale nationale

BANQ-M   Bibliothèque et Archives nationales du Québec, centre de Montréal

CÉA-M   Centre d'études Acadiennes [Acadian Studies Centre], Université de Moncton

CRCCF   Centre de recherche en civilisation canadienne-française

CRLG   Centre de recherche Lionel-Groulx

CVFA   Conseil de la vie française en Amérique

FSSJBO   Fédération des Sociétés Saint-Jean-Baptiste de l'Ontario

LAC   Library and Archives Canada

Notes

Introduction

Translation of epigraph:
How can the centuries severing languages from meanings be abolished? (Perrault)

1 The term "symbolic order," as we use it, refers to those symbols used to give meaning to the concept of nationhood or statehood. States and nations have flags, mottos, and other symbols that rally and inspire individuals. When states or nations alter these symbols, some individuals and groups will oppose these transformations if they do not or cannot recognize themselves in the new formulations.

1. From religion to language: 1539-1848

1 Quoted in Guy Bouthillier and Jean Meynaud, *Le choc des langues au Québec, 1760-1970*, Montreal, Presses de l'Université du Québec, 1972, pp.139, 141. See also Chantal Bouchard, *La langue et le nombril: Histoire d'une obsession québécoise*, Montreal, Fides, 1998, p.67. Translation of: "*le fond de population et l'immense majorité est partout française"…"ont une ressemblance frappante avec nos villes de province*" … "*manquent particulièrement de distinction [et] parlent français avec l'accent normand des classes moyennes.*"

2 Francis Maseres, *Occasional Essays on Various Subjects, Chiefly Political and*

Historical, London, Robert Wilks, 1809, pp.341-42.

3 Bouthillier and Meynaud, *Le choc des langues au Québec*, p.106. Translation of: "*[ce] que deviendroit le Bien général de la colonie, si ceux qui en composent le corps principal en deviendroient des membres inutiles par la différence de la Religion.*"

4 The Parliamentary Register, vol. 28, London, J. Devrett, 1791, p.514.

5 Quoted in Jim McCue, *Edmund Burke and Our Present Discontents*, London, Claridge Press, 1997, p.23.

6 Parliamentary Register, vol. 29, 1791, pp.379-80.

7 Edmund Burke, "A Letter to Sir Hercules Langrishe on the Catholics of Ireland, January 3rd, 1792," in Edmund Burke, *The Works of the Right Honourable Edmund Burke*, vol. 1, London, Holdsworth and Corner, 1839, pp.303-6.

8 Parliamentary Register, vol. 29, 1791, pp.379-80.

9 *The Quebec Gazette*, Feb. 14, 1793, p.3, quoted in French in Réal Bélanger, Richard Jones, and Marc Vallières, *Les grands débats parlementaires, 1792-1992*, Sainte-Foy (Quebec), Presses de l'Université Laval, 1994, pp. 54-56.

10 *The Quebec Gazette*, Feb. 21, 1793, p.1, quoted in French in John Hare, *Aux origines du parlementarisme québécois, 1791-1793*, Sillery (Quebec), Septentrion, 1993, p.91. See also Michael Dorland and Maurice

Charland, *Law, Rhetoric, and Irony in the Formation of Canadian Civil Culture*, Toronto, University of Toronto Press, 2002, pp.101-2.

11   Bélanger, Jones, and Vallières, *Les grands débats parlementaires*, pp.54-56. Translation of Lotbinière: *"Le plus grand nombre de nos Électeurs étant placés dans une situation particulière, nous sommes obligés de nous écarter des règles ordinaires et sommes contraints de réclamer l'usage d'une langue qui n'est pas celle de l'empire; mais aussi équitables envers les autres, que nous espérons qu'on le fera pour nous-mêmes, nous ne voudrions pas que notre langage vint à bannir ceux des autres Sujets de Sa Majesté; mais demandons que l'un et l'autre soient permis."*... *"Nous sommes persuadés que les nouveaux Sujets [les Canadiens] lui sont aussi chers [au roi George III] que les autres...Quand une partie de nos constituants [les sujets canadiens] seront en état d'entendre la langue de l'Empire, alors le moment sera arrivé de passer toutes nos loix dans le texte anglois, le faire avant seroit une cruauté, que le meilleur des rois, ni son parlement ne voudroit jamais permettre."* Translation of Taschereau: *"qui nous constitue libres ... commande aux deux premières puissances de la Législation [les conseils exécutif et législatif] de concourir avec nous"*... *"de manière à répondre aux intentions bienfaisantes de sa Majesté et de son Parlement."*

12   Quoted in Gaston Deschênes, *Une capitale éphémère: Montréal et les événements tragiques de 1849*, Sillery (Quebec), Septentrion, 1999, p.104.

13   *La Minerve*, Feb. 16, 1832, p.1.

14   Quoted in Jean-Paul Bernard, ed., *Assemblées publiques, résolutions et déclarations de 1837-1838*, Montreal, VLB, 1988, pp.278, 284. Translation of: *"Dieu ne créa aucunes distinctions artificielles entre l'homme"*... *"seule source légitime de tout pouvoir"*... *"de quelqu'origine, langue ou religion."*

15   *The Quebec Gazette*, Jan. 15, 1801.

16   John Lambton (Lord Durham), *The Report and Dispatches of the Earl of Durham, Her Majesty's High Commissioner and Governor-General in British North America*, London, Ridgways, 1839, p.16.

17   Ibid., pp. 47-48.

18   Ibid.

19   Ibid., p.225.

20   Quoted in Bruce Curtis, "Irish Schools for Canada: Arthur Buller to the Bishop of Quebec, 1838," *Historical Studies in Education/ Revue d'histoire de l'éducation*, vol. 13, no 1 (2001), p.54.

21   Translation of "A-t-il [J.H. Dunn] oublié déjà que j'appartiens à une origine si horriblement maltraitée par l'Acte d'Union?

22   Bélanger, Jones, and Vallières, *Les grands débats parlementaires*, p.57. Translation of: *"Je dois informer l'honorable membre, et les autres honorables membres, et le public du sentiment de justice duquel je ne crains pas d'en appeler, que quand même la connaissance de la langue anglaise me serait aussi familière que celle de la langue française, je n'en ferais pas moins mon premier discours dans la langue de mes compatriotes canadiens-français, ne serait-ce que pour protester contre cette cruelle injustice de cette partie de l'Acte d'Union qui tend à proscrire la langue maternelle d'une moitié de la population du Canada. Je le dois à mes compatriotes, je le dois à moi-même."*

2. The first language tremors: The school crises in Canada, 1848-1927

Translation of epigraph:
Oh our History! Casket of pearls ignored!
I lovingly caress your revered pages.
Everlasting register; luminous poem
That France wrote with the purest of its blood! (Fréchette)

1   Matteo Sanfilippo, "Essor urbain et création de nouveaux diocèses dans l'ouest: la correspondance des délégués apostoliques, 1902-1918," *Canada e Italia verso il Duemila:*

Metropoli a Confronto, Milan, Schena Editore, 1992, p.269. Translation of: "*des évêques de langue anglaise.*"

2 In this case, bilingualism means that the priest or members of a religious order mastered a second language as well as French. Robert Painchaud, "Les exigences linguistiques dans le recrutement d'un clergé pour l'ouest canadien, 1818-1920," *Société canadienne d'histoire de l'Église catholique, sessions d'étude 1975*, pp. 43-64.

3 Henri Bourassa, "La langue française et la religion catholique," in Guy Frégault, Michel Brunet, and Marcel Trudel, eds., *Histoire du Canada par les textes*, Montreal, Fides, 1952, p.236.

4 Letter from Mgr. Ignace Bourget to Godefroi Lamarche, May 27, 1872, quoted in Roberto Perin, *Ignace de Montréal: Artisan d'une identité nationale*, Montreal, Boréal, 2008, p.204. Translation of: "*tout faire et tout sacrifier pour que les faibles soient protégés contre les forts.*"

5 Letter from L.-F. Laflèche to J.-A. Chapleau, May 12, 1890, reproduced in Robert Rumilly, *Monseigneur Laflèche et son temps*, Montreal, Éditions B.D. Simpson, 1945, p.338. Translation of: "*C'est au nom du pacte fédéral que la minorité du Manitoba vient demander protection contre une loi injuste qui viole ce pacte fédéral, car ce pacte [lui] garantit l'usage officiel de la langue française sur le même pied que la langue anglaise, et le maintien des écoles séparées, conditions sans lesquelles la population catholique et francologue [sic] du Manitoba n'aurait jamais consenti à entrer dans la Confédération. Or, c'est cette garantie que la loi [manitobaine] vient de fouler aux pieds, pour dépouiller injustement, sans même l'ombre d'un prétexte, cette minorité du droit auquel un peuple tient le plus, le droit de conserver la langue et la foi de ses pères.*"

6 Rumilly, *Monseigneur Laflèche et son temps*, pp.339-40. Translation of: "*Les cours de justice, si elles rendaient un arrêt décrétant l'illégalité de cette mesure, met-*

traient fin à cette question sans donner lieu à une agitation politique que l'acte officiel du gouvernement fédéral ne manquerait pas de soulever. Supposons le veto du gouverneur général en conseil publié contre la loi [manitobaine]; [le gouvernement de cette province] ne manquerait pas de soulever une agitation qui, même limitée à la province du Manitoba, conduirait sûrement à une dissolution de la législature, et un appel électoral ne laisse pas de doute sur son issue. La nouvelle législature passerait la même loi en l'accentuant encore, appuyée qu'elle serait par un élément aussi puissant que violent dans tout le pays. ... Une décision judiciaire ne saurait au contraire provoquer d'agitation populaire. Confirmée par les autorités légales de l'Empire, elle s'imposerait même aux plus remuants, la passion politique ne pouvant y trouver prise."

7 Edmund A. Aunger, "Justifying the End of Official Bilingualism: Canada's North-West Assembly and the Dual-Language Question, 1889-1892," *Canadian Journal of Political Science*, vol. 34, no. 3 (September 2001), pp.451-86; Bouthillier and Meynaud, *Le choc des langues au Québec*, p.255.

8 LAC, Royal Commission on Dominion-Provincial Relations Fonds, C6987, *Mémoire des Canadiens français de l'Alberta*, March 14, 1938, p.3.

9 Paul-E. Gosselin, *Le Conseil de la vie française*, Quebec, Éditions Ferland, 1967, p.4.

10 Michel Verrette, *L'Alphabétisation au Québec, 1660-1900: En marche vers la modernité culturelle*, Sillery (Quebec), Septentrion, 2002, pp.92, 101.

11 Ibid., p.119.

12 Quoted in Bouthillier and Meynaud, *Le choc des langues au Québec*, p.207. Translation of: "*que notre langue reste véritablement française.*"

13 Ibid., p.231. Translation of: "*l'anglicisme nous déborde, nous inonde, nous défigure et nous dénature.*"

14 Ibid., pp.355-57; Yvan Lamonde, *Histoire sociale des idées au Québec, 1896-1929*, Montreal, Fides, 2004, pp. 62-63, 145.

15 Quoted in Bouthillier and Meynaud, *Le choc des langues au Québec*, p.281.

16 Ibid., p.294. Translation of: "*la mauvaise opinion du langage qui se parle chez nous.*"

17 Translation of: "*Laissez-les partir, c'est la canaille qui s'en va.*"

18 Quoted in Lamonde, *Histoire sociale des idées au Québec*, p.54. Translation of: "*qu'il est de l'intérêt et du bonheur de la Confédération, et dans l'esprit du pacte fédératif de 1867, que la langue française, officielle en vertu de la Constitution, soit mise dans les affaires publiques, notamment la frappe des monnaies et l'administration des postes, sur un pied d'égalité avec la langue anglaise.*"

19 Napoléon-Antoine Belcourt, "De l'exercice des droits reconnus à la langue française au Canada," *Premier Congrès de la langue française au Canada: Compte rendu*, Quebec, Imprimerie de l'Action sociale, 1913, pp.288-307; Henri Bourassa, "La langue française et l'avenir de notre race," ibid., pp.370-89.

20 Ibid., p.78. Translation of: "*château fort*" ... "*tout ce qui contribue à la grandeur de [sic] Québec contribue à la force et à la grandeur des groupes français du dehors. ... tout ce qui fortifie les avant-postes tourne à la gloire et à la force de [sic] Québec.*"

21 Belcourt, "De l'exercice des droits reconnus à la langue française au Canada," p.302. Translation of: "*c'est vous dire que la survivance du français dans [l']Ontario sera le prix d'une vigilance constante, d'un combat de tous les instants, exigeant de grands sacrifices d'argent et de temps, une détermination finale et irréductible à parler le français et à la [sic] faire parler à nos enfants.*"

22 CRCCF, Fonds de l'ACFÉO, c2/236/2, Statuts & Règlements du Comité permanent du Congrès de la langue française au Canada. Translation of: "*le développement de la langue et de la littérature françaises au Canada et en général chez les Acadiens et les Canadiens français de l'Amérique du Nord.*"

3. All quiet on the front: from the repeal of Regulation 17 to the Laurendeau-Dunton Commission, 1927-63

Translation of epigraph:
There are some who did not want to leave
Who wanted not to leave, but remain
We look at them we don't understand
We don't belong to the same race ...
We have nothing to say and don't hear the
    voice of a companion. (Garneau)

1   "I'll Stay in Canada," in Stephen Leacock, *On the Front Line of Life: Memories and Reflections, 1935-1944*, Toronto, Dundurn Group, 2004, p.177.

2   Quoted in "Canada and the Monarchy," ibid., p.198.

3   AVQ, Fonds du CVFA, P52/D5.6, *Acte d'adhésion officielle des Franco-Ontariens au Congrès de la langue française à Québec*, June 1937; letter to Mgr. Camille Roy from P.-E. Rochon, director general of the ACFÉO, and J.-M. Laframboise, director general of the Association Saint-Jean-Baptiste d'Ottawa, Dec. 14, 1936. Translation of: "*Nous avons réussi à briser la vague d'anglicisation qui, par intermittence, pour ne pas dire d'un mouvement continu, menaçait de déferler sur le Québec, et à l'instar des héros de Verdun nous avons la légitime fierté de pouvoir affirmer que nos communs envahisseurs n'ont pas franchi la ligne interprovinciale qui nous sépare, nous éprouvons, par ailleurs, un vif besoin d'être secourus dans la mise en pleine valeur de notre victoire decisive.*"

4   Mgr. Émile Yelle, "La langue et l'esprit français dans le Manitoba et dans l'Ouest canadien," *Deuxième Congrès de la langue française au Canada, Québec, 27 juin-1er juillet 1937, Compte rendu*, Quebec, Imprimerie L'action catholique, 1938, p.239. Translation of: "*ont conservé leur héritage français parce qu'ils l'ont défendu, ils entendent, sans se faire illusion sur les difficultés de demain, continuer à se défendre pour conserver leur héritage français.*"

5   Bouthillier and Meynaud, *Le choc des langues au Québec*, pp.485–87, 622–25.

6   Karim Larose, *La langue de papier: Spéculations linguistiques au Québec*, Montreal, Les Presses de l'Université de Montréal, 2004, pp.40–41.

7   Jean-Pierre Charland, "L'instruction chez les Canadiens français," in Michel Plourde, dir., *Le français au Québec: 400 ans d'histoire et de vie*, Saint-Laurent et Sainte-Foy (Quebec), Fides et Publications du Québec, 2000, p.180.

8   Ibid., pp.181–82.

9   Debates in the Quebec Legislative Assembly, April 25, 1947. Translation of: "*auprès du gouvernement d'Ottawa contre l'injustice dont est victime la minorité canadienne-française de ce pays ... à l'esprit de la constitution.*"

10 Translation of: "*Ce projet de loi a été adopté par le Parlement du Canada en avril 1938. ... Aucune nomination permanente ou temporaire ne doit être faite à un emploi local dans une province, et aucun employé ne doit être transféré d'un emploi dans une province à un emploi local dans la même ou une autre province, qu'il soit permanent ou temporaire, jusqu'à ce que le candidat ou l'employé se soit qualifié, par voie de concours, dans la connaissance et l'usage de la langue de la majorité des personnes avec lesquelles il est tenu de traiter; toutefois, cette langue doit être le français ou l'anglais. ... Chaque examen prévu par la présente loi doit avoir lieu en anglais ou en français, au choix du candidat; avis de chaque examen doit être publié en anglais et en français dans la Gazette du Canada, et cet avis doit indiquer le nombre d'emplois qu'il est projeté de remplir, les emplois alors vacants et, dans chaque cas, les qualités exigées pour ces emplois.*"

11 AVQ, Fonds CVFA, p52/D7-4, Letter from the Conseil, September 1939; AVQ, Fonds CVFA, P52/D7-5, letter from Paul-Émile Gosselin to Jules Castonguay, director of the Bureau of the Census, Oct. 8, 1940; CRCCF, Fonds de l'ACFÉO, c2/457/2,

Mémoire du Conseil de la vie française en Amérique à Paul Comtois, ministre des Mines et des Relevés techniques du Canada, sur l'Atlas du Canada et sur d'autres publications de son ministère (1958).

12 AVQ, Fonds CVFA, P52/D7-9, letter from Paul-Émile Gosselin to Jules Castonguay, Chief Registrar of Canada, March 5, 1942; letter from Association catholique franco-canadienne de la Saskatchewan to Jules Castonguay, April 8, 1942.

13 *Le Devoir*, Feb. 7, 1962, p.1.

14 LAC, Fonds de la Commission royale des relations entre le Dominion et les provinces, c6987, *Mémoire des Acadiens et des Canadiens français des provinces maritimes*, April 11, 1938. Translation of: "*Quelle folie eût été celle des "Pères" [de la Confédération] en décrétant cet usage du français au Parlement et devant les tribunaux fédéraux si leur intention n'avait pas été de rendre possible partout au Canada l'emploi du français?*" ... "*de façon à ce que les minorités françaises des provinces maritimes jouissent des droits et privilèges que la province de Québec accorde actuellement à ses minorités anglaises et protestantes.*"

15 Ibid., *Mémoire des Canadiens français de l'Alberta*, March 14, 1938. Translation of: "*la reconnaissance officielle de la religion catholique et de la langue française dans les écoles de chacune des provinces du Canada et ... que la langue française soit officielle dans tous les Parlements et devant tous les tribunaux du pays.*"

16 Conseil de la vie française en Amérique, *Troisième Congrès de la langue française, Québec, 18-26 juin 1952, Compte rendu*, Quebec, Éditions Ferland, 1953, pp.446–47. Translation of: "*Que nos postes de radio s'appliquent de plus en plus à soigner la langue française, en vue de se constituer eux-mêmes les gardiens et les propagateurs de la culture française au Canada, de l'Atlantique au Pacifique; que la télévision de demain, respectant les lois de la morale, devienne aussi une école de bon goût et de bon langage; que le même souci de culture*

française anime les producteurs et les propagandistes du film canadien."

17 CRCCF, Fonds de la FSSJBO, c19-3/1/12, *Réunion régulière du Conseil*, March 13, 1959.

18 CRCCF, Fonds de l'ACFÉO, c2/229/5, letter from the ACFÉO to Premier Leslie Frost, Feb. 5, 1961.

19 Normand Labrie, *La construction linguistique de la Communauté européenne*, Paris, Honoré Champion, 1993, pp.28–29. Translation of : "*influencer, ou ayant pour effet d'influencer, le comportement des autres, en ce qui concerne l'acquisition, la structure et la répartition fonctionnelle de leurs codes linguistiques.*"

20 "M. Hees élimine tout espoir: Le recensement 61 sabotera l'équilibre franco-anglais," *La Presse*, Nov. 19, 1960.

21 Richard Arès, "Positions du français dans l'Ouest canadien," *Relations*, no. 163 (July 1954), p.195; "Positions du français aux Maritimes," *Relations*, no. 161 (May 1954); "Positions du français en Ontario et au Québec," *Relations*, no. 164 (August 1954). Translation of: "*que le recensement de 1961 révèle des pertes encore plus brutales.*"

22 Larose, *La langue de papier*, p.102.

23 [Jean-Paul Desbiens], *Les impertinences du Frère Untel*, Pref. by André Laurendeau. Translation of: "*Il est question d'un office provincial de la linguistique. J'en suis. La langue est un bien commun, et c'est à l'État comme tel de la protéger. L'État protège les orignaux, les perdrix et les truites. On a même prétendu qu'il protégeait les grues. L'État protège les parcs nationaux, et il fait bien: ce sont là des biens communs. La langue aussi est un bien commun, et l'État devrait la protéger avec autant de rigueur. Une expression vaut bien un orignal, un mot vaut bien une truite.*"

24 Translation of: "*Cette minorité francophone est déjà engagée dans un processus avancé d'anglicisation rapide et massive et, si la situation scolaire ne change pas rapidement et radicalement, le français disparaîtra totalement dans un avenir rapproché.*"

25 CRCCF, Fonds de l'ACFÉO, c2/342/1, Gaston Dulong, *L'état actuel du français au Manitoba*, May and June 1963.

26 Georges-Émile Lapalme, *Le vent de l'oubli: Mémoires*, t. 2, Ottawa, Leméac, 1970, p.241; *Pour une politique: Le programme de la Révolution tranquille*, Montréal, VLB, 1988, pp.76–98. Translation of: "*est venu de concevoir l'État provincial comme un phénomène culturel.*"

27 Jean-Louis Roy, *Les programmes électoraux du Québec: Un siècle de programmes politiques québécois*, t. 2, *1931-1966*, Ottawa, Leméac, 1971, pp.378–79. Translation of: "*Dans le contexte québécois, l'élément le plus universel est constitué par le fait français que nous nous devons de développer en profondeur. C'est par notre culture plus que par le monde que nous nous imposerons; conscients de nos responsabilités envers la langue française, nous lui donnerons un organisme qui soit à la fois protecteur et créateur; conscients de nos responsabilités envers les trois ou quatre millions de Canadiens-français et d'Acadiens qui vivent au-delà de nos frontières, en Ontario, dans les Maritimes, dans l'Ouest, dans la Nouvelle-Angleterre et la Louisiane, le Québec se constituera la mère patrie de tous. Dans le domaine des arts, tout en participant au mouvement universel, nous tenterons de développer une culture qui nous soit propre en même temps que, par l'urbanisme, nous mettrons en valeur ce qui reste de notre profil français. C'est par la langue française et la culture que peut s'affirmer notre présence française sur le continent nord-américain.*"

28 Édouard Duc, "La langue française dans les relations entre le Canada et la France (1902-1977): De la 'survivance' à l'unilinguisme français au Québec," history dissertation, Université Paris-IV Sorbonne, 2007, t. 2, pp.671-73. Translation of: "*en matière d'affichage public pour faire en sorte que la langue française y soit prioritaire.*"

29 Quebec, *Rapport de la Commission royale d'enquête sur l'enseignement dans la province de Québec*, 2e partie ou t. ii, 1964,

http://classiques.uqac.ca/contemporains/
quebec_commission_parent/
rapport_parent_3/rapport_parent_vol_3.doc.
Translation of: "*L'école aura beau faire,
le français sera sans cesse menacé
d'effritement et de disparition au Québec si
l'enseignement qu'on en donne ne s'appuie
pas sur de solides et profondes motivations
socioéconomiques. ... Le ministère de
l'Éducation n'est pas le seul en cause ici. Le
gouvernement du Québec tout entier doit,
tout en veillant à ne pas isoler le Québec en
un ghetto, adopter des mesures très fermes
pour protéger le français non seulement
dans les écoles et universités, mais dans
toute la vie publique. C'est particulièrement
urgent à Montréal.*"

4. Action-reaction: Commissions of inquiry and agitation, 1963-69

Translation of epigraph:
Someday I will have accepted where I was
born. (Miron)

1   Paul Daoust, "Les jugements sur le joual
(1959-1975) à la lumière de la linguistique
et de la sociolinguistique," dissertation,
Université de Montreal, Departement of
Linguistics and Philology, 1983, quoted in
Bouchard, *La langue et le nombril*, p.231.
Translation of: "*2 523 articles et ouvrages
rédigés par 1303 auteurs différents sont
publiés sur cette question.*"
2   Gérald Godin, "Les colombes séparatistes,"
1974, quoted in Larose, *La langue de papier*,
p.175. Translation of: "*la lingua del pane, au
Quebec, c'est l'anglais. C'est la langue de
travail, c'est la langue de la piastre, c'est
la langue des affaires.*" "*Lingua del pane*"
means "language of bread."
3   Gérald Godin, "Le joual et nous," *Parti
pris*, vol. 2, no. 5 (January 1965); "La
Langue au Québec: entretien avec Wilfrid
LeMoyne, extraits," November 1975, pp.33,
78, quoted in Larose, *La langue de papier*,
p.175. Translation of: "*décalque parfait de
la décadence de notre culture nationale*"

et représenterait le "*décalque de la réalité
économique et politique du Québec.*"
4   André Major, "À joual donné, il faut (quand
même) regarder les dents," *Le Devoir*, Nov.
14, 1969, p.6. Translation of: "*le joual, chez
[lui], vient d'une réaction contre un théâtre
de compromis, à la [Marcel] Dubé, ni tout
à fait français ni tout à fait joual, entre
les deux.*"
5   Quoted in Larose, *La langue de papier*,
p.243; Robert Yergeau, *Art, argent,
arrangement: Le mécénat d'État*, Ottawa,
Éditions David, 2004. Translation of: "*Qu'on
commence à donner à manger aux gens.
On n'a pas d'affaire à leur dire comment
parler. Les campagnes de bon parler sont
les choses les plus stupides qui existent.
Bien parler, c'est se respecter: c'est faux, ça.
Bien manger, c'est se respecter! Faut être
colonisé pour sortir des slogans pareils.*"
6   Joël Belliveau, "Tradition, libéralisme
et communautarisme durant les 'trente
glorieuses': les étudiants de Moncton et
l'entrée dans la modernité avancée des
francophones du Nouveau-Brunswick, 1957-
1969," history dissertation, Université de
Montréal, 2008, pp.293-98. Translation of:
"*des bâtards culturels.*"
7   Mark V. Levine, *La reconquête de Montréal*,
Montreal, VLB, 1997, pp.91-92. Translation
of: "*de faire de Montréal, métropole
naturelle des Canadiens français, une ville
de langue et de culture françaises.*"
8   Duc, "La langue française dans les relations
entre le Canada et la France," pp.841,
851, 915.
9   *Les États généraux du Canada français:
Assises nationales tenues à la Place des
Arts de Montréal du 23 au 26 novembre
1967*, Montreal, Éditions de l'Action nationale, 1968, pp.125-26. Translation of: "*à la
condition que le français soit prioritaire.*"
10   Donat J. Taddeo and Raymond C. Taras,
*Le débat linguistique au Québec: La
communauté italienne et la langue
d'enseignement*, Montreal, Presses de
l'Université de Montréal, 1987; Michel
Plourde, *La politique linguistique du
Québec, 1977-1988*, Quebec, IQRC, 1988.

11 Nicolas Landry and Nicole Lang, *Histoire de l'Acadie*, Sillery (Quebec), Septentrion, 2001.

12 Richard Arès, "La grande pitié de nos minorités françaises," *Relations*, no. 267 (March 1963), p.65. Translation of: *"fort coûteuse à la langue française: non seulement cette dernière n'a pas réussi à conserver tous ses adhérents, mais elle doit encore accuser une perte de plus de 400 000 parmi ceux qui normalement auraient dû la parler."*

13 Ibid., p.68. Translation of: *"Le drame des minorités françaises au Canada est aussi celui de toute la Confédération canadienne; le destin de celle-ci est lié au sort de celles-là. Si les premières meurent, il ne restera plus à la seconde qu'à descendre, elle aussi, dans la tombe."*

14 "En l'absence de politiques appropriées: La situation démographique des francophones au Québec et à Montréal d'ici l'an 2000," *Le Devoir*, Nov. 4, 1969, p.5.

15 Paul Cappon, *Conflit entre les Néo-Canadiens et les francophones de Montréal*, Quebec, Presses de l'Université Laval and Centre international de recherche sur le bilinguisme, 1974, p.17. Translation of: *"existe un biais d'ordre économique qui agit contre l'assimilation des immigrants à la communauté francophone ... l'assimilation au groupe qui domine économiquement la société québécoise."*

16 Duc, "La langue française dans les relations entre le Canada et la France," t.2.

17 André Laurendeau, "A Letter to the Reader of Le Devoir," translated and reprinted as "Equality of Biculture Group Praised," *The Gazette* (Montreal), July 24, 1963, http://news.google.com/newspapers?nid=1946&dat=19630724&id=nJMtAAAAIBAJ&sjid=j54FAAAAIBAJ&pg=7038,4010823.

18 Royal Commission on Bilingualism and Biculturalism, *Preliminary Report*, Ottawa, Queen's Printer, 1965, p.133.

19 CRCCF, Fonds de l'ACFÉO, c2/454/11, Lettre adressée à toutes les cellules du Canada de l'Ordre concernant la commission sur le bilinguisme et le biculturalisme, July 2, 1963.

20 Conseil de la vie française en Amérique, *Bilinguisme et biculturalisme*, Quebec,

Éditions Ferland, 1964, p. 99. Translation of: *"Nous sommes heureux de la présence au Canada de milliers de concitoyens dont les ascendances culturelles diffèrent des nôtres et constituent pour nous un enrichissement. Nous estimons cependant qu'il existe en ce pays une culture anglo-canadienne et une culture canadienne-française, distinctes de celles de la France et de l'Angleterre, mais nous ne croyons pas qu'on puisse soutenir qu'il y a chez nous une culture germano-ou italo-canadienne, canado-ukrainienne ou israélienne, pour ne citer que quelques exemples."*

21 Société Saint-Jean-Baptiste de Montréal, *Le Bilinguisme et l'union canadienne*, Montreal, 1964, p.54. Translation of: *"Impossible pour un Canadien français de 1964, conscient des véritables problèmes de la nation à laquelle il appartient, de se remémorer l'histoire du bilinguisme dans l'administration fédérale sans éprouver un sentiment de lassitude ou de révolte."*

22 LAC, MG 31 E 38, vol. 11, file 14, letter from the Voice of Canada League, n.d.; letter from the Canadian National Association, n.d.; LAC, MG 32 B35, vol. 133, file S.O.S. Bilinguisme notes, letter from the Voice of Canada League, Feb. 3, 1969.

23 *The Globe and Mail*, March 20, 1965.

24 LAC, MG 31 H188, vol.3, file 6, letter from Neil Morrison, English-language Secretary of the Royal Commission on Bilingualism and Biculturalism, to Charles E. Dojack, President of the Canada Ethnic Press Federation, Feb. 6, 1965.

25 Tricia Hong, "Redefining the Storyline: Immigrant/Ethnic Briefs to the Royal Commission on Bilingualism and Biculturalism," Major Research Paper, History Department, York University, December 2006.

26 *Le Devoir*, Dec. 3, 1967, editorial; "The 'Third Group' Looks at Bilingualism and Biculturalism," *The Ottawa Citizen*, vol. 11, no. 1 (February 1965), p. 1; LAC, MG 32 C67, vol. 98, file on the 1969 Official Language Bill, letter from Senator Paul Yuzyk to federal members of Parliament, May 21, 1969.

27 LAC, MG 30 C72, vol.7, file Briefs to the B&B Commission, Statement of the Canadian Jewish Congress, Western Division, n.d.; *Toronto Daily Star*, editorial, March 31, 1965.

28 Michael Oliver, "Réflexion sur la Royal Commission on Bilingualism and Biculturalism," *Isuma: Revue canadienne de recherche sur les politiques*, vol. 2, no. 2 (Summer 2001), p.131. Translation of: *"plus de temps à la recherche en sciences sociales ... plus d'importance que toute autre commission, à l'exception de la Commission Rowell-Sirois."*

29 Royal Commission on Bilingualism and Biculturalism, *Report*, Book 1: *The Official Languages*, Ottawa, Queen's Printer, 1968, p.198.

30 Robert Comeau, "André Laurendeau et la Commission royale d'enquête sur le bilinguisme et le biculturalisme," in Robert Comeau, dir., *André Laurendeau: Un intellectuel d'ici*, Montreal, Presses de l'Université du Québec, 1990, p.203. Translation of: *"à l'extérieur et de près – en des pays comme la Belgique et la Suisse – la façon dont des sociétés aux prises avec les mêmes questions [que les nôtres] les ont résolues."*

31 Royal Commission on Bilingualism and Biculturalism, *Report*, Book 1, 1967, p.xxxv.

32 Ibid., p.199.

33 LAC, RG 146, vol. 2378, *Mouvement pour l'unilinguisme français au Québec*, Quebec (Prov.), file 1; RG 146,vol.2621, *Protests and Demonstrations Against Bill 63, Province of Quebec*, files 1–6.

34 Translation of : *"Commission d'enquête sur la situation de la langue française et sur les droits linguistiques des francophones, Mandat, arrêté en conseil (9 décembre 1968). ... Considérant une enquête sur la situation de la langue française au Québec et les mesures à prendre pour en assurer le plein épanouissement, ainsi que les droits linguistiques des citoyens du Québec; Vu la complexité du problème linguistique au Québec et l'urgence d'y apporter des solutions; Vu les responsabilités du Québec à l'égard de la langue de la majorité de ses citoyens; Vu la nécessité d'une politique linguistique qui tienne compte du caractère du Québec en Amérique du Nord et de ses relations avec les autres provinces du Canada et le gouvernement fédéral; Attendu qu'il est essentiel de faire enquête sur la situation de la langue française au Québec; Attendu que pour les mêmes motifs, il est essentiel de rechercher les moyens les plus aptes à garantir l'exercice des droits linguistiques de la majorité dans le respect des droits de la minorité; Il est ordonné, en conséquence, sur la proposition du premier ministre: Que soit constituée ... une commission pour faire enquête et rapport sur la situation du français comme langue d'usage au Québec, et pour recommander les mesures propres à assurer: a) les droits linguistiques de la majorité aussi bien que la protection des droits de la minorité; b) le plein épanouissement et la diffusion de la langue française dans tous les secteurs d'activité, à la fois sur les plans éducatif, culturel, social et économique."*

35 BANQ-Q, E140, Fonds de la Commission d'enquête sur la situation de la langue française et sur les droits linguistiques au Québec, 1960-01-520/1, Kahn-Tineta of Caughnawaga Indian Land, Quebec, Feb. 20, 1969, pp.1–2.

36 BANQ-Q, E140, Fonds de la Commission d'enquête sur la situation de la langue française et sur les droits linguistiques au Québec, 1960-01-520/2, transcript of the meetings on the theme "Immigrants et groupes ethniques," April 28, 1970, June 4, 1970.

37 Quebec, *Rapport de la Commission d'enquête sur la situation de la langue française et sur les droits linguistiques au Québec*, Livre I : *La langue de travail. La situation du français dans les activités de travail et de consommation des Québécois*; Jean-Claude Gémar, "Les grandes commissions d'enquête et les premières lois linguistiques," in Michel Plourde, dir., *Le français au Québec: 400 ans d'histoire et de vie*, pp.247–53.

38 Translation of: *"il en coûte plus à un travailleur francophone pous [sic] monter dans*

la hiérarchie de travail qu'à un anglophone. Au premier on demande le bilinguisme, au second on concède l'unilinguisme."

39 Serge Carlos, *L'Utilisation du français dans le monde du travail du Québec: Analyse sociolinguistique du monde du travail québécois*, study for the Commission d'enquête sur la situation de la langue française et sur les droits linguistiques au Québec, Quebec, 1973, p.216.

40 See Martin Pâquet, *Tracer les marges de la Cité: Étranger, immigrant et État au Québec, 1627-1981*, Montreal, Boréal, 2005.

41 Royal Commission on Bilingualism and Biculturalism, *Report*, Book II: *Education*, p.139.

42 Daniel Bourgeois, *Canadian Bilingual Districts: From Cornerstone to Tombstone*, Montreal and Kingston, McGill-Queen's University Press, 2006, pp.36-38.

43 Duc, "La langue française dans les relations entre le Canada et la France," pp.789, 841.

44 Larose, *La Langue de papier*, pp.204-5.

45 BANQ-Q, E6, Fonds du ministère de la Culture, des Communications et de la Condition féminine, box 3, file Quebec-Paris-Ottawa, Association canadienne des éducateurs de langue française, *Mémoire à la Commission royale d'enquête sur le bilinguisme et le biculturalisme*, October 1964; report by G.-H. Dagneau to the Minister of Cultural Affairs, Dec. 16, 1963; brief accompanying the Director's report, Dec. 2, 1963.

46 Translation of: "*Confier le sort des minorités à un ministère de l'Éducation fédéral, c'est confier leur sort au pouvoir politique fédéral. L'histoire de la Confédération nous apprend que le seul gouvernement canadien qui a voulu rendre justice aux minorités a été défait et que pas un parti n'a voulu risquer son avenir ensuite sur cette question."*

47 AVQ, Fonds CVFA, D366, box 19847, letter from P.-É. Gosselin to members of the Conseil de la vie française en Amérique, Feb. 25, 1966.

48 Royal Commission on Bilingualism and Biculturalism, *Report*, Book II, p.193.

49 LAC, MG 31 D77, vol. 44, *Verbatim Report of Proceedings, Ontario Advisory Committee on Confederation*, March 1965, p.19.

50 AO, RG3-26, box 455, file French Language Ontario Correspondence Ontario Govt. June-December 1968, letter from R. Glen Hodgson, MPP, Government Whip, to John Robarts, Feb. 2, 1968; PAO, RG3-26, box 454, file French Language Ont. – General-Ontario Government, January-December 1969, "Main points made in letters on bilingualism, 1968."

51 AO, F1017, box 5312, file Source papers 1965, *Statement of the Cultural Sub-Committee on the Status of French in Ontario*, Jan. 21, 1966; Jon Sufrin, "The Canadian Apocalypse: Nationalists and the End of Canada, 1963-1983," dissertation, Graduate Program in History, York University, 2009, pp. 370-73.

52 AO, F1017, box 5311, file Notices and Agendas 1967, *Thoughts for a Position Paper on the Question of Bilingual Districts Resulting from a Discussion at the February 17 Meeting of the OACC.*

53 See the study by Marcel Martel, *Le deuil d'un pays imaginé: Rêves, luttes et déroute du Canada français: Les rapports entre le Québec et la francophonie canadienne (1867-1975)*, Ottawa, Presses de l'Université d'Ottawa, 1997.

54 Rolande Faucher, *Jean-Robert Gauthier: "Convaincre ... sans révolution et sans haine,"* Sudbury, Prise de parole, 2008, pp.98-100.

55 Michel Doucet, *Le discours confisqué*, Moncton, N.B., Éditions d'Acadie, 1995, pp.27-36; Belliveau, "Tradition, libéralisme et communautarisme durant les 'trente glorieuses,'" pp.256-61.

5. Action: language laws, 1969-82

Translation of epigraphs:
  We know
  that we are not alone. (Lalonde)
  We no longer want to be like
  those who accept us
  on condition that we erase
  all traces of our personal history. (Leblanc)

1   Patrick Tomlinson, "The Debate on Bill C-120: An Evaluation of the Parliamentary Dialogue of the Official Languages Act," Graduate Program in History, York University, November 2007.

2   LAC, MG 31 E38, vol. 18, file 11, letter from Carol Joy Feldsted Wilson to J. T. Thorson, Dec. 3, 1970; letter from A.J. Bolsby to J.T. Thorson, March 21, 1971; letter from J.T. Thorson to Hugh MacPhail, Oct. 11, 1972; *The Globe and Mail*, Jan. 21, 1972, p.2, June 1, 1972, p.3, Jan. 23, 1974, p.10, Feb. 12, 1974, p. 9, April 3, 1974, p.9; Leonard Jones, "The Bigot," speech at the Alliance for the Preservation of English in Canada, Nov. 20, 1978, http://www.freedominion.ca/phpBB2/viewtopic.php?t=63219&start=0.

3   Jon Sufrin, "The Canadian Apocalypse," pp.134, 377-82, 425-29.

4   Ibid., pp.429-34.

5   CRCCF, Fonds de l'ACFÉO, C2-38/5/14, projet de lettre de l'ACFÉO au premier ministre P.E. Trudeau, n.d.; CRCCF, Fonds de l'ACFÉO, C2/528/4, The Dynamic of the Franco-Ontarian Heritage: Brief to Heritage Ontario, June 1972 (translation).

6   LAC, MG 30 D 387, vol. 1, file 21, speech by H. J. Syrnick, Vice-President of the Ukrainian Canadian Committee, July 1, 1970.

7   CRCCF, Fonds de l'ACFÉO, C2-38/5/14, draft letter from the ACFÉO to Prime Minister P.-E. Trudeau, n.d.; CRCCF, Fonds de l'ACFÉO, C2/528/4, The Dynamic of the Franco-Ontarian Heritage: Brief to Heritage Ontario, June 1972 (translation), p.5.

8   BANQ-M, E 47, Fonds du ministère de l'Immigration, 16 9.12, *Multiculturalisme*, letter from Robert Bourassa to Pierre Elliott Trudeau, Quebec, Oct. 11, 1971, pp.1-3; BANQ-Q, E 42, Fonds du ministère des Affaires intergouvernementales, 154, *Communiqués – général – 1970-71*, file 1971 – Robert Bourassa, "Le principe de la politique du multiculturalisme m'oblige à apporter des réserves sérieuses," Robert Bourassa, Quebec, Nov. 16, 1971, p.3. Translation of: "*difficilement compatible avec la réalité québécoise, où il y a une présence dominante de langue et de culture françaises, en plus d'une minorité importante de langue et de culture anglaises, ainsi que de nombreuses minorités d'autres langues et d'autres cultures … le rôle de premier responsable sur son territoire de la permanence de la langue et de la culture françaises dans le contexte nord-américain … tous les moyens à sa disposition … qu'il puisse y avoir la moindre discrimination envers les autres cultures.*"

9   BANQ-Q, E5, Fonds du conseil exécutif 2.1, *Minutes 1960-1980*, 1996-01-007/1, Conseil des ministres, Feb. 24, 1971, p.6.

10 AO RG3-26, 544, file "Bilingualism in Public Service Billing. Dists. Advisory Board Civil Service Commission," memorandum from W.A.B. Anderson to Robert Welch, Provincial Secretary and Minister of Citizenship, July 20, 1970.

11 LAC, MG 30 D 387, vol. 1, file 21, speech by Dr. I. Hlyka, President of the Taras Shevchenko Foundation, July 1, 1970.

12 Derick McNeil, "Et la lutte reprendra le 17 avril 1982: Québec, Ottawa et la Fédération des francophones hors Québec: Leurs luttes pour l'éducation en langue minoritaire, 1976-1982," master's thesis, University of Ottawa, 1994, pp.13, 27, 32.

13 Fédération des francophones du Québec, *Les Héritiers de Lord Durham*, Ottawa, 1977, vol. 1, p.7. Translation of: "*le Québec a décidé de participer activement à l'élaboration de son destin. En ce sens, son attitude est exemplaire et les francophones hors Québec la respectent et veulent s'en inspirer.*"

14 *The Globe and Mail*, March 18, 1976.

15 Ibid., June 16, 1976.

16 Ibid., June 25, 1976.

17 Quebec, *Rapport de la Commission d'enquête sur la situation de la langue française et sur les droits linguistiques au Québec*, livre 1; Jean-Claude Gémar, "Les grandes commissions d'enquête et les premières lois linguistiques," p.154.

18 Plourde, *La politique linguistique du Québec*, pp.13-16.

19 LAC, RG 146, vol. 2622, file Protests and Demonstrations – Reaction to Language

Bill 22, Quebec, vol.5, from 15-11-74, n.d., *Rapport sur les réactions face au bill 22 (analyse)*, Sept. 22, 1974.

20 *Débats de l'Assemblée nationale du Québec, 26 août 1977*, used again by Camille Laurin in *Une traversée du Québec*, Montreal, L'Hexagone, 1999, p.116. Translation of: "*un geste décisif pour la libération et la promotion des travailleurs québécois ... pour toutes les petites gens de chez nous ... la langue nationale est une condition de vie.*"

21 Charter of the French Language, S.Q. 1977, c.7, Preambule.

22 Charter of the French Language, Preamble; BANQ-Q, E5, Fonds du ministère du conseil exécutif, 3.4, *Cabinet du ministre d'État au Développement culturel*, 2005-03-001/ 242,101M, Camille Laurin to Billy Diamond, Montreal, June 3, 1997, pp.1-2.

23 BANQ-Q, E5, Fonds du Conseil exécutif, 2.1. *Minutes 1960-1980*, 2005-10-001/10, Conseil des ministres, *Séance du 23 mars 1977*, p.4. Translation of: "*que le gouvernement se doit de traiter [la communauté anglophone] de façon civilisé ... se comporter en agresseur vis-à-vis [de] la minorité.*"

24 *Débats de l'Assemblée nationale du Québec, 26 août 1977*, used again by Camille Laurin in *Une traversée du Québec*, p.114. Translation of: "*la main tendue du député de D'Arcy McGee ... nous respectons et apprécions trop, en effet, la communauté anglophone du Québec pour ne pas faire montre à son égard de la plus grande amitié et ouverture d'esprit possible.*"

25 *La Politique québécoise de développement culturel, vol. I: Perspectives d'ensemble: de quelle culture s'agit-il?*, Quebec, Ministère d'État au Développement culturel, 1978, p.6. Translation of: "*un projet commun, collectif, d'une société moderne et démocratique.*"

26 BANQ-Q, E42, Fonds du ministère des Relations internationales, 2002-04-003/44, Pierre-É. Laporte, *L'Expérience de planification linguistique en Israël et son intérêt pour le Québec: Rapport de mission*, [1979], pp.4, 8. Translation of: "*un consensus général touchant le statut de l'hébreu comme langue nationale ... au Québec ce n'est pas encore le cas [avec le français] ... les aspects politiques et techniques de la question linguistique restent entremêlés ... l'existence d'une seule autorité étatique souveraine donne aux travaux de normalisation terminologique une uniformité de résultats qui n'est pas toujours atteinte chez nous à cause du chevauchement des juridictions [sic].*"

27 Martin Weger, "A Canadian Company? Canadian Tire in Quebec and Western Canada," chapter on "A Relationship of Trust: Canadian Tire and Canadian Consumers, 1922-2000," history dissertation, York University, 2010.

28 McNeil, "Et la lutte reprendra le 17 avril 1982," pp.20-24; Marcel Martel, "L'intervention du gouvernement fédéral auprès des groupes minoritaires francophones," in Conseil de la langue française, *Pour un renforcement de la solidarité entre francophones au Canada: Réflexions théoriques et analyses historique, juridique et sociopolitique*, Sainte-Foy, Publications du Québec, 1995, pp.111-18.

29 McNeil, "Et la lutte reprendra le 17 avril 1982," pp.23-27; Michael D. Behiels, *Canada's Francophone Minority Communities: Constitutional Renewal and the Winning of School Governance*, Montreal and Kingston, McGill-Queen's University Press, 2004, pp.40-42.

30 AO, RG3-26, 503, file Official Language Act Federal government Jan. 70-Dec. 70, *Government of Ontario: Policy and Projects Undertaken in the Field of Bilingualism since 1967*, Office of the Co-ordinator on Bilingualism, Oct. 1, 1970.

31 Ibid.; AO,RG3-26,544, file Bilingualism in Public Service Jan.71-Feb.71, *Memorandum to All Cabinet Ministers from Prime Minister of Ontario*, Dec. 23, 1970.

32 LAC, RG146, vol. 3046, *The New Brunswick Area Commander Security Service, Re: Pressure Groups – General – Canada, Moncton District Unit Security Service*, Moncton, Dec. 11, 1978.

33 *The Moncton Times*, May 1, 1972.

34 CÉA-M, Fonds du comité pour le bilinguisme à Moncton (1921-1972), 152.16, Yves Roberge, Jérôme Pelletier and Gilbert Doucet, *Visage français de l'Acadie*, Moncton, n.d.. Our thanks to Julien Massicotte for having attracted our attention to the Comité pour le bilinguisme à Moncton.

35 CÉA-M, Fonds Donatien-Gaudet, 70-16, *Congrès des francophones du N.-B./Conférence de Léon Thériault*, Léon Thériault, *Les Acadiens du Nouveau-Brunswick et le phénomène politique*, [1972], p.6. Translation of: "*Dans son cheminement pour une société plus juste ... peuple acadien du Nouveau-Brunswick ... acadianiser l'appareil politique, là où cela nous concerne, est devenu aussi important que d'acquérir des écoles françaises, des hôpitaux français, etc.*"

36 Michel Doucet, *Le discours confisqué*, pp.59-62, 77-94.

37 José E. Igartua, *The Other Quiet Revolution: National Identities in English Canada, 1945-71*, Vancouver, University of British Columbia Press, 2006, p.210; Raymond-M. Hébert, *Manitoba's French-Language Crisis: A Cautionary Tale*, Montreal and Kingston, McGill-Queen's University Press, 2004, pp.19-20.

38 CRLG, P2/C228, letter from Fred E.Walden to André Laurendeau, Co-Chair of the B & B Commission, June 2, 1966; Igartua, *The Other Quiet Revolution*, p.216.

6. Law and language since 1982

Translation of epigraphs:
Tell us about your Charter
about the crimson beauty of your autumns
of dismal October
and of Noblet too ...
we are a hundred peoples who came from far away
to tell you that you are not alone. (Micone)
Silence. I hear words. (Bacon)

1 McNeil, "Et la lutte reprendra le 17 avril 1982," pp.36-49.

2 José Woehrling, "Convergences et divergences entre les politiques linguistiques du Québec, des autorités fédérales et des provinces anglophones: le noeud gordien des relations entre les Québécois francophones, la minorité anglo-québécoise et les minorités francophones du Canada," in Conseil de la langue française, *Pour un renforcement de la solidarité entre francophones au Canada*, p.253.

3 Official Languages Act, http://www.pch.gc.ca/pgm/lo-ol/legisltn/bill_s3_fact-eng.cfm.

4 Tina Chui, Kelly Tran, and Hélène Maheux, *Immigration in Canada: A Portrait of the Foreign-Born Population, 2006 Census*, Ottawa, Statistics Canada and Minister of Industry, December 2007, pp.11-12, http://www12.statcan.gc.ca/english/census06/analysis/immcit/pdf/97-557-XIE2006001.pdf.

5 Woehrling, "Convergences et divergences," p.272.

6 *Le Devoir*, April 1, 2005. Translation of: "*l'embrouillamini juridique ... difficultés d'application baliser la souplesse.*"

7 *Le Devoir*, Dec. 4, 2009.

8 *Le Devoir*, May 22, 1986. Translation of: "*solution raisonnable.*"

9 Woehrling, "Convergences et divergences," p.274.

10 United Nations, Human Rights Committee, *Constatations au titre du paragraphe 4, de l'article 5 du Protocole facultatif se rapportant au Pacte international relatif aux droits civils et politiques – Quarante-septième session*, Communications Nos. 359/1989 and 385/1989, John Ballantyne and Elizabeth Davidson, and Gordon McIntyre v. Canada, May 5, 1993, art. 11.2 and 11.5. Translation of: "*n'ont fait l'objet d'aucune discrimination fondée sur leur langue.*"

11 Stéphane Dion, *Straight Talk: Speeches and Writings on Canadian Unity*, Montreal and Kingston, McGill-Queen's University Press, 1999.

12 *The Gazette*, April 1, 2005.

13 *La Presse*, March 13, 1996. Translation of: "*Dans le débat sur la langue ... les deux grands groupes linguistiques du Québec sont maintenant sortis de l'ère des*

*bouleversements pour entrer dans une
période d'intérêt mutuel."*

14 *The Gazette*, Sept. 11, 1996. Translation of:
"*Nous sommes entre démocrates. Nous
avons la responsabilité – en fait, l'obligation
– de protéger les droits fondamentaux de
nos citoyens ... de concevoir un aménagement linguistique juste, stable, qui assure
la pérennité du français à Montréal et au
Québec, qui assure une meilleure intégration des nouveaux arrivants ... au dyna-
misme de la communauté anglophone."*

15 Commission des États généraux sur la
situation et l'avenir de la langue française
au Québec, *Le Français, une langue pour
tout le monde: Une nouvelle approche
stratégique et citoyenne*, Quebec, Quebec
government, 2001, p.21. Translation of:
"*l'approche historique canadienne qui
divise l'identité québécoise suivant une
ligne de partage ethnique, la canadienne
française et la canadienne-anglaise ... une
approche civique qui fonde l'identité du
peuple du Québec sur l'accueil et l'inclusion
grâce à une langue commune, le français, et
à une culture commune formée des apports
de toutes ses composantes."*

16 *Le Soleil*, Jan. 27, 2003. Translation of:
"*l'apprentissage de l'anglais est une nécessité pour le progrès individuel et collectif
des Québécois."*

17 Gérard Bouchard and Charles Taylor,
*Building the Future: A Time for Reconcilia-
tion, Report*, Consultation Commission
on Accommodation Practices Related to
Cultural Differences, 2008, p.217.

18 Quebec, *Declaration of the Gouvernement
du Québec respecting Québec's participation in international forums dealing with
education, language, culture and identity*,
Quebec, March 24, 1999, pp.498, 500,
http://www.saic.gouv.qc.ca/publications/
Positions/Part3/Document39_en.pdf.

19 *Québec's International Policy: Working in
concert*, Quebec, Ministère des Relations
internationales, 2006, p.89,
http://www.mri.gouv.qc.ca/en/informer/
publications/Fiche_desc/pol_inter_force_
action.asp.

20 "*Anna braillé ène shot*" is joual for *Elle a
beaucoup pleuré*; *Ta mé tu là?* is joual for *Ta
mère est-elle là?*

21 The Société des Acadiens du Nouveau-
Brunswick was founded in 1972. This organization became the Société des Acadiens
et des Acadiennes du Nouveau-Brunswick
(SAANB) in 1988; and in 2008 the Société
de l'Acadie du Nouveau-Brunswick (SANB).

22 Richard Julien, "Les Franco-Albertains et
la gestion de leurs écoles," *Cahiers franco-
canadiens de l'Ouest*, vol. 7, no. 1 (1995),
pp.119–54.

23 Quoted in Woehrling, "Convergences
et divergences," p.306. See
http://www.thecanadianencyclopedia.com/
index.cfm?PgNm=TCE&Params=A1A
RTA0010099.

Conclusion

Translation of epigraph:
But why speak
Of what exists only to question words
The silence of an entire people
Is the one that poems regret. (Dumont)

1 Eugénie Brouillet, *La négation de la
nation: L'identité culturelle québécoise et
le fédéralisme canadien*, Sillery (Quebec),
Septentrion, 2005, p.343. Translation of:
"*la survie et l'épanouissement de l'identité
culturelle québécoise à travers notamment
la protection de la langue française constituent des aspirations communes, donc un
droit collectif des Québécois."*

2 Pierre Bourdieu, *Ce que parler veut dire:
L'économie des échanges linguistiques*,
Paris, Fayard, 1982, p.101. Translation of:
"*Dans la lutte pour l'imposition de la vision
légitime ... détiennent un pouvoir propor-
tionné à leur capital symbolique, c'est-à-dire
à la reconnaissance qu'ils reçoivent
d'un groupe."*

3 Lise Gauvin, *La fabrique de la langue: De
François Rabelais à Réjean Ducharme*,
Paris, Seuil, 2004, p.338. Translation of:
"*théorie également centralisatrice et
normalisatrice de la langue."*

4   Joseph Yvon Thériault, *Faire société:*
     Société civile et espaces francophones,
     Sudbury, Ont., Prise de parole, 2007. Trans-
     lation of *"faire société."*

5   Fernand Dumont, "Peuple sans parole
     (poèmes)," *Liberté*, vol. 7, no. 5 (41),
     1965: p.406, republished in "La mémoire
     réconciliée," *La part de l'ombre: Poèmes
     1952-1995*, Montreal, L'Hexagone, 1996,
     p.125. Translation of: *"le silence d'un peuple
     tout entier/est celui-là que regrettent
     les poèmes."*

Bibliography

For the convenience of readers this book provides a simplified set of notes. The bibliography includes all the documents and studies used in the book, and in particular those whose author is quoted in the body of the text.

Archival Sources

Archives de la ville de Québec
Fonds du Conseil de la vie française en Amérique

Archives of Ontario
George Gathercole fonds (F1017)
Premier John P. Robarts fonds, General
    Correspondence (RG3-26)

Library and Archives Canada
Walter Bossy fonds (MG 30 C72)
Modest-Orest-Cmoc fonds (MG 30 D 387)
Royal Commission on Dominion Provincial
    Relations fonds
Donald Creighton fonds (MG 31 D 77)
Walter Dinsdale fonds (MG 32 B35)
Charles Dojack fonds (MG 31 H188)
Royal Canadian Mounted Police fonds (RG 146)
Joseph Thorson fonds (MG 31 E 38)
Paul Yuzyk fonds (MG32 C67)

**Bibliothèque et Archives nationales du
Québec (Centre de Québec)**
Fonds de la Commission d'enquête sur la situa-
    tion de la langue française et sur les droits
    linguistiques au Québec (E-140)
Fonds du conseil exécutif (E-5)

Fonds du ministère de la Culture, des Communi-
    cations et de la Condition féminine (E-6)
Fonds du ministère des Affaires intergouverne-
    mentales (E-42)
Fonds du ministère des Relations internatio-
    nales (E-42)

**Bibliothèque et Archives nationales du
Québec (Centre de Montréal)**
Fonds du ministère de l'Immigration (E-47)

**Centre d'études acadiennes Anselme-
Chiasson, Université de Moncton**
Fonds du Comité pour le bilinguisme à Moncton
Fonds Donatien-Gaudet

**Centre de recherche en civilisation
canadienne-française, University of Ottawa**
Fonds de l'association canadienne-française
    d'éducation d'Ontario
Fonds de la Fédération des Sociétés Saint-Jean-
    Baptiste de l'Ontario

Centre de recherche Lionel-Groulx, Montréal
Fonds de la commission
    Laurendeau-Dunton (P2/C)

Newspapers and Magazines
Le Devoir
La Minerve
La Presse
Parti pris
The Quebec Gazette
Relations
Le Soleil

The *Gazette* (Montreal)
The *Globe and Mail*
The *Moncton Times*
The *Toronto Star*

Databanks

Lexum (for Supreme Court of Canada decisions), Université de Montréal, Faculté de droit, http://scc.lexum.org/en/index.html.
CanLII (for decisions relating to federal, provincial and territorial legislation), Federation of Law Societies of Canada, www.canlii.org/fr/index.php.

Studies

Andrade, Michel Simão, "La commission des écoles catholiques de Montréal et l'intégration des immigrants et des minorités ethniques à l'école française de 1947 à 1977," *Revue d'histoire de l'Amérique française*, vol. 60, no. 4 (Spring 2007), pp.455-486.
Aunger, Edmund A., "Justifying the End of Official Bilingualism: Canada's North West Assembly and the Dual-Language Question, 1889-1892," *Canadian Journal of Political Science*, vol. 34, no.3 (September 2001), pp.451-486.
Barbaud, Philippe, *Le choc des patois en Nouvelle-France. Essai sur l'histoire de la francisation au Canada*, Quebec, Presses de l'Université Laval, 1984.
Bastien, Frédéric, *Relations particulières. La France face au Québec après de Gaulle*, Montréal, Boréal, 1999.
Beaudin, Maurice, Nicolas Béland and Éric Forgues, "Inégalités selon le bilinguisme: un parcours différencié entre les travailleurs francophones et anglophones du Québec et du Nouveau-Brunswick de 1970 à 2000," paper presented at the Canadian Economics Association, Toronto, University of Toronto, May 28-31, 2009.
Bédard, Éric, "McGill français: un contexte de fébrilité étudiante et nationaliste," *Bulletin d'histoire politique*, vol.9, no. 1 (automne 2000), pp.148-152.
Bédard, Théophile-Pierre, *Histoire de cinquante ans (1791-1841). Annales parlementaires et politiques du Bas-Canada depuis la Constitution jusqu'à l'Union*, Quebec, Léger-Brousseau, 1869.
Behiels, Michael D., *Canada's Francophone Minority Communities: Constitutional Renewal and the Winning of School Governance*, Montreal and Kingston, McGill-Queen's University Press, 2004.
Bélanger, Réal, *Wilfrid Laurier. Quand la politique devient passion*, Second Edition, Quebec, Presses de l'Université Laval, 2006.
Bélanger, Réal, Richard Jones and Marc Vallières, *Les grands débats parlementaires, 1792-1992*, Sainte-Foy, Presses de l'Université Laval, 1994.
Belcourt, Napoléon-Antoine, "De l'exercice des droits reconnus à la langue française au Canada," *Premier Congrès de la langue française au Canada. Compte rendu*, Quebec, Imprimerie de l'Action sociale, 1913, pp.288-307.
Belkhodja, Chedly, "Une réaction de droite au changement: le refus des réformes Robichaud au Nouveau-Brunswick," in *L'ère Louis J. Robichaud, 1960-1970. Actes du colloque*, Moncton, N.B., Institut canadien de recherche sur le développement régional, 2001, pp.127-141.
Belliveau, Joël, *Tradition, libéralisme et communautarisme durant les 'trente glorieuses'. Les étudiants de Moncton et l'entrée dans la modernité avancée des francophones du Nouveau-Brunswick, 1957-1969*, history dissertation, Université de Montréal, 2008.
Bernard, Jean-Paul (ed.), *Assemblées publiques, résolutions et déclarations de 1837-1838*, Montreal, VLB, 1988.
Bouchard, Chantal, *La langue et le nombril. Histoire d'une obsession québécoise*, Montreal, Fides, 1998.
Bouchard, Gérard and Charles Taylor, *Building the Future: A Time for Reconciliation, Report*, Consultation Commission on Accommodation Practices Related to Cultural Differences, 2008.
Bourassa, Henri, "La langue française et l'avenir de notre race," *Premier Congrès de la langue française au Canada. Compte rendu*, Quebec, Imprimerie de l'Action sociale, 1913, pp.370-389.

Bourdieu, Pierre, *Ce que parler veut dire. L'économie des échanges linguistiques*, Paris, Fayard, 1982.

Bourgeois, Daniel, *Canadian Bilingual Districts: From Cornerstone to Tombstone*, Montreal and Kingston, McGill-Queen's University Press, 2006.

Bouthillier, Guy, and Jean Meynaud. *Le choc des langues au Québec, 1760-1970*, Montreal, Presses de l'Université du Québec, 1972.

Breton, Raymond, "Institutional Completeness of Ethnic Communities and the Personal Relations of Immigrants," *American Journal of Sociology*, vol. 70 (1964), pp.193-205.

Brouillet, Eugénie, *La négation de la nation. L'identité culturelle québécoise et le fédéralisme canadien*, Sillery (Quebec), Septentrion, 2005.

——, "La charte de la langue française et la charte canadienne des droits et libertés: la difficile conciliation des logiques majoritaire et minoritaire," in Marcel Martel and Martin Pâquet (eds.), *Légiférer en matière linguistique*, Quebec, Presses de l'Université Laval, 2008, pp.359-388.

Brun, Henri, *La formation des institutions parlementaires québécoises, 1791-1838*, Sainte-Foy (Quebec), Presses de l'Université Laval, 1971.

Bureau, Brigitte, *Mêlez-vous de vos affaires. 20 ans de luttes franco-ontariennes*, Ottawa, Association canadienne-française de l'Ontario, 1989.

Burke, Edmund, *The Works of the Right Honourable Edmund Burke*, vol. 1, London, Holdsworth and Corner, 1839.

Cameron, David, and Richard Simeon (eds.), *Language Matters: How Canadian Voluntary Associations Manage French and English*, Vancouver, University of British Columbia Press, 2009.

Canada, Royal Commission on Bilingualism and Biculturalism, *Preliminary Report*, Ottawa, Queen's Printer, 1965.

——; *Report*, Book I, *The Official Languages*, Ottawa, Queen's Printer, 1968.

——; *Report*, Book II, *Education*, Ottawa, Queen's Printer, 1968.

——; *Report*, Book III, *The Work World*, Ottawa, Queen's Printer, 1969.

Cappon, Paul, *Conflit entre les néo-Canadiens et les francophones de Montréal*, Quebec, Presses de l'Université Laval, Centre international de recherche sur le bilinguisme, 1974.

Carlos, Serge, *L'Utilisation du français dans le monde du travail du Québec. Analyse sociolinguistique du monde du travail québécois*, study for the Commission d'enquête sur la situation de la langue française et sur les droits linguistiques au Québec, Quebec, 1973.

Castonguay, Charles, "Assimilation linguistique et remplacement des générations francophones et anglophones au Québec et au Canada," *Recherches sociographiques*, vol. 43, no.1 (2002), pp.149-182.

Certeau, Michel de, Dominique Julia, and Jacques Revel, *Une politique de la langue. La Révolution française et les patois: l'enquête de Grégoire*, Paris, Gallimard ("Folio Histoire" 117), 2002 [1975].

Charland, Jean-Pierre, "L'instruction chez les Canadiens français," in Michel Plourde (ed.), *Le Français au Québec. 400 ans d'histoire et de vie*, Montreal and Quebec, Fides and Publications du Québec, 2000, pp. 177-183.

Chui, Tina, Kelly Tran and Hélène Maheux, *Immigration in Canada: A Portrait of the Foreign-born Population, 2006 Census*, Ottawa, Statistics Canada and Minister of Industry, December 2007.

Colley, Linda, *Britons: Forging the Nation*, 1707-1837, London, Pimlico, 1992.

Comeau, Robert, "André Laurendeau et la Commission royale d'enquête sur le bilinguisme et le biculturalisme," in Robert Comeau (ed.), *André Laurendeau. Un intellectuel d'ici*, Montreal, Presses de l'Université du Québec, 1990.

Conseil de la vie française en Amérique, *Troisième Congrès de la langue française. Québec 18-26 juin 1952. Compte rendu*, Quebec, Éditions Ferland, 1953.

——; *Bilinguisme et biculturalisme*, Quebec, Éditions Ferland, 1964.

Cook, Ramsay, *The Regenerators: Social Criticism in Late Victorian English Canada*, Toronto, University of Toronto Press, 1985.

——, Canada, Québec, and the Uses of Nationalism, Second Edition, Toronto, McClelland & Stewart, 1995 [1986].

Corbeil, Jean-Claude, L'embarras des langues. Origine, conception et évolution de la politique linguistique québécoise, Montreal, Québec Amérique, 2007.

Couturier-LeBlanc, Gilberte, Alcide Godin and Aldéo Renaud, "L'enseignement français dans les Maritimes, 1604-1992," in Jean Daigle (ed.), L'Acadie des Maritimes, Moncton, Centre d'études canadiennes, 1993, pp.543-586.

Curtis, Bruce, "Irish Schools for Canada: Arthur Buller to the Bishop of Quebec, 1838," Historical Studies in Education / Revue d'histoire de l'éducation, vol.13, no. 1 (2001), pp.49-58.

Débats de l'Assemblée législative du Québec, 1867-1968.

Débats de l'Assemblée nationale du Québec, as of 1968.

Denis, Wilfrid B., "Ethnicité et conflits scolaires en Saskatchewan de 1905 à 1980," in Linda Cardinal (ed.), Une langue qui pense. La recherche en milieu minoritaire francophone au Canada, Ottawa, Presses de l'Université d'Ottawa ("Actexpress"), 1993, pp.77-100.

Desbiens, Jean-Paul, The Impertinences of Brother Anonymous, Preface by André Laurendeau, translation by Miriam Chapin. Montreal, Harvest House, 1966, c1962.

Deschênes, Gaston, Une capitale éphémère. Montréal et les événements tragiques de 1849, Sillery (Quebec), Septentrion, 1999.

Dickason, Olive, Les Premières Nations du Canada, Sillery (Quebec), Septentrion, 1996.

Dion, Stéphane, Straight Talk: Speeches and Writings on Canadian Unity, Montreal and Kingston, McGill-Queen's University Press, 1999.

Dorland, Michael, and Maurice Charland, Law, Rhetoric, and Irony in the Formation of Canadian Civil Culture, Toronto, University of Toronto Press, 2002.

Doucet, Michel, Le discours confisqué, Moncton, Éditions d'Acadie, 1995.

Duc, Édouard, La langue française dans les relations entre le Canada et la France (1902-1977). De la 'survivance' à l'unilinguisme français au Québec, history dissertation, Université Paris-IV Sorbonne, 2007.

Dumont, Fernand, "Peuple sans parole (poèmes)," Liberté, vol. 7, no. 5 (41), 1965: p.406, republished in "La mémoire réconciliée," La part de l'ombre: Poèmes 1952-1995, Montreal, L'Hexagone, 1996.

——, Genèse de la société québécoise, Montreal, Boréal, 1993.

Les États généraux du Canada français. Assises nationales tenues à la Place des Arts de Montréal du 23 au 26 novembre 1967, Montreal, Éditions de l'Action nationale, 1968.

Farina, Annick, "Lingua e identità: il dilemma del joual durante la 'Rivoluzione tranquilla'," Rivista di Studi canadesi, no. 20 (2007). pp.105-111.

Faucher, Rolande, Jean-Robert Gauthier, Convaincre... sans révolution et sans haine, Sudbury (Ontario), Prise de parole, 2008.

Fédération des francophones hors Québec, Les Héritiers de Lord Durham, vol. 1, Ottawa, Fédération des francophones hors Québec, 1977.

——, Pour ne plus être... sans pays. Rapport du comité politique de la Fédération des francophones hors Québec, Ottawa, Fédération des francophones hors Québec, 1979.

Ferretti, Lucia, Brève histoire de l'Église catholique au Québec, Montreal, Boréal, 1999.

Francis, Daniel, National Dreams: Myth, Memory and Canadian History, Vancouver, Arsenal Pulp Press, 1997.

Fraser, Graham, Sorry I Don't Speak French, ou Pourquoi quarante ans de politiques linguistiques au Canada n'ont rien réglé... ou presque, Montreal, Boréal, 2007.

Frégault, Guy, Michel Brunet and Marcel Trudel (eds.), Histoire du Canada par les textes, Montreal, Fides, 1952.

Frenette, Yves, Les Anglo-Normands dans l'est du Canada, Ottawa, Société historique du Canada ("Les groupes ethniques du Canada," 21), 1996.

Frenette, Yves (in collaboration with Martin Pâquet), Brève histoire des Canadiens français, Montreal, Boréal, 1998.

Gaffield, Chad, *Aux origines de l'identité franco-ontarienne. Éducation, culture, économie*, Ottawa, Presses de l'Université d'Ottawa, 1993.

Gauvin, Lise, *La fabrique de la langue. De François Rabelais à Réjean Ducharme*, Paris, Seuil, 2004.

Gémar, Jean-Claude, "Les grandes commissions d'enquête et les premières lois linguistiques," in Michel Plourde (ed.), *Le français au Québec. 400 ans d'histoire et de vie*, Montreal and Quebec, Fides and Publications du Québec, 2001, pp.247-253.

Gendron, Jean-Denis, *D'où vient l'accent des Québécois? Et celui des Parisiens? Essai sur l'origine des accents. Contribution à l'histoire de la prononciation du français moderne*, Quebec, Presses de l'Université Laval, 2007.

Goodfriend, Joyce D., *Before the Melting Pot: Society and Culture in Colonial New York City, 1664-1730*, Princeton, N.J., Princeton University Press, 1992.

Gosselin, Paul-E., *Le Conseil de la vie française*, Quebec, Éditions Ferland, 1967.

Greenwood, F. Murray, *Legacies of Fear: Law and Politics in Quebec in the Era of the French Revolution*, Toronto, University of Toronto Press and Osgoode Society, 1993.

Guest, Dennis, *Histoire de la sécurité sociale au Canada*, Montreal, Boréal, 1993.

Hamelin, Jean, and André Côté, *Analyse du contenu des mémoires présentés à la Commission Gendron*, Quebec, Éditeur officiel, 1974.

Hare, John, *Aux origines du parlementarisme québécois, 1791-1793*, Sillery (Quebec), Septentrion, 1993.

Harvey, Louis-Georges, *Le printemps de l'Amérique française: Américanité, anticolonialisme et républicanisme dans le discours politique québécois, 1805-1837*, Montreal, Boréal, 2005.

Hayday, Matthew, *Bilingual Today, United Tomorrow: Official Languages in Education and Canadian Federalism*, Montreal and Kingston, McGill-Queen's University Press, 2005.

Hébert, Raymond M., *Manitoba's French-Language Crisis: A Cautionary Tale*, Montreal and Kingston, McGill-Queen's University Press, 2004.

Helly, Denise (in collaboration with Marie McAndrew and Judy Young), "Le financement des associations ethniques par le programme du Multiculturalisme canadien," in Altay Manço, Joseph Gatugu and Spyros Amoranitis (eds.), *La Vie associative des immigrants: quelles valorisations politiques? Perspectives européennes et canadiennes*, Paris, L'Harmattan ("Compétences Interculturelles"), 2004, pp.223-248.

Hong, Tricia, "Redefining the Storyline: Immigrant/Ethnic Briefs to the Royal Commission on Bilingualism and Biculturalism," major research paper (history), York University, December 2006.

Igartua, José E., *The Other Quiet Revolution: National Identities in English Canada, 1945-71*, Vancouver, University of British Columbia Press, 2006.

Isambert, François-André et al. (eds.), *Recueil général des anciennes lois françaises depuis l'an 420 jusqu'à la Révolution de 1789, Troisième race, Ordonnances des Valois, Règne de François Ier*, Paris, Velin-Leprieur et Verdière, 1827.

Joy, Richard J., *Languages in Conflict*, Montreal, published by the author, 1967.

Julien, Richard, "Les Franco-Albertains et la gestion de leurs écoles," *Cahiers franco-canadiens de l'Ouest*, vol.7, no.1 (1995), pp.119-154.

Kelley, Ninette, and Michael Trebilcock, *The Making of the Mosaic: A History of Canadian Immigration Policy*, Toronto, University of Toronto Press, 1998.

Labrie, Normand, *La construction linguistique de la Communauté européenne*, Paris, Honoré Champion, 1993.

Lacoste, Paul, "André Laurendeau et la Commission royale d'enquête sur le bilinguisme et le biculturalisme," in André Laurendeau, *Journal tenu pendant la Commission royale d'enquête sur le bilinguisme et le biculturalisme*, Montreal, VLB, 1990, pp.25-43.

Lafleur, Jacques, *L'aménagement linguistique dans le monde*, en ligne: www.tlfq.ulaval.ca/axl/

Lambton, John (Lord Durham), *The Report and Dispatches of the Earl of Durham, His Majesty's High Commissioner and Governor-General in British North America*, London, Ridgways, 1839.

Lamonde, Yvan, *Histoire sociale des idées au Québec. 1896-1929*, vol.2, Montreal, Fides, 2004.

Landry, Nicolas, and Nicole Lang, *Histoire de l'Acadie*, Sillery (Quebec), Septentrion, 2001.

Lang, George, "Voyageur Discourse and the Absence of Fur Trade Pidgin," *Canadian Literature*, 131 (winter 1991), pp.51-63.

Lang, Stéphane, *La communauté franco-ontarienne et l'enseignement secondaire, 1910-1968*, history dissertation, University of Ottawa, 2003.

Lapalme, Georges-Émile, *Le vent de l'oubli. Mémoires*, t.2, Ottawa, Leméac, 1970.

——, *Pour une politique. Le programme de la Révolution tranquille*, Montreal, VLB, 1988.

Larose, Karim, *La langue de papier. Spéculations linguistiques au Québec*, Montreal, Presses de l'Université de Montréal, 2004.

Laurin, Camille, *Une traversée du Québec*, Montreal, L'Hexagone, 1999.

Leacock, Stephen, *On the Front Line of Life: Memories and Reflections, 1935-1944*, Toronto, Dundurn Group, 2004.

LeBel, Marie, "Montfort, de l'affaire à la cause. Un moment charnière dans les stratégies de défense des droits des francophones," in Martin Pâquet (ed.), *Faute et réparation au Canada et au Québec contemporains. Études historiques*, Quebec, Nota Bene, 2006, pp.289-318.

Legault, Josée, *L'invention d'une minorité. Les Anglo-Québécois*, Montreal, Boréal, 1992.

Levine, Mark V., *La reconquête de Montréal*, Montreal, VLB, 1997.

Lijphart, Arendt, *The Politics of Accommodation: Pluralism and Democracy in the Netherlands*, Berkeley, University of California Press, 1968.

——, *Democracies: Patterns of Majoritarian and Consensus Government in Twenty-one Countries*, New Haven (Conn.), Yale University Press, 1984.

Linteau, Paul-André, "The Italians of Quebec: Key Participants in Contemporary Linguistic and Political Debates," in Roberto Perin and Franc Sturino (eds.), *Arrangiarsi: The Italian Immigration Experience in Canada*, Montreal, Guernica, 1989, pp.179-207.

Mackey, Eva, *The House of Difference: Cultural Politics and National Identity in Canada*, Toronto, University of Toronto Press, 2002.

Mandel, Michael, *La Charte des droits et libertés et la judiciarisation du politique au Canada*, Montreal, Boréal, 1996.

Martel, Marcel, "L'intervention du gouvernement fédéral auprès des groupes minoritaires francophones," in Conseil de la langue française, *Pour un renforcement de la solidarité entre francophones au Canada. Réflexions théoriques et analyses historique, juridique et sociopolitique*, Sainte-Foy, Publications du Québec, 1995, pp.111-118.

——, *Le deuil d'un pays imaginé. Rêves, luttes et déroute du Canada français. Les rapports entre le Québec et la francophonie canadienne (1867-1975)*, Ottawa, Presses de l'Université d'Ottawa, Centre de recherche en civilisation canadienne-française ("Amérique française,"5), 1997.

Martel, Marcel, and Martin Pâquet (eds.), *Légiférer en matière linguistique*, Quebec, Presses de l'Université Laval, 2008.

Maseres, Francis, *Occasional Essays on Various Subjects, Chiefly Political and Historical*, London, Robert Wilks, 1809.

McCue, Jim, *Edmund Burke and Our Present Discontents*, London, Claridge Press, 1997.

McKay, Ian, "The Liberal Order Framework: A Prospectus for a Reconnaissance of Canadian History," *Canadian Historical Review*, vol. 81, no. 4 (December 2000), pp.617-645.

——, *Rebels, Reds, Radicals: Rethinking Canada's Left History*, Toronto, Between the Lines, 2005.

McLaren, Angus, *Our Own Master Race: Eugenics in Canada, 1885-1945*, Toronto, McClelland & Stewart, 1990.

McNeil, Derick, *Et la lutte reprendra le 17 avril 1982. Québec, Ottawa et la Fédération des* francophones hors Québec : leurs luttes pour l'éducation en langue minoritaire, 1976-1982, master's thesis in history, University of Ottawa, 1994.

McRae, Kenneth (ed.), Consociational Democracy: Political Accomodation in Segmented Societies, Toronto, McClelland & Stewart, 1974.

McRoberts, Kenneth, Quebec: Social Change and Political Crisis, Toronto, McClelland & Stewart, 1988.

——, Un pays à refaire. L'échec des politiques constitutionnelles canadiennes, Montreal, Boréal, 1999.

Michaud, Nelson, "La doctrine Gérin-Lajoie," in Stéphane Paquin and Louise Beaudoin (eds.), Histoire des relations internationales du Québec, Montreal, VLB ("Études québécoises,"75), 2006, pp.263-277.

Miller, James R., Equal Rights: The Jesuits' Estates Act Controversy, Montreal and Kingston, McGill-Queen's University Press, 1979.

Montpetit, Éric, "La démocratisation de la gestion des risques," Lien social et politiques-RIAC, t.50 (2003), pp.91-104.

Mossman, Mary Jane, "The Charter and Access to Justice in Canada," in David Schneiderman, David and Kate Sutherland (eds.), Charting the Consequences: The Impact of the Charter Rights on Canadian Law and Politics, Toronto, University of Toronto Press, 1997, pp.271-302.

Mougeon, Raymond, "Le français s'impose en Nouvelle-France," in Michel Plourde (ed.), Le français au Québec. 400 ans d'histoire et de vie, Montreal and Quebec, Fides and Publications du Québec, 2000, pp.33-38.

Nadeau, Jean-François, Bourgault, Montreal, Lux, 2007.

Noël, Lucie, Les enjeux juridiques et sociopolitiques des conflits linguistiques au Québec, Quebec, Centre international de recherche sur le bilinguisme, 1987.

Norris, Mary Jane, "Langues autochtones au Canada : nouvelles tendances et perspectives sur l'acquisition d'une langue seconde," Tendances sociales canadiennes, no. 11-008 (May 2007), pp.21-29.

Oliver, Michael, "Réflexion sur la Commission royale d'enquête sur le bilinguisme et le biculturalisme," Isuma, Revue canadienne de recherche sur les politiques, vol. 2, no.2 (summer 2001), pp.130-134.

Otis, Alain, "La traduction des lois au gouvernement du Canada 1841-1935," Revue parlementaire canadienne, vol. 28, no.2 (summer 2005), pp.26-32.

Painchaud, Claude, and Richard Poulin, Les Italiens au Québec, Hull, Éditions Asticou, 1989.

Painchaud, Robert, "Les exigences linguistiques dans le recrutement d'un clergé pour l'Ouest canadien, 1818-1920," Société canadienne d'histoire de l'Église catholique, sessions d'étude 1975, pp.43-64.

Pâquet, Martin, Vers un ministère québécois de l'Immigration, 1945-1968, Ottawa, Société historique du Canada ("Les groupes ethniques du Canada," 23), 1997.

——, Tracer les marges de la Cité. Étranger, immigrant et État au Québec, 1627-1981, Montreal, Boréal, 2005.

——, "Pensée scientifique et prise de décision politique au Canada et au Québec," Bulletin d'histoire politique, vol.17, no.1 (fall 2008), pp.175-192.

The Parliamentary Register, vol. 29, London, J. Devrett, 1791.

Perin, Roberto, Rome in Canada: The Vatican and Canadian Affairs in the Late Victorian Age, Toronto, University of Toronto Press, 1990.

——, Ignace de Montréal. Artisan d'une identité nationale, Montreal, Boréal, 2008.

Pichette, Robert, "Culture et langues officielles," in L'ère Louis J. Robichaud, 1960-1970. Actes du colloque, Moncton, Institut canadien de recherche sur le développement régional, 2001, pp.69-89.

Plourde, Michel, La politique linguistique du Québec, 1977-1988, Quebec, IQRC, 1988.

Poirier, Claude, et al., Le trésor de la langue française au Québec, online: www.tlfq.ulaval.ca

Québec, Bureau de la statistique, Démographie québécoise, Rapport, Quebec, Éditeur officiel, 1987.

Québec, Commission d'enquête sur la situation de la langue française et sur les droits linguistiques au Québec, *La situation de la langue française au Québec*, vol. 1, Quebec, Government of Quebec, 1972.

Québec, Commission des États généraux sur la situation et l'avenir de la langue française au Québec, *Le français, une langue pour tout le monde. Une nouvelle approche stratégique et citoyenne*, Québec, Gouvernement du Québec, 2001.

Québec, Commission royale d'enquête sur l'enseignement dans la province de Québec, *Rapport de la Commission royale d'enquête sur l'enseignement dans la province de Québec*, Québec, La commission, 1963-1966, 5 vol.

Québec, Ministère d'État au Développement culturel, *La politique québécoise de développement culturel*, vol.1, *Perspectives d'ensemble: de quelle culture s'agit-il?*, Quebec, Éditeur officiel, 1978.

Québec, Ministère des Relations internationales, *La politique internationale du Québec. La force de l'action concertée*, Quebec, Government of Québec, 2006.

Québec, *Déclaration du gouvernement du Québec concernant la participation du Québec aux forums internationaux traitant d'éducation, de langue, de culture et d'identité*, Quebec, Marche 24, 1999.

Québec, *Rapport de la Commission d'enquête sur la situation de la langue française et sur les droits linguistiques au Québec*, livre 1: *La langue de travail. La situation du français dans les activités de travail et de consommation des Québécois*, Québec, Éditeur officiel, décembre 1972.

Ramirez, Bruno, *La ruée vers le sud. Migrations du Canada vers les États-Unis, 1840-1930*, Montreal, Boréal, 2003.

Resnick, Philip, *Thinking English Canada*, Toronto, Stoddart, 1994.

——, *The European Roots of Canadian Identity*, Toronto, Broadview Press, 2005.

Rivard, Adjutor, *Études sur les parlers de France au Canada*, Quebec, J.-P. Garneau éditeur, 1914.

Roby, Yves, *Les Franco-Américains de la Nouvelle-Angleterre. Rêves et réalités*, Sillery (Quebec), Septentrion, 2000.

Roy, Jean-Louis, *Les programmes électoraux du Québec. Un siècle de programmes politiques québécois*, tome II: 1931-1966, Ottawa, Leméac, 1971.

Rumilly, Robert, *Monseigneur Laflèche et son temps*, Montreal, Éditions B.D. Simpson, 1945.

Sanfilippo, Matteo, "Essor urbain et création de nouveaux diocèses dans l'Ouest: la correspondance des délégués apostoliques, 1902-1918," in *Canada e Italia verso il duemila. Metropoli a confronto*, vol. 1, Milan, Schena Editore, 1992, pp.261-280.

Saussure, Ferdinand de, *Cours de linguistique générale*, Paris, Payot, 1995 [1913].

Savard, Pierre, "Relations avec le Québec," in Cornelius J. Jaenen (ed.), *Les Franco-Ontariens*, Ottawa, Presses de l'Université d'Ottawa ("Ontario Historical Studies Series"), 1993, pp.231-263.

Savard, Stéphane, '*Je t'aime, moi non plus*': réceptivité et identités des membres des élites franco-ontariennes vis-à-vis du gouvernement Trudeau, 1968-1984, master's thesis, Université Laval, 2005.

——, "Pour 'une politique globale, précise, cohérente et définitive de développement.' Les leaders franco-ontariens et les encadrements politiques fédéraux, 1968-1984," *Politique et Sociétés*, vol. 27, no.1 (2008), pp.129-155.

Seymour, Michel, "Le Canada reconnaît-il l'existence des droits collectifs linguistiques du peuple québécois?," in Marcel Martel and Martin Pâquet (eds.), *Légiférer en matière linguistique*, Québec, Presses de l'Université Laval, 2008, pp.423-446.

Société Saint-Jean-Baptiste de Montréal, *Le bilinguisme et l'union canadienne*, Montreal, 1964.

Spolsky, Bernard, *Language Management*, Cambridge (UK), Cambridge University Press, 2009.

Stevenson, Don, and Richard Gilbert, "Municipal Associations," in David Cameron and Richard Simeon (eds.), *Language Matters:*

How Canadian Voluntary Associations Manage French and English, Vancouver, University of British Columbia Press, 2009, pp.74–94.

Stevenson, Garth, *Community Besieged: The Anglophone Minority and the Politics of Quebec*, Montreal and Kingston, McGill-Queen's University Press, 1999.

Sufrin, Jon, *The Canadian Apocalypse: Nationalists and the End of Canada, 1963-1983*, history dissertation, York University, 2009.

Taddeo, Donat J., and Raymond C.Taras, *Le débat linguistique au Québec. La communauté italienne et la langue d'enseignement*, Montréal, Presses de l'Université de Montréal, 1987.

Thériault, Joseph Yvon, *Faire société: Société civile et espaces francophones*, Sudbury, Ont., Prise de parole, 2007.

Thériault, Léon, "L'Acadie, 1763-1978. Synthèse historique," in Jean Daigle (ed.), *L'Acadie des Maritimes. Études thématiques des débuts à nos jours*, Moncton, Université de Moncton, Centre d'études acadiennes, 1993, pp.49–94.

Tomlinson, Patrick, *The Debate on Bill C-120: An Evaluation of the Parliamentary Dialogue of the Official Languages Act*, Graduate Program in History, November 2007.

Turk, Danilo, "Le droit des minorités en Europe," in Henri Giordan (ed.), *Les minorités en Europe. Droits linguistiques et droits de l'Homme*, Paris, Éditions Kimé, 1992, pp.447–469.

United Nations, Human Rights Committee, *Constatations au titre du paragraphe 4, de l'article 5 du Protocole facultatif se rapportant au Pacte international relatif aux droits civils et politiques*
——, *Quarante-septième session*, Communications Nos. 359/1989 and 385/1989, John Ballantyne and Elizabeth Davidson, and Gordon McIntyre v. Canada, May 5, 1993.

Valverde, Mariana, *The Age of Light, Soap, and Water: Moral Reform in English Canada, 1885-1925*, Toronto, McClelland & Stewart, 1991.

Vandycke, Robert, "Le statut de minorité en sociologie du droit. Avec quelques considérations sur le cas québécois," *Sociologie et Sociétés*, vol. 26, no.1 (Spring 1994), pp.87–97.

Verrette, Michel, *L'alphabétisation au Québec, 1660-1900. En marche vers la modernité culturelle*, Sillery (Quebec), Septentrion, 2002.

Vipond, Mary, "One network or two? French-Language Programming on the Canadian Radio Broadcasting Commission, 1932-36," *Canadian Historical Review*, vol. 89, no.3 (September 2008), pp.319–343.

Waddell, Eric, "State, Language, and Society: The Vicissitudes of French in Quebec and Canada," in Alan Cairns and Cynthia Williams (eds.), *The Politics of Gender, Ethnicity, and Language in Canada*, Toronto, University of Toronto Press, 1986, pp.67–110.

Walzer, Michael, *Thinking Politically: Essays in Political Theory*, New Haven (Conn.), Yale University Press, 2007.

Warren, Jean-Philippe, *Une douce anarchie. Les années 68 au Québec*, Montreal, Boréal, 2008.

Weger, Martin, *A Relationship of Trust: Canadian Tire and Canadian Consumers, 1922-2000*, history dissertation, York University, 2010.

Weil, François, *Les Franco-Américains, 1860-1980*, Paris, Belin, 1989.

Woehrling, José, "Convergences et divergences entre les politiques linguistiques du Québec, des autorités fédérales et des provinces anglophones: le nœud gordien des relations entre les Québécois francophones, la minorité anglo-québécoise et les minorités francophones du Canada," in Conseil de la langue française, *Pour un renforcement de la solidarité entre francophones au Canada. Réflexions théoriques et analyses historique, juridique et sociopolitique*, Sainte-Foy, Publications du Québec, 1995, pp.209–344.

——, "La Charte de la langue française: des ajustements juridiques," in Michel Plourde (ed.), *Le français au Québec. 400 ans d'histoire et de vie*, Montreal and Quebec, Fides and Publications du Québec, 2000, pp.285–291.

Yelle, Émile, "La langue et l'esprit français dans le Manitoba et dans l'Ouest canadien,"

Deuxième Congrès de la langue française au Canada. Québec, 27 juin - 1ᵉʳ juillet 1937, Compte rendu, Quebec, Imprimerie L'Action catholique, 1938, pp.225-243.

Yergeau, Robert, *Art, argent, arrangement. Le mécénat d'État*, Ottawa, Éditions David, 2004.

Index

Aboriginal languages, 16, 49, 154, 229-31, 238; death of, 229, 246; rights of, 230; threatened, 229

Aboriginal peoples: abandonment of traditional values, 48; acculturation of, 154; assimilation of, 48-49, 154; "civilization" of, 48-49; claims of, 7; confinement of to reserves, 49; cultural survival and vitality of, 229; enfranchisement of, 48-49; financial support for, 154; French policies towards, 16; future well-being of, 7, 10; marginalization of, 229; negotiations with in New France, 16; presence of prior to European colonization, 123; and private property, 48-49; in Quebec, 196, 230-31; and residential schools, 49; social exclusion of, 6, 229; sovereignty of, 16; special status for, 158; and spoken word, 15, 16-17; status of as minors, 49; treaties of, 130; will to live together of, 6

Acadia: activism, 180-81; anaemic nature of French language, 78; civil society, 78; clergy, 50; economic underdevelopment, 142; international standards vs. spoken language, 111; mirroring of Irish experience, 22; national project, 50; presentation of language issue, 78; use of French, 4

Acadians, 9, 76, 91, 93, 225; alienation of, 111; assimilation in language and school policies, 47, 116, 181; and battle for French-Canadian nation, 71-72; creation of institutional network, 72; cultural colonization of, 9; deportation of, 5, 17, 22, 23, 36; elite, 9; equivalent of Brother Anonymous among, 101; illiteracy among, 141; as "intellectual bastards," 111; language and school policies,

47; language tensions between anglophones and, 121; limited access to higher education for, 36; linguistic rights of, 8, 46, 223; migration of to United States, 236, 244; minority of, 6, 46, 72, 73, 97-98, 174; mobilization of, 180-81; and New Brunswick school issue, 52; organizations promoting rights of, 86; patois of, 68; precariousness of rights of, 72-73; reception of school reform among, 141-42; recognition of as people, 182; resentment of towards bilingualism, 180-81; rights of, 86; school boards, 142, 180-81; socio-economic progress of, 217; solidarity shown by, 80; struggles of, 81; student activists, 111, 114, 178, 180; subsistence economy of, 36; tensions between anglophones and, 121; Vatican and, 50

accent, 15; of Versailles of Louis XIV, 15

accommodation: erosion of culture of, 107; and how to live together, 9; mutual, 6, 76, 216, 237; reasonable, 208-9; strategies of, 72, 236

Acheson, Archibald, 38

Act for the Preservation and Enhancement of Multiculturalism in Canada (1988), 193-94

L'Action française, 67

L'Action nationale, 84, 112, 135

activism: Acadian, 180; anglophone, 63, 162, 180, 182, 196; citizen, 142, 199, 243; civil society, 64, 85; of courts, 188; judicial, 217, 221; language, 94; in language planning, 45; political, 158; around provision of French services, 175; state, 140, 179; student, 107, 111, 114-15

Act of Union: of 1840, 41; of England and Scotland, 20; of England and Wales, 17

245; income of male salaried workers, 127; institutional networks, 72, 81, 86, 90, 98, 105, 136, 153, 227-28, 238; and integration of French language, 5; interprovincial migration of, 81; linguistic rights of, 8, 46, 80, 118; literacy among, 65; in Manitoba, 53-57, 68; maternal duties of, 65; migration of to United States, 65-66, 68, 236, 244; militant, 49; minority of, 6, 72, 98; mission of to establish Catholic faith and French language in North America, 68; mobilization of, 65; mobilization of bishops, 56; and nationalism, 71; and nationalization of language, 236; in Ontario, 61-62, 64, 68; organizations promoting rights of, 86; patois of, 68; political colonization of, 109; precariousness of rights of, 72-73; prejudices against, 92; reduction in number of in Manitoba, 53; reduction in number of in Northwest Territories, 58; relations with English Canadians, 71; resistance of, 75; respect for rights of, 80, 85, 88; solidarity shown by, 70-72, 80; struggles of, 73, 81; underrepresentation of in federal civil service, 86-87; Vatican and, 50; weak qualifications of teachers, 60; in West, 81

French immersion programs, 156, 175, 181, 222-23

French language: access to education in, 132, 174, 175-76, 181, 190-91; as administrative language of New France, 4; anaemic nature of, 78; anglicisms in, 37, 66, 68, 82, 98, 101; anxiety about, 1; as barrier to success, 236; co-existence of with English, 98; as common good, 101, 237; as common language of New France, 2; as common language of Quebec, 1, 160, 161, 188; conferences on, 78, 81-82, 105; contamination of by English, 37; demeaning notion of, 98; disappearance of regional languages in favour of, 14; encouragement of "blossoming" of in provinces, 112; enhancement of standing of, 104; entrenchment of as official language, 46; equality of English and, 148, 179; establishment of by French Canadians, 68; as foreign language in Northwest Territories, 58; fragility of, 66; guaranteed use of in provinces, 91; homogeneous authorities in, 228; as idiom of diplomacy, 20; inadequacy of opportunity to communicate in, 158; international standard, 111; as language of communication and work, 85, 104, 121, 134,

161, 162, 238; as language of legislation and courts in Quebec, 168; as language of power and administration, 13; as language of use in United Province of Canada, 46; laxity in methods used to teach, 210; in Lower Canada, 5; in Manitoba, 53-57, 72, 101, 218-21; in media, 210-11; mother's role in teaching rudiments of, 65; nationalization of, 41-42, 236; in New Brunswick, 52-53, 178-82; as not simply a mode of communication, 41; in Ontario (see under Ontario); on outdoor signage, 112, 134, 201-4; of Parisian colleges, 15; Parisian standard, 111; poor quality of, 66, 67-68, 78, 82, 97-98, 99-102, 105, 108, 210-11, 244-45; precariousness of, 115-18; predominance of, 201; preservation of, 64-66; as primary language in Quebec, 134, 209; prohibition of in House of Assembly, 32; promotion of, 9, 10, 12, 108, 132, 162, 209; protection of, 238; provision of services in, 64, 86, 90, 121, 128, 132, 133, 140, 146, 156, 175, 177-80, 182, 184, 193-94, 213-14, 216-20, 231-32, 237; public use of, 42, 111, 209; reassurance about future of, 166; reduction in proportion of Catholics and French Canadians in, 53; refusal to declare official language, 157-58; regression in usage of, 95; revaluation of status of, 9; rightful use of, university attention to, 108; rights related to use of in Quebec, 168-72; right to receive education in, 80, 242; right to trial in, 212; right way to speak, 82, 110-11, 134; school boards, 176, 180, 191, 212-13, 223; standards of, 66, 85, 109-11; survival of speakers of, 71; training programs for immigrants, 83-84; use of in air traffic control, 159-60; viability of, 168, 184; vitality of, 78, 80, 96, 101-2, 106, 118, 142, 223, 229

French Revolution, 5, 17, 24, 26, 244
"Frère Untel." See Desbiens, Jean-Paul
Front du Québec français, 128, 135
fur trade, 16

Gaffield, Chad, 64
Gagnon, Lysiane, 200
Gagnon-Tremblay, Monique, 210
Galganov, Howard, 207
Garneau, Hector de Saint-Denys, 75
Garneau, Michel, 3
Gaudet, Donatien, 181